Sacrifice and Violence

Violence is at the heart of the sacrifice, despite its denial in the texts. For the participants and observers, it materialises in the exposure of everyone and everything to the 'fountains of blood'. The specificity of this public and holistic violence, orchestrated in Nepal by the highest dignitaries and aimed at the rejuvenation of the cosmic, political and social order, allows us to see sacrifice as the ultimate model of legitimate violence. At the same time, observation reveals its oxymoronic nature through the opposite effect its violence has on its participants. As such, sacrifice is not only the organiser of society, but also the revelator of its internal tensions and fault lines. The book explores the complex aspects of royal ceremonies, their contestation by different groups, and finally the contours of the new legitimacy that sacrifice found during the revolutionary period under its most extreme form of human sacrifice.

Marie Lecomte-Tilouine is research director at the Centre national de la recherche scientifique (CNRS), Paris, and member of the Laboratoire d'anthropologie sociale, CNRS/EHESS/Collège de France, Paris. Author of *Hindu Kingship, Ethnic Revival and Maoist Rebellion in Nepal* (2009), she has extensive fieldwork experience in the Himalayas, a region on which she has coordinated several collaborative research programmes. The most recent of these resulted in the volume *Encounters with the Invisible: Revisiting Spirit Possession in the Himalayas* (co-edited with Anne de Sales, 2024).

Sacrifice and Violence

Reflections from an Ethnography in Nepal

Marie Lecomte-Tilouine

Translated from the French original by the author

CAMBRIDGE
UNIVERSITY PRESS

CAMBRIDGE
UNIVERSITY PRESS

Shaftesbury Road, Cambridge CB2 8EA, United Kingdom

One Liberty Plaza, 20th Floor, New York, NY 10006, USA

477 Williamstown Road, Port Melbourne, VIC 3207, Australia

314–321, 3rd Floor, Plot 3, Splendor Forum, Jasola District Centre, New Delhi – 110025, India

103 Penang Road, #05–06/07, Visioncrest Commercial, Singapore 238467

Cambridge University Press is part of Cambridge University Press & Assessment, a department of the University of Cambridge.

We share the University's mission to contribute to society through the pursuit of education, learning and research at the highest international levels of excellence.

www.cambridge.org
Information on this title: www.cambridge.org/9781009537490

First published 2024

Printed in India by Avantika Printers Pvt. Ltd.

A catalogue record for this publication is available from the British Library

ISBN 978-1-009-53749-0 Hardback

Contents

Map and figures

Map

Figures

Note on transliteration

Nepali terms are transliterated according to the conventions adopted by Turner (1932).

Acknowledgements

Anthropology is a collective work, one which is entirely dependent on the generosity of those who agree to welcome us and partake in our discussions. These people are too numerous to be thanked here other than by paying a general tribute to the incredible humanity of the inhabitants of Nepal. I would particularly like to express my gratitude to Purna Bahadur Rana Magar, Prem Shahi, Mohan Singh and Krishna Rana Magar, Prem Bahadur Sris, Chitra Bahadur, Narmati and Ashok Gharti Magar, Bhim Rai, Surakshya Thapa Magar, Bijuli Magar, Mahes Raj Pant, C. K. Lal and Krishna Hacchethu. This work owes a great deal to Salvatore D'Onofrio, who encouraged me to write it, and to Monique Jeudy-Ballini and Marie Mauzé, who offered to read it. I am indebted to Charlotte Willis-Jones for her careful revision of the English translation of the text. Finally, I would like to thank Jacques, for listening and reacting to these pages in the making, as well as Adele, Darius and Jacob for their inspiring presence.

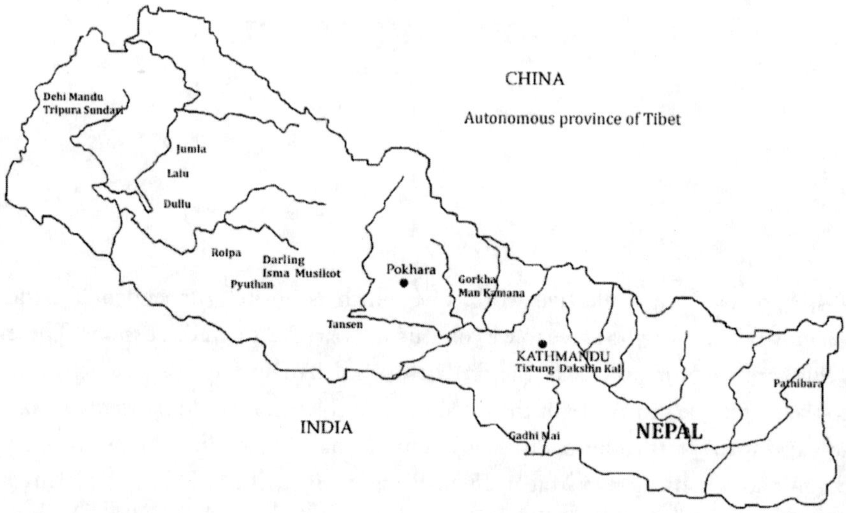

Map 1 Locations of the main places mentioned in the text

Source: Author.

Introduction

Nepal is one of the few contemporary contexts where blood sacrifice is still a common, authorised and official practice, one which is closely associated with political power. As such, it forms an ideal framework for studying the relationship between sacrifice and violence, which is here considered in terms of a relationship between legitimate violence and transgressive violence.

In a stroke of fortuitous timing, my first visits to Nepal took place during the great buffalo sacrifices of the autumn. I thus found myself, due to politeness, unable to decline invitations and having to stand as close as possible to the scene, holding my camera close to my face like a screen to protect me from the violence of the spectacle and the spurts of blood which resulted from it.

Sacrifice and violence operate in this context in their most absolute form – killing – thereby diminishing the importance of the usual care needed in the use of these categories for wider meanings. Killing constitutes the core of violence, *hiṃsā*, for speakers of Indo-Aryan languages, who see in it its primary definition. It also forms the constituent act of blood sacrifice, *bali dān*, regardless of the intentions or logic behind it, the context in which it is performed or any practices which may come to take its place.

In the pages that follow, we shall reconsider the sacrificial device by considering it from its core trait of violence, which is so visible in the unfolding of the ritual itself and yet so hidden in the texts devoted to it. In order to do so, we will attempt to tread the tightrope between an analytical distance, which has often denied the violent nature of such rituals, and a sensitive proximity, which enables one to measure their importance but does not allow understanding the mindsets of those who perform them. One way of getting around these two pitfalls is to consider the sacrifice in terms of its framing and acting out of violence, how violence is transformed by the sacrificial rituals, but also how they themselves are transformed, either when caught up in a violent movement or, alternatively, when the legitimacy of their violence is contested. Nepal offers all of these possibilities.

Questioning the violence of sacrifice is another way of looking at its effects – on those who practise it or attend the ceremony, on those who are enthusiastic about it or those who are so repulsed by it that both parties are likely to go into a trance. As the object of both fervour and horror, sacrifice evokes passionate feeling on both sides. Its intensity forces us to question what messages are conveyed by the brutality of the killing, as well as the strangeness of an oxymoronic practice that associates spirituality and bestiality, devotion and butchery, and which, as the Nepalis say, 'makes laugh and cry'.

Sacrifice in Nepal appears to be a device that creates both order, whereby each person is assigned a role according to his or her status, and disruption, as these roles can often be turned on their head throughout the course of ritual, and because it provokes opposite effects in the group. Despite the tensions it generates, sacrifice seems to hold an unstable equilibrium at its core, through its capacity to renew and replenish itself from the multiple threads of its construction. Such a multiplicity leaves questions about its nature unanswered: is sacrifice about offering something precious or about depriving oneself of it? Is it about eliminating an evil force or releasing one accumulated by the rite? Is it about showing brute force and arbitrary violence in order to consolidate power? Or is it to establish some sort of collective organisation through a bloody pact? Is it used to put everyone in their rightful place in a dramatic way? Or to publicly ostracise those who are excluded from the sacrifice? Is it an exchange? The settlement of a debt? A trial? The execution of an innocent being or of a guilty party? A military exercise? A butchery? Is it about offering one's own life through an *alter*? What links the person who offers the sacrifice, the person who sanctifies it, the one who executes it, the one who is offered and the one to whom the sacrifice is addressed? How do these roles merge, combine or oppose each other? Do they combine in a system where any and all arrangements are possible? How are substitutions carried out, based on which criteria? What relationships link sacrifice with myth and with the event, with the repetitive and with the contingent? Does the rite retain meaning when considered without the presence of the invisible? And how to admit the invisible without producing a new theology of sacrifice, or how not to admit it without producing a moral of sacrifice?

Our investigation will provide detailed answers to these questions, based on the practices observed among the caste groups and the indigenous peoples who inhabit the mountainous region of central and western Nepal, between the great Himalaya and its foothills. In the variety of forms that sacrifice takes there, where each group, each caste, and each religious community, clan or patrilineage cultivates its own ways of doing things, attention will focus on a practice long imposed on all by the government: the national festival of Dasaĩ, a bloody ceremony dedicated to the goddess Durgā (or *Durgā pūjā*), which calls for the decapitation of thousands of kid goats and culminates in the sacrifice of buffaloes.

Dasaĩ is a royal, civic and holistic sacrifice that involves the entire population in one way or another. In the region studied, the buffalo is only killed on this occasion, and all males of this species end up under the sacrificial cutlass. Dasaĩ can thus be considered a holistic sacrifice for humans and buffaloes alike. As ‘impure’ animals, they are seen as demons, incarnations of evil forces, and are killed as enemies. In this respect, the buffalo is opposed to the goat, which represents a pure offering whose death is mourned, and is presented to the Goddess in the name of the family, lineage or clan, rather than the community. The relationships that the sacrifice establishes with the categories of victims thus divide the world of the living into many spheres, where relationships of identity and power are played out.

In Nepal, buffalo sacrifice is linked to the history of the ancient warlike kingdoms that occupied the territory until their military conquest by the Gorkhā army in the late eighteenth century and the subsequent creation of the unified Kingdom of Nepal. Even today, in the capital as well as in each of the localities that once housed a palace or fort, great sacrificial gatherings are held at the time of Dasaĩ. These are solemn occasions that celebrate victory in war, and more especially the great battle led by the Goddess over the demonic forces headed by a buffalo-shaped demon. They take place to the sound of drums and brass instruments, in the midst of a dense crowd, where everyone puts on their finery or even their military decorations and where the ‘great men’ of the community squeeze into the front row. These rituals reveal the nature of power relations, in the distribution of roles, traditions and respects that must be correctly observed, while simultaneously reaffirming the status of each group through the various ritual tasks assigned to them. This sumptuous display of protocol and organisation draws attention away from the murderous act that forms the heart of the ceremony.

Sacrificial killing, an exemplary form of violence, is nevertheless a subject that has divided the Hindu world since ancient times and has contributed to the development of religious currents such as Buddhism. Nepal differs from neighbouring India in this respect, since despite the population being made up of approximately 10 per cent Buddhists, the practice of blood sacrifice here has never abated, while it has gradually disappeared in most parts of India. Vegetarian Vaishnavism and Shaivism never managed to develop in any meaningful sense in Nepal, a country strongly attached to the values of Śakta, which confer pre-eminence to the divine energy, *śakti*, which is materialised in the figure of the Goddess and maintained by sacrifice. Almost all gods receive blood sacrifices in Nepal, including Śiva, and the practice has been the subject of royal protection since ancient times. As far back as the seventeenth century, a local chronicle edited by Daniel Wright[1] reports that the king of Kathmandu had covered up an image of a ferocious form of Śiva to which blood sacrifices were offered so as to prevent the mockery of Indian visitors (Wright 1877: 214). It thus seems that it was preferable to conceal the identity of the god rather than to conform to an Indian orthodoxy.

It is only very recently, after 1990, that a movement challenging blood sacrifice has emerged in Nepal. Its arguments are certainly not new, but they simply did not have the means to be heard before the political liberalisation of the country, which, in that same year, put an end to the various authoritarian regimes that had muzzled the population: the Rana regime from 1846 to 1951 and then the partyless Panchayat regime (1961–1990), instituted by King Mahendra, under which Hinduism held the status of state religion and many sacrificial rites were financed by public funds.

With the political liberalisation of 1990, the legitimacy of sacrifice experienced its first challenges from two distinct groups: first, the newly created indigenous associations, whose attacks were aimed more at the national festival of Dasaĩ as a symbol of state Hinduism than at sacrifice as such and, second, a less formal but more pervasive group, who condemned the violence of animal sacrifice in general. The latter emerged during a period of influx of neo-Hindu currents from India and the rise of groups supported by international animal rights associations. Their campaigns, which are increasingly ubiquitous in Nepal, denounce cruelty towards animals, the unhygienic conditions of ritual slaughter, the impact of the violent spectacle on young people and even the damage to the image of the divine that blood sacrifice causes. Their voice in the ongoing public debate has continued to grow louder since the transformation of the Hindu kingdom into a republic 'without religious parties' in 2008. These groups do not, however, advocate for the abolition of sacrificial ritual entirely, but instead suggest substituting it with derivative forms, ranging from the execution of coconuts (which, ironically, often accompanies blood sacrifice already, as a substitute for human sacrifice) to the offering of flowers or money. Proponents of the non-violent ritual today find new ways to express themselves in a ritualised way, through women possessed by the

Goddess, who speak with the divine voice of She to whom the sacrifice is offered to condemn such rites at the great sacrificial sites.

As the protest against animal sacrifice started to take on a militant form, blood sacrifice found a particularly spectacular and highly valued resurgence in the martyrdom glorified by Maoist revolutionaries during the People's War from 1996 to 2006. During this ten-year period, the movement sought to equate its own bloody repression at the hands of forces of law and order with a symbolic sacrifice of the people perpetrated by the king, and proposed martyrdom, the supreme sacrifice, as a counter-sacrifice by which the victims become the agents of their own death and thus divert its meaning.

Much like the sacrifice of the buffalo, which is presented as the killing of an enemy, the sacrifice of the martyr is a tool of war, with the key difference being that the former has long obliged all men to take on roles determined by caste, rank and gender, whereas martyrdom is offered as a possibility which is open to all, regardless of social status. From being a holistic practice aimed at reaffirming political power and social organisation, with the personalisation of martyrdom, sacrifice has to all intents and purposes become the instrument of its deconstruction, in a kind of antithetical transformation. Self-sacrifice has undermined the 'royal' sacrifice with a more radical violence, by getting rid of substitutes – animal or vegetable – as well as any clearly defined temporal or spatial framework and specific divine recipients, thus becoming universal.

Armed violence, when understood as a magnified form of sacrifice, allows the usually limited, regulated and controlled domain of the sacrificial rite to invade the social field. This adds an exciting force to the effectiveness of religious forms while opening channels of projection into a transcendent domain – that of higher forces or causes – which both determines the form of the violence and gives it meaning. Within its framework, each participant takes part in an enterprise whose disturbing nature – since there is an unavoidable loss of life at the heart of any sacrificial rite – is overcome in order to achieve a goal relating to the wider world order, whether it is to strengthen it, as in royal sacrifice, or to transform it, as in revolutionary sacrifice.

In the case of royal sacrifice, the form is ceremonial, the killing is limited and targeted, the time is fixed and each role is determined. The revolutionary context seems, on the other hand, to be informal, ruled by unorganised spontaneity and popular impulse, and the associated sacrificial death becomes generalised and thus possible, albeit not certain, for all. If revolutionary martyrdom borrows from the former, notably in its vocabulary, it is still not entirely conditioned by long-held traditions of ideas relating to sacrifice. Certainly, the Hindu religious domain is so vast that it could well include any form of sacrifice, including the sudden expansion of the sacrificial register through war. However, it must be made clear that the revolutionary movement differs from war in that it formalises the confrontation between two opposing societal models, each carrying a form of sublimated violence called 'sacrifice': one based on a hierarchical social organisation, the other its disorganisation; one which stages sacrificial violence in a limited, codified and controlled manner as an expression of its power over others, the other which deploys it in all foreseeable directions to put an end to the former, requiring self-sacrifice in order to achieve this aim.

The importance of examining the reciprocal links between violence and sacrifice is thus incumbent on anyone working on the contemporary period in Nepal. Blood offerings are to be found everywhere in the country, in the ordinary practices of the householder as well as in collective ceremonies or even certain regional cults, where the killings can reach astronomical figures, such as the 250,000 to 500,000 animals offered to the goddess Gaḍhī Māī during her cultic ceremonies held once every five years, not to mention the 20,000 (human) deaths of the People's War, whose entire ideology was couched in sacrificial terms.

Despite the numerous manifestations of this close link between sacrifice and violence in Nepal, following such a thread is a departure from the 'traditional' Hindu view, which does not recognise the violence of sacrifice as such. For conservative or traditional pandits, sacrifice, much like wars fought for so-called just causes, does not make use of 'ordinary' violence, but of what they call 'Vedic violence'. Similarly, for the Maoists, violence is primarily considered to be the social oppression that develops in times of peace, whereas the sacrifice of revolutionaries is a form of renunciation necessary to bring about a better, classless society.

To posit violence as the essential character of sacrifice also departs from most anthropological theories on such a practice, which rarely discuss violence or, when they do take it into account, see sacrifice as a means of expunging it. This is not a question, however, of adopting the type of ethical approach that tends to associate animal sacrifice with a form of terror or barbarism, in line with views expressed before the rise of anthropology. The central contribution of the discipline, since the publication of the founding essay by Hubert and Mauss, has been the effort anthropologists have made to get inside the sacrificers' heads, and such a decentred approach remains fundamental. However, anthropology has not fully considered the divisive nature of sacrifice within the very group that practises it, nor the variety of perceptions associated with it. Observation of rituals in Nepal, and, crucially, listening to what the Nepalis have to say about them, suggests that the perspective of the sacrificers is not hegemonic, even within contexts of holistic sacrifice.

It further appears that the different views on sacrifice are not randomly distributed, and that their correlations – to the position of the group within society and of the individual within the group, to local and national history, to thc realities of myth, to particular collective circumstances and situations – all form some of the constitutive characters of sacrifice. In this field, as in so many others, sacrifice is nebulous and difficult to pin down. It is seen as an effective device and its fundamental principles are rarely contested beyond the reservations expressed about killing. This means that anyone can make use of sacrificial rites should they need to, despite what they may say or think about them. Finally, there is the more troubling idea that sacrifice is an imposed reality, because the world is ultimately a vast sacrificial scene from which there is no escape.

One day, while seated on the steps above the temple of the bloody goddess Dakṣiṇ Kālī, next to pastry sellers who had set up their stall there, I observed devotees in the distance approaching the shrine, pulling their goats towards the place of sacrifice (see Figure I.1). They were slaughtered by three muscular priests, soundtracked to a macabre chorus of bleating. In the midst of all this were to be found a few couples decked in brocaded garments, since Dakṣiṇ Kālī is also a shrine where lovers come to marry in secret. Pointing to the scene, which seemed so unreal to me, I asked the pastry sellers, 'What do you think?' Both of them answered vehemently: 'We don't want to see that and that's why we have set up shop here, even if we have fewer customers.' – 'Don't you think the goats offered to the Goddess go to heaven, *svarga*?' – 'To heaven? By dying like this? No, they probably go to hell, *narka*. Only flowers and incense should be offered. Look, some of them are still babies!' A couple passed us, and I told them that they should buy something from the stall, making the women laugh. They suggested that we go down the stairs for a cup of tea, and we talked about other things, in front of the big trees of the forest surrounding the Goddess. Becoming suddenly pensive and pointing her cup in the direction of the woods, one of them blurted out: 'Last year, one of these trees fell and killed two people. If you don't sacrifice to the Goddess, she does it herself.' She was correcting herself on the subject of sacrifice, suggesting that, after all, it exists whether we like it or not, whether we want it or not, and that there is a global economy of sacrifice according to which humans become the victims when they stop sacrificing animals.

When Nepalis are asked about their reasons for offering sacrifice, they often mention a promise made to the deity, *bhākal*, or what can be referred to as their 'religiosity' or 'trust', *biśvās*, their respect for tradition, *pāraṃpara*, and,

Figure I.1 Pastry sellers who expressed their dislike of sacrifice, Dakshin Kali, 2009

Source: Author.

more generally, the need to sacrifice in order to please the gods. Put together, these motives mean that sacrifice is considered a matter of trust, a need to satisfy invisible powers through communication channels established long ago. More precisely, those who practise sacrifice consider it the most effective way to please the invisible powers. This is done to obtain something from them in return or, more often, in thanks for a request already granted, or to appease them and contain their wrath. Whatever the ritual occasion at which it is practised, be it collective or individual, regular or extraordinary, blood sacrifice takes place only after the animal has been purified, a gesture which the Nepalis explain as a way to test whether the deity to whom they address themselves is duly satisfied. Is she or he *khuśiyālī*, happy? Is she or he *prasanna*, satisfied? She or he will say so by causing the animal's body to tremble before it is put to death and will further inscribe the fate of humans in its liver, to be read upon its removal. The priests and sacrificators are purported to gain merit and prestige from the sacrifice, and the sponsors (or sacrifiers) the fulfilment of their wishes and, for a minority of those I interviewed, the victim itself will gain a better fate, whether it be by being transported to a heavenly abode, obtaining immortality or a higher rebirth. (I use the term 'sacrificator' to specifically designate the person who puts the animal to death in order to restore its centrality in the context of the study, where the practice often happens without any other officiant. Sacrifier ['sacrifiant' in French] is used for the person who offers an animal as a sacrifice, while the meaning of the term 'sacrificer' is less defined. Here, I use it in a general sense for the adepts of blood sacrifice and, in a more restricted one, for those who are directly involved in such a ritual.)

For a long time, scholars who have studied sacrifice have not radically departed from the above perspective, proposing interpretations that do not acknowledge the violence of the act at the heart of the ritual and the role that it might play for the group, but have instead emphasised the benefits that they might derive from it, through the notions of exchange, gift, communion, mediation or distancing. All these perspectives, from practitioners and academics alike, focus on the ultimate effect of sacrifice, its teleology, with the main difference being that the practitioners of the rite emphasise the effect it produces on the gods, whereas the analytical perspective disregards invisible recipients, reducing sacrifice to a practice aimed at producing a positive effect on the human collective. In the first (religious) perspective, the 'community' involved in sacrifice can encompass humans and the world they inhabit as a whole, but it can also be reduced to a circumscribed unit, ranging from the individual to the village, a particular domestic group or members of a neighbourhood, whereas the second (scholarly) perspective sets the group as an abstract entity, without taking its various configurations, the contrasting ways in which sacrifice operates within it, the affects observable during the sacrifice or what the various participants may say about it into consideration.

And yet sacrifice is something whereby everyone is impressed. We might even be tempted to use a definition from the world of art and say that blood sacrifice is a religious practice which aims at producing an effect, any effect. This is due not only to the brutal exhibition of death, but also to the contradictions which inform blood sacrifice. What could be more disturbing than non-violent violence, the execution of an innocent-yet-condemned being, a life-giving murder and a joyful death?

Faced with such sacrificial oxymorons, with this sacred horror, we might be tempted to proceed, as Kierkegaard did with Abraham's sacrifice, by proposing a series of readings offering a stream of different possible scenarios, without choosing any one in particular, because each only proffers a partial image. To consider blood sacrifice solely as an exercise aimed at reaffirming the cohesion of the group or its communion with the divine strips it of its repulsive, even terrorising, character for certain factions of the population. Conversely, to consider it purely as an instrument of terror or domination disregards its devotional aspect and its festive framework.

However, as anthropologists, we have other paths to follow, beyond the study of texts which describe either past or codified forms of sacrifice, or contemporary writings that denounce its violence. We can, for instance, explore the relations between the narrative form of the sacrificial model and its ceremonial actualisations, and between the latter and larger socio-political organisations. We can investigate the performance of the ritual itself, in terms of its micro-events, the body language observed, the remarks or the views expressed. In Nepal, one often hears people say that the beheading of victims, especially buffaloes, 'gets them used to the sight of blood' and thus allows them to wage war. Sometimes, too, during the performance of such sacrifices, one overhears snippets from women who quietly lament that humans behave towards animals like *rākṣas*, those bloodthirsty demons who feast on human flesh. Such impassioned reactions are often diametrically opposed to the joy expressed by these same people a few hours later at the banquet, something I myself experienced.

These differing reactions of community members thus illustrate the oscillatory movement that sacrifice produces, by presenting it at a given moment as a practice which is so disturbing as to transform the character of those who engage in it. These idle words underline how sacrifice acts on the ontology of humans, blurring ordinary categories, by framing the man who kills a 'demon' as a 'demon' himself, one who kills an animal, or as a man now capable of killing his fellow man. The demonic or brutal transformations mentioned here form a counterpoint to the transportation of the sacrifier towards a celestial abode as mentioned in the Brahmanic texts, and its associated danger of not being able to return to his human and earthly condition at the end of the sacrifice, for which he must protect himself by paying a sacrificial fee (Malamoud 1980). These conflicting comments and the viewpoints they represent open up to a baser realm of sacrifice, which coexists with its more celestial counterpart, in changing imbrications according to which participants are partaking in different circumstances.

While distanced views on sacrifice all tend to whitewash its violence, many archetypal forms of killing are attributed a sacred and foundational character, notably in the case of myths. The disciplines that study them have also drawn up mythico-historical schemes aimed at explaining the root of all human societies by one original, unique and universal sacrificial phenomenon. This is particularly true among authors who could be qualified as 'mythical', for the vaunted place they occupy in the pantheon of human sciences. Consider the murder of the father by the primitive horde which, for Freud (1960 [1912–13]), is the origin of the rules of social and religious life, or else the killing of the king which, for Frazer and, following him, Maurice Hocart, is the origin of royalty itself, or the elimination of the scapegoat which, for René Girard, is the engine of social cohesion. Even Claude Lévi-Strauss's 'exchange' of women (1949) could be read in this way, at least from a Hindu perspective, where the gift of a daughter by her father on the occasion of her marriage is clearly akin to her sacrifice.

The murder of the father is an imaginary figure which can be used as a model of liberating, transgressive violence. Freud himself did so, when he saw in the Russian Revolution and the assassination of the tsar the realisation of the myth of the primitive horde where the brothers join together to kill the father. For Hocart, on the other hand, the death of the king seems to have neither a sponsor nor an executor and does not take on a liberating character: its value lies in its capacity to confer the sacredness necessary for kingship to be constituted in the first place, even if it does not explain why death, which affects all living beings, should lead to such a concentration of sacredness in the person of a particular deceased individual. The important thing for Hocart is to show that kingship, like a society organised around the principle of a caste system, is purely ritualistic in nature. This is a thesis that deserves to be discussed in the light of the data from Nepal, the only Hindu kingdom that has never been placed under the tutelage of a foreign power and where the caste organisation remained enshrined in law until 1963. In contrast to these models, where the identity of the person killed is primordial (be it the father or the king), other theorists give primacy to the very act of killing itself in the emergence of the sacred, such as Burkert (1972/1986), who posits hunting as the archetypal model of sacrifice. René Girard's approach (1972) continues along this path with the killing of a scapegoat by a community, which he in turn sets up as the archetype of ritual and sacrificial violence.

In these models, there is no room for personal initiatives and strategies, for discordant voices or even for the particularities of social organisation. The drama takes place in a world peopled by interchangeable beings, and the killing of the king, the father, the game or the scapegoat assumes a singular role, that of social regulator, without any explicit mention of violence. Indeed, even the Girardian approach, which seems to acknowledge the centrality of violence, accords with most theories of sacrifice, which see it primarily as a procedure aimed at ensuring the unity of the group. This contradiction is clearly expressed when, following René Girard, Lucien Scubla (1999) suggests breaking with the long tradition of denial of sacrificial violence by opposing it with a conception of sacrifice as a violent act. However, the thesis he develops then seems to merge with the very idea he is fighting against, since he goes on to explain that sacrifice ultimately comes to contain the violence that would otherwise threaten to spread exponentially in the absence of formal control mechanisms. The author attaches so much value to this principle that he suggests that the 'bloodier' (or more violent) the sacrifice, the more effective it is, so that the sacrifice of plants, which would not fulfil this function, would 'again' expose a community to the spread of violence.

Underlying this idea of the control of collective violence with the help of sacrifice, there is the notion of the danger of the war of all against all, an imaginary monstrosity of generalised violence invented by Hobbes, in the name of which all 'ordering' violence is seen as a healthy mechanism of regulation. The opposite scenario is hardly ever considered, although there is an abundance of examples where conflicts or wars have been initiated by a sacrifice, not to mention the many armed movements which present themselves as sacrificial crusades.

It is not, however, a question of defending the idea that sacrifice necessarily propagates violence, but of abandoning a binary vision based on a careful selection of facts to demonstrate that sacrifice is a machine for either absorbing violence or, on the contrary, generating it. We are then left with a ritual device which resorts to violence, by both exercising and exposing it, and which also seems able to act upon it. Of these three actions, the last is of particular interest. Sacrifice, both in its narrative forms and in its ritual expressions, indeed seems to be able to act upon violence through the use of violence itself, in a range of different ways.

The Brahmins, these 'gods on earth' whose killing carries the heaviest of karmic burdens, have spread the threat of righteous suicide in an effort to put an end to violence, conflict or abuse of power. The practice of hunger strike follows the same line of thought in a more inclusive and universal manner. It is used today in Nepal with success. For example, in February 2019, the surgeon Govinda K. C. (who is not a Brahmin but represents a modern-day equivalent, as an embodiment of righteousness) began his sixteenth hunger strike in order to obtain medical sector reforms from the Nepalese government. In contrast, buffalo sacrifice has long served as a prelude to war in Nepal and, in some regions, still takes the form of a massacre where sacrificators fight among themselves for the privilege of being recognised as the killers of the buffaloes released into the crowd. This emphasises how sacrifice can trigger generalised forms of violence, either during the ritual itself or in its aftermath. The two examples cited mirror one another:

the self-sacrificial 'one against all' aimed at putting an end to a situation of general violence is in contrast to the sacrificial 'all against one' which initiates generalised violence.

The violence of 'all against one' seems to represent the very image of sacrifice, if we simplify it to an opposition between a group and a victim. This structure manifests itself in the murder of the father as exposed by Freud, where the violence of the brothers converges towards their progenitor, who subordinates them all, at least from a generational point of view. This configuration is also found in the violence towards the king, who, like the father, subjugates the others, and then more generally in the elimination of the 'model-obstacle to the desire of all', as René Girard puts it.

In Hindu mythology, the convergence of divine forces to defeat a higher entity is the fundamental architecture behind the creation of the Supreme Power, or Adi Śakti, who manifests in the form of the Goddess. Created by the gods to destroy the buffalo-demon that they cannot defeat, she channels their combined forces and annihilates the enemy. This is also the model of royal sacrifice in Nepal, which symbolically plays out this fight each year by the killing of the buffalo.

However, when this mythical model is transposed into the sacrificial ceremonies at the heart of the former royal capitals and in the main sanctuaries dedicated to the Goddess, it undergoes a number of transformations. The most notable of these is the shift of roles of the Goddess, who, from being the executor of the killing in the myth, becomes its recipient in the ritual, leaving her original place vacant. The king, or whoever serves in his stead, seizes it, and this move reorders the sacrifice according to the local organisation of power. This is achieved either by concentrating it, that is, by the 'king' carrying out the killing himself, like the Goddess in the myth, as is the case in the ancient royal capital of Musikot; or by delegating the right to kill to a representative, to a champion from the warrior caste, which is the most common case; or by distributing this right to all the Kshatriyas; or even by granting this right to all the men without distinction of caste or rank. This last practice, observed in far western Nepal, is in strict opposition to the concentration which gives birth to the Goddess in the original myth, since instead of an attribution of all weapons and all forces to a single figure, we witness here a distribution en masse by the king of the power to kill.

In the abstract model of the convergence of forces, of all against one, sacrificial violence affects a realm situated outside of the group, which determines and constrains it, leading to a reconfiguration of reality. Conversely, when this model of all against one is imported from outside the group and moves from being a mythical model to a socio-political reality, it swells to fit its local organisation and becomes a conservatory factor, thereby assuring its own renewal.

Indeed, the buffalo sacrifice renews all – it opens a new cycle of annual time, a new season, and restarts all individual karmas and all inter-individual relations. By its blood, or the vermilion that takes its place, the peasants restore vigour to their tools, the workers to their machines, the drivers to their cars, the pilots to their planes, the schoolchildren to their slates and the pandits to their texts. In the same way, all hierarchical relations are similarly revived, starting with the public sphere, before continuing within each lineage and each household.

This foundational gesture of the killing of the buffalo, repeated every year, thus initiates the renewal of all things, from the reign of the king to the cycle of nature, as well as the occupations and status of each individual, in a model that perpetually self-reproduces. Could it be, as Edmund Leach (1976: 83) puts it, because the killing of the animal causes a principle or a soul to escape, and that this soul alone is able to pass from the world of ordinary reality to another world? But then, in this case why would this passage cause a renewal of the world of ordinary reality, in contrast with natural death that also liberates the soul? Is it because it is manmade? Could it be, as Hubert and Mauss (1899) thought, that the death of the animal unloads the energies accumulated by the consecration onto or into the person of the sacrifier and the community he represents? We must therefore ask: Is this process universal or only present during the royal buffalo sacrifice? Could this renewal be due to the sacrifice being a repetition of a divine model? But is not every sacrifice, by definition, the repetition of a model?

The temporal cycles generated by the iterative actualisation of the creation of Supreme Power by the buffalo sacrifice have something in common with the 'rebounding violence' identified by Maurice Bloch (1992). This process is aimed at denying the natural process of the weakening of the organism through old age and death and is constituted by a double cycle of violence expressed in the rituals: a first form of violence, such as fasting, aimed at weakening the person's vital energy, followed by a second form of violence exerted on an external being or thing, which would restore energy in superabundance. This rebounding violence would make it possible to create a process which is autonomous from reality and thus able to act upon it.

In the sacrifice of the buffalo, the annual actualisation of the mythical sacrifice brings about the fusion of the present with a timeless, abyssal and foundational time. These two temporalities merge at the precise moment of the killing of the animal, which, like a quilting point, to paraphrase Lacan, connects one with the other. This eternal youth created by sacrificial violence prevents time from slipping away and tethers it to its starting point. The moment of fusion is determined by humans, who calculate the auspicious moment to conduct the ceremony, triangulated from their position in time and space. They thus ensure control over the degradation of the time which passes through the sacrificial 'loop', thereby making time cyclical. However, the effect of the sacrifice is not just temporal.

During the ceremony, violence itself traverses the different planes of reality – the real, the ritual (or the intersection of the real and the invisible) and the invisible – which it binds together and acts upon. This action causes the real, which has become the ritual, to actualise the invisible.

While it binds these planes together, sacrificial violence also reinforces the reality of each of these planes individually, and this to a greater degree than any other ritual practice.

Sacrificial killing, as an act of visible, factual and definitive violence, subjects ordinary reality to an extreme intensification by solemnly revealing its ultimate end point, through the figure of the being whose life is taken. The death of a living being is a *nitya pralaya*, an 'individual end of the world', which is an expression of the end of time itself. Sacrificial killing also reinforces the reality of the rite, making it a matter of life or death, stripping it of its semblance of masquerade, of its pomp and circumstance. Finally, putting a living creature to death as a gift confers a very strong reality on the invisible for whom a being is deprived of its life.

Everything which occurs in the course of the sacrificial ceremony contributes to this intensification process that the killing inflicts on the three realities that it brings together: the tightened circle that forms as the execution approaches, the powerful, haunting beating of the drums, the silence and attentiveness of the participants in expectation of the quivering of the animal as a sign of acquiescence, the 'spontaneous' possessions that occur in the audience and, finally, the shock of the decapitation.

The effects of the sacrifice are then very real, not only for the victim, of course, but also on those who participate in the ceremony. The crowd, which has gathered silently until this point, starts moving in all directions as soon as the act is accomplished, some to trace a bloody enclosure on the ground with the rest of the victim's blood, by dragging its beheaded, still bleeding body around the sacrificial post or the temple, the others to mark their foreheads with its blood or to plunge their hands into it and mark their bloody imprint on the temple; one seizes the head and lays it down as an offering; others run away with cutlass, logs, basins and leaf-plates and head to where the animal will be cut up. Between the extreme concentration that precedes the killing and the agitation that follows, the moment of the execution itself exists in a sort of suspended time, where the expression of emotions is momentarily obscured by everyone's attention to the act in progress. Yet a wide range of emotions are expressed in the crowd, from an explosion of joy to a pout of horror, a gaze alternately fixed and averted, with faces sometimes even covered by hands.

The contrast between the different emotional and bodily affects aroused by sacrificial killing suggests that the all-against-one model only gives an artificial image of the sacrifice, since it indiscriminately blends the participants into a single unit, where in fact there is diversity, even if only in terms of body language (see Figure I.2). In some localities, the reactions of the crowd are even presented by the ritual's participants as being diametrically opposed, so as to highlight the division of the assembly in 'those who laugh and those who cry', which exposes the opposition of pure and impure castes. This contrasting effect the buffalo sacrifice has on the different categories of participants reveals the chiasmus at the heart of the act of violence. But there is nothing which is either definitive or consensual, and this rift of affect often lasts only a brief moment, or flits in and out of existence like a flame, in the same way as the rules of sacrifice are always determined, but change depending on each particular context.

The case of Sita, a medium woman in her forties, introduces one of the common modalities of sacrifice. Possessed by a bloodthirsty form of the Goddess, Sita holds consultations in the city of Pokhara. As I tried to get her to talk about the blood sacrifices her patron deity demands, her answers to my questions were always the same: Kālīkā eats meat and she must be fed. It does not matter whether the animal consents to the sacrifice, whether it is better for it to end up this way or in some other way, Kālīkā is hungry. And, 'as we eat rice and lentils, she needs blood sacrifices'. The more one offers sacrifices, the more she is satisfied and the more she sends her blessings. Sita, even though she is a Brahmin, told me that one day the Goddess asked her to offer her a *pañcabali*, a set of five sacrifices. She had no choice but to comply, but with apprehension because Kālīkā is especially fond of buffalo meat, which is polluting to high-caste people like Sita. 'I couldn't offer her a buffalo, she would have said to me: eat it,' she specified.

As Sita's embarrassment illustrates, blood sacrifice violates the natural order of things and puts humans in something of a dilemma. Sita is in direct relationship with the Goddess who takes possession of her body and speaks both to her and through her daily. If she were to offer her the forbidden meat, she feels she would have no choice but to accept the *prasād*, 'ritual remains', of the Goddess and eat them, which would cause her to lose her social status. Faced with this challenge, this sort of double-edged sacrifice that the Goddess demanded of her, Sita chose

Figure I.2 The effects of sacrifice. The top photograph shows a he-goat and its vegetable double, both placed next to the sacrificial post. The policeman on the left laughs as he watches the scene. The bottom image shows a detail from the next photo taken during the execution of the goat. The same policeman grimaces, while his colleague, staring at the horizon, smiles.

Source: Author.

to evade it by offering five beings who were acceptable to both her and her divine Mother, while still fearful of transgressing the Goddess's demands. Nothing happened, but to hear Sita justify herself, we understand that, for her, there is still the threat of danger. The possible deferred consequences of her evasiveness obviously continue to haunt her and are likely to give a deeper meaning to the vagaries of her personal history.

The act of sacrifice thus subjects humans to the test of transgression. In the form we are looking at, where the victim is a buffalo, it consists of offering an impure animal who is likely to lead to a particularly repulsive fate, that of being transformed into an 'untouchable'. This danger threatens the sacrifier when the rule followed is 'the one who offers must eat'. Sometimes, especially in mythical narratives, the danger is transferred to the sacrificator, with the rule 'he who kills must eat'. In a few rare localities, an exception is made for impure sacrificed meat, which can be consumed, but, most often, the buffalo meat remains impure, and it is neither the one who offers the animal nor the one who kills it who takes the impurity of the sacrifice upon themselves. Those who are impure by birth and excluded from either making offerings or sacrificing consume the blessed but impure meat. In this way, only a collective which brings together individuals of different castes can carry out the buffalo sacrifice while respecting the rules and without affecting anyone's status.

There do exist many more absolute forms of sacrificial transgression demanded by certain deities, such as requests for the sacrifice of bulls or even human beings, but to stick to the 'royal' sacrifice of the buffalo, only an association of castes can adequately carry out its execution. This necessity means that the buffalo sacrifice is an activity of a collective, complementary and even political nature, since it requires the coordination of at least three major caste groups: Brahmin priests, Kshatriya sacrificators and Untouchable recipients of the impure offerings.

The ability to organise sacrifice therefore demonstrates a power over society in its entirety, and its importance in the sphere of political power, which is nourished and perpetuated by blood sacrifice, is therefore not accidental. In one fell swoop, the buffalo sacrifice reinforces the power of action over others, both as a practice that reconfirms individuals' position in society and as the ultimate form of legitimate violence. Coming perilously close to transgressive violence, it is situated in a troubled hinterland, where something out of the ordinary is conferred upon the person who has been given the right to kill, as if the rule of law no longer applied to them. We can better understand why some participants cry while others laugh by examining how this right to kill an animal is experienced indirectly as a form of killing of themselves by certain categories of the population.

Before we delve further into this issue, we first need to justify the association we make here between violence and sacrifice, because the latter does not necessarily involve the killing of a living being – at least not in any real sense – and is defined in its most general sense as a gift or an abnegation. Indeed, the term 'sacrifice', whose Latin etymology means 'to make sacred', covers a vast semantic field. However, in the Nepalese context of our current study, this field is classified into different categories, such as renunciation, or *tyāg*, donation, or *dān*, sacrifice to the sacred fire, or *hom*, Brahmanic sacrifice, or *jagge* or *yagya* (which Nepalis define as a 'ceremony under a pavilion', a building called a *jagge* in Nepali); finally, the notion most commonly translated as 'sacrifice', *bali dān*, is defined as the offering of a living being through its killing. All of these fields are intertwined, but *bali dān* is distinguished by the clarity of its definition.

In the majority of cases, *bali dān* is a sudden killing, by decapitation. The execution is preceded by a period of suspense, while waiting for a sign of acceptance from the victim. They must visibly shiver after having been doused with water on their neck by the sacrifier, or sometimes by the Brahmin priest if it is a collective rite. This process distinguishes the sacrifice from the gift, *dān*, which is also accompanied by a libation, in the case of a gift of land for example, but where no sign of the acceptance of the thing offered is expected in return. In the *bali dān*, the libation has numerous dimensions: it is at once a purification, the moment when the sacrifier mentally announces his intention to offer the sacrifice and when he forms a particular request to the deity in his mind, and it also represents that decisive moment when the possibility of offering the animal is put into question. The execution is contingent on the visible trembling of the victim, and whether this trembling is understood as a response from the animal or from the deity to whom it is offered, the blood sacrifice cannot be accomplished without this communication.

If this sign is not observed, the victim is spared, which means that the giver's intentionality is not sufficient for the sacrifice to take place and that another, non-human, intentionality, takes precedence over the first and must be evidenced in supplement. Thus, strictly speaking, only blood sacrifice corresponds to the definition of sacrifice given by Hubert and Mauss (1994 [1899]: 302), as 'a process that consists of establishing communication between the sacred world and the profane world through the intermediary of a victim'. In the Nepalese context, communication is a sine qua non condition for sacrifice. It humanises and sets the victim apart within the category of its fellows. For those who believe that it is the victim who responds to the question asked through the libation, its response even qualifies the sanctified animal as a conscious subject, who offers itself willingly to die. This view, which is often found in the writings of ethnologists, is not, however, unanimously accepted in Nepal, and is in fact a rather uncommon opinion. Most of the Nepalis I interviewed, on the contrary, consider that it is the deity who manifests their acceptance of the animal presented to them, while only a small minority see a simple, kneejerk reaction to contact with water, which forces the victim to attempt to shake it off. All interviewees, and this is most striking, were surprised when asked this question. They apparently had no preconceived ideas about the issue and needed time to mull it over before answering. The problem of the extent to which communication is constitutive of the blood sacrifice thus seems doubly uncertain, but as much as the question 'Will there be an answer?' is very much at stake, the question of 'Who is answering?', which is devoid of consequence, is never asked. The agency of the being who communicates by the trembling, an act which conditions the sacrifice, thus remains undetermined, the important thing being that it manifests in the first place. If it does not, the reason will be searched for in a number of lines of enquiry: is the animal defective, or is the sacrifier pure, or is the sacrifice blocked by another power that has not yet received a previously promised sacrifice?

Unlike the Brahmanic *jagge* ceremonies, conducted by Brahmin priests with the help of ritual manuals that set out the ingredients, acts and words to be used, as well as explaining the various stages to be followed, blood sacrifice in Nepal does not follow a single set of instructions. It instead follows inherited rules, sometimes rather unique, and unfolds in a cloud of unknowing, where paradoxes are left unresolved. For example, it aims to materially nourish entities whose corporeality is immaterial without the practitioners dwelling on this quandary. They offer the divinity a victim whose flesh is actually polluting for the priests, the sacrifiers and the sacrificators alike, seemingly without any questioning of this contradiction. These unanswered questions are, however, sufficiently disturbing for some to seek to resolve them by mobilising intermediary entities between humans and the divinity, that is, demons, to whom animal sacrifice would be exclusively addressed, in order to make sure they are satisfied when honouring the divinity they accompany.

Sacrifice can be requested by the deity in order to test the devotee, as one of the terms of a devil's bargain, where the devotee is given the choice between a sacrifice with harmful consequences for him or her, such as degradation or death, and the realisation of their dearest wish. And in desperate situations, Nepalis promise sacrifices in exchange for divine intervention, without always properly assessing the consequences, since these commitments, *bhākal*, lead to madness or misfortune for those who do not honour their word. In this way, the sacrificial contract becomes a test equal to the ordeal it is answering to. The binding nature of the sacrifice is finally expressed in the compulsory participation in the buffalo sacrifice, imposed on the entire population of Nepal, including Indigenous peoples (*janajāti*), Buddhists and Muslims. In all such cases, sacrificial violence is therefore one which responds to or uses another type of violence to come to fruition, through the use of ordeal and coercion.

Violence thus informs blood sacrifice from all sides: through the enforcement of various ordeals or by coercion, then by having to put a living being to death and, finally, through the terrorising and stigmatising effects sacrifice has on some members of the population. Violence, in its derivative form of coercion, spares no one in the collective rite where participation is mandatory for all. It then becomes selective and absolute, when the victim is targeted, alone against a crowd, by the ultimate act of killing itself. Blood sacrifice then produces, through the execution of the victim in the middle of the entire community, a prismatic effect whose spectrum follows the partition lines of a caste-based society, lines which divide the pure and impure, men and women, Hindus and Indigenous peoples, as we shall examine in the pages which follow.

With violence as our guiding thread, we will first seek to identify the difficulties that it raises as a category of analysis and the specific characteristics that are attributed to violence in a sacrificial context. We will then examine the place given to violence in the main theories of sacrifice, focusing more specifically on the founding essay by Hubert and Mauss and on the works of Charles Malamoud devoted to Vedic India. Thereafter we will examine ethnographic material, approaching it through the various narratives which expose the patterns of sacrifice and form the framework of thought, and also through the performance of the vernacular epic, which generates emotion and further highlights the effect of violence. After examining the partition lines that sacrifice traces in society, we will focus on the sacrificial rite of Dasaĩ, using a comparative description, so as to contrast the different ways in which violence is processed and distributed, perceived and received within the community. Rather than concentrating on the details of the procedures of the rite itself, we propose to consider the back and forth between the practices and what is said about them by ordinary participants and then also by the groups who are today making their voices heard in contesting the validity of the sacrifice. Finally, we will follow the evolution of sacrifice in its contemporary forms, through the Maoist mystical sacrifice, or martyrdom, as expressed in the stories and writings of the fighters who waged the People's War.

The ways in which revolutionary self-sacrifice has been constructed to garner support for the cause and as a tool for delegitimising animal sacrifice deserves attention, not only because it has led to the most important restructuring of Nepal's political history in modern times, but also for the possibility it offers of studying the concrete ways in which it was disseminated throughout the region.

Although it was not possible to conduct an ethnography within the Maoist armed organisation, alternative approaches, such as the study of its clandestine literature, observation in localities under Maoist control and interviews with party members, were used. Finally, my close relationship with the villagers of the locality where I resided for a long time in the 1980s, which had become a 'Maoist model village', provided a privileged gateway to investigate the fate of sacrifice during the People's War.

Note

1. A British doctor who stayed in Kathmandu from 1866 to 1876 (Bajracharya and Michaels 2012: 85).

1

A violence that is not violence

To offer in sacrifice or to offer oneself in sacrifice are both rendered by the Nepali phrase 'to offer a *bali dān*', *bali dān caḍāune*.[1] In this compound, *dān* designates the gift, while the meaning of *bali* is less well defined.[2] It derives, according to the majority of the villagers I interviewed, from *bal*, which means 'strength'. This is a popular etymology, far from its attested meaning in Sanskrit, where the term simply means 'offering'. The local interpretation thus sheds light on sacrifice as it is understood in contemporary Nepal, as a 'gift of strength', through the death inflicted on a 'breathing being', *prāṇi*, whether it be animal or human. The phrase sometimes also applies to the sacrifice of plants, such as squash or coconuts, insofar as these are explicitly presented as substitutes for *prāṇi* beings.

Bali dān refers to death inflicted in two specific contexts: sacrifice and war. In the former, death is inflicted upon another being, while in warfare *bali dān* refers to the act of offering one's own life. At least, this is the meaning which prevails today. The more ancient, reciprocal version of this transaction in the context of war, where both killing and being killed were equated with sacrifice, no longer holds true. This reciprocity can still be found in the oral epics of western Nepal and is also found in a number of testimonies dating from the pre-unification period (before the nineteenth century), when the captured enemy was offered in sacrifice. For instance, a chronicle of the second half of the nineteenth century reports that in 1660, the king of Bhaktapur attacked a stronghold of the king of Kathmandu and captured twenty-one prisoners, whom he had beheaded as a sacrifice to the deities of his kingdom the following day (Wright 1877: 244). A century later, a Capuchin father also witnessed the offering of enemies at the temple of a goddess in the Kathmandu Valley. And the inhabitants of Pyuthan (mid-western Nepal) have to this day kept the memory alive of the old practice of collecting the enemy's blood in *pokhāri*, ritual ponds which are today filled with water but still have a sacrificial post staked in their centres.[3]

We may add that if the warlike *bali dān* is now understood as the offering of one's own life, it is nevertheless seen as a gift that strengthens the group, instead of weakening it, and which therefore follows the sacrificial principle stating that benefit derives from destruction.

The term *bal* found in *bali dān* refers to muscular strength and, by extension, also denotes an armed force. But it is not so much this strength that is at play in *bali dān*, for when the Nepalis are questioned on this point, they specify that sacrificial execution requires not so much physical strength as 'strength of heart'. One officiant insisted on its importance and I asked him what a 'strong-hearted' person, *muṭu baliyo*, could accomplish. He answered: 'It enables the person to kill, to climb rock faces or not to be afraid to speak.' This particular strength, the courage needed in order to sacrifice a being, brings in return a force of another kind, namely *śakti*.

Depicted as a divine force or energy that manifests itself in everyday life and in every endeavour of all beings, for the Nepali scholar Satyamohan Joshi, *śakti* is defined as the vital force which animates the living: 'In the minds of people, without *śakti*, no one could take a step, speak or reflect upon anything' (Joshi 1982: 34). It is thus inherent to the life of all sentient beings, but it is in the movement of inanimate things, such as water or air, that the most indisputable proof of its existence is revealed in the eyes of the Nepalis. The power of *śakti* becomes all the more noticeable in the most violent natural phenomena, such as hail or thunderstorms, landslides and earthquakes, as illustrated, among many other examples, by the following excerpt from Khadananda Sharma's account of the 1933 earthquake (1959: 10): 'On all sides, there were thousands of deaths. Very many men and women lost their lives at the same time. By the *śakti* of the Goddess, living beings met their death.'

As the text makes clear, *śakti* is especially attached to the figure of the Goddess, who concentrates within herself the *śakti* of all the gods. Her warlike form is commonly called the 'form of the *śakti*' (*śaktirupī durgā bhavānī*). The worship of the Goddess undertaken during Dasaĩ is thus described as the main *śakti pūjā*, a formulation which can equally be understood as the main ritual addressed to the *śakti* as much as the main ritual aimed at obtaining *śakti*, thereby emphasising the circularity of this force in the ritual context.[4]

When men are *śaktiśālī*, 'endowed with *śakti*', they too are said to be animated by this external force, by this power which confers upon them a capacity to act and to make others act, in speech or in deed. The power of politicians, in particular, is designated as such, and it is therefore not surprising that blood sacrifice is one of the ways used by them to obtain or strengthen it. Until the abolition of the monarchy in 2008, it was through such a circulation of forces that the sovereign renewed his reign each year during the annual Dasaĩ celebrations, at the end of a vast synchronised slaughter of buffaloes offered to the Goddess at all the holy places and the 'seats of the *śakti*' (*śakti pīṭh*) of his kingdom.

In the *bali dān* ritual, the transmutation of the inner force into active power is achieved by the killing of a 'breathing being'. It is this violence that determines the sacrificial gift and confers on it the proper meaning of sacrifice. Yet, despite its core determining role, the violence at the heart of sacrifice is also its most obscure dimension, due in part to the fluctuating definition of violence in the ordinary context, and also to the specific nature and properties attributed to it in the sacrificial context.

In its lay sense, violence may be depicted as a force that constrains, damages or destroys.[5] Understood in this way, it qualifies the use of force in at least three registers – physical, verbal and moral – without presenting a precise image for any of them. Physical violence extends from simple bodily contact to killing; verbal violence, from crossed words to death threats; while the field of psychological or moral violence is even broader.

Wherever it is expressed, violence thus covers such a wide spectrum that it seems to escape any attempt at its characterisation. It is also surprisingly versatile: the same word, the same gesture is just as likely to be qualified as violence or as something else, depending on the context of its occurrence and the point of view adopted by those attempting to describe it. Here, we do not aspire to discuss conceptions and definitions of violence in an abstract way, but rather to pinpoint properties which apply to what the Nepalis understand by *hiṃsā* and its relation to what we consider violence. *Hiṃsā* is a term which is in fact so close to violence that its official definition in Nepali by the Nepal Academy could be taken from a Western dictionary: '1. To take the life of a living being or kill. 2. To bring affliction to others by any means' (Parajuli et al. 1983: 1417, my translation).

Among the three forms of *hiṃsā* which are commonly distinguished in Nepal – *hiṃsā* in action, *hiṃsā* in speech and *hiṃsā* in spirit – a difference does emerge. *Hiṃsā* in spirit not only is a psychological violence inflicted upon others as it would be understood in the West, but also constitutes a 'deterioration' of the mind of the one from whom it emanates, who may be jealous of others or wish them misfortune, without it even being strictly necessary that these 'violent' thoughts come to affect others. Likewise, *hiṃsā* in speech includes malicious gossip, which does not necessarily affect the person it concerns, although it does require the presence of a third party. These three forms of *hiṃsā* are presented as follows by the Nepali scholar Bhimabhakta Man Simha Varma in his 'Good Instructions' (n.d.: 58, my translation):

> Whosoever speaks ill of others, who engages in malicious gossip, commits *hiṃsā* by speech. Whosoever is jealous of others, wishes them misfortune, commits *hiṃsā* by spirit. Whosoever kills or strikes the other commits *hiṃsā* by deeds. These three kinds of *hiṃsā* are to be renounced. *Hiṃsā* gives rise to anger in the human, destroys the good thoughts of the mind, increases [karmic] fault, and prevents one from obtaining peace in this world and in the hereafter.

There is a strong reflexivity of *hiṃsā* in the above extract, to the point that verbal violence, *hiṃsā* by speech, does not even include any direct verbal interaction. Yet the latter also falls in this category, and when discussing with people it is clear that *hiṃsā* has the same faculty to evade an absolute definition, being instead dependent on context. The concept of *hiṃsā* in contemporary Nepal is thus very close to violence.

Both subjective and socially constructed, the definition of violence by its various qualifications is the source of endless controversy, to the point that we might even go so far as to consider that features intrinsic to violence hinder the possibility of exercising complete control over it, or even that minority views on violence could be created by the act of violence itself. It is therefore not only a subjective force, but a divisive one, constructed through collective imaginings.

In Nepal as elsewhere, there is general agreement on what constitutes violence, in the form of the *doxa* which is both carved out by and expressed in the law, customs and practices. There is an entire process of rendering certain forms of violence more or less visible taking place here, whether in their condemnation, naturalisation or instrumentalisation in one way or another. Yet such normalised forms of violence are fragile constructions for several reasons. First, they reflect the views and interests of those who govern, broadly speaking. The grip these individuals exert on the definition of violence can be seen on occasion, in particular during times of political regime change, which are often accompanied by the sudden transformation of the conception of violence. In Nepal we can cite, for instance, high treason, which was evidently abolished with the dissolution of the monarchy.[6] The existence of such shifting categories of violence suggests that the ways in which its definitions are divided up depend on the particular pressure points of a given socio-political organisation which is presiding over it at that time.

However, the changing definitions of violence have more profound effects than on their specific contexts alone, in that they introduce some relativity into the otherwise absolute nature of the law and, of particular interest to us, into the characterisation of violence itself. If that which was considered violent yesterday is no longer so today, or vice versa, then the foundation upon which the understanding of what violence is starts to crack, making it a topical issue. The relativity of violence has especially come to the fore since the dawn of modern globalisation, which has revealed the variety of its definitions, but it has also contributed, conversely, to a unification of meaning, by eradicating some of its conceptions – in an official way at least. This is what happened in Nepal, where the kingdom had sanctioned a caste-based society by law until the 1960s.[7]

The Muluki Ain, or 'code of the country', in force from 1854 to 1963, posited the contamination of others as a fundamental form of violence and sanctioned its many variations.[8] Under this law, an interaction such as offering water to someone could constitute a crime, depending on the caste of the protagonists. In this type of context, where the degree of social purity determines a person's position in the social hierarchy, impurity can be transmitted by contact or, in the case of an ingested substance, through a 'conductor', of which water is seen as the most sensitive of all. Thus, when it is offered by a person of 'impure caste' to someone of a 'pure caste', the interaction is akin to a wilful contamination of the other, the consequences of which are dramatic for the 'victim', who is subsequently condemned to be excluded from his or her family, functions and village. The transmission of impurity is analogous to the idea of passing a virus from one person to another who is not a carrier. In 1963, a decade after Nepal 'opened up' to the world in 1951, despite the penalisation of violence being mainly focused on inter-caste relationships, any matter relating to caste was suddenly declared illegal. In theory, the Hindu construction of violence was made to simply vanish overnight.

Nepal is therefore a remarkable example of a sudden and radical transformation in the nature of violence. It is important to note, however, that the old customs have nevertheless persisted, particularly in the religious domain, and while access to education and labour migration to foreign countries have enabled some Untouchables to transcend the conditions imposed upon them, in a religious context they are still expected to not defile that which is sacred and pure. In this way, religious spaces are in effect centres of exclusion, nuclei from which the holistic rite is spread into the public space, thereby making the entire population complicit actors in the scheme, each playing roles specific to their castes. The Nepalese legal reforms in fact ended up having this major side effect, that the rite was reinforced as a singular moment, a time of demonstration of a now-illegal organisation in all its violence. The People's War tackled this situation head-on, and the Maoist party did send Untouchables to desecrate holy places and defile Brahmins by forcing them to ingest food prepared by them. The Maoists identify these techniques as the most formidable weapons of war, because they reversed the very principles of Hindu violence instead of simply putting them aside from the legal framework, and used them on their opponents in an unprecedented way.

Beyond the conditioning of violence brought about by the socio-political context, other reasons, more intrinsic to the very nature of violence, seem to hinder any attempts at creating a hegemony of definition and, even more importantly, unanimity in terms of its perception.

The subjective chiasmus at the heart of violence

If we consider that violence is not a fact itself, but rather a qualification of the factual, as such it must seek to reduce the complexity of a given situation in order to adequately characterise it. In particular, this act of definition cannot admit the opposing points of view which form the tangled Gordian knot of violence, at the risk of annihilating both, as in the concept of 'word against word'.[9] The qualification of violence must take a side and arbitrate between the divergent points of view at the heart of violence, for without divergence, there is no violence, to the point that any consent between protagonists about a fact which could be qualified as violent means that it effectively can no longer be qualified as an instance of violence.[10] Thus, violence conceals within itself a subjective chiasmus which is objectified by attempts to qualify violence. Any kind of utopian views on a unified conception of violence is faced with this fundamental paradox, which brings parties into opposition, dividing them into aggressors and victims, each with their respective perceptions. The opposing polarities represented by these newly cast subjects-in-violence open up an infinite field of possibility, where anyone can position themselves and relate the event in question to elements located on a temporal and/or spatial line of flight[11] that has no limit. In this sense, the differentiating force of violence is total, with the potential to encompass all parties, all space and all time, from its minimal starting point of intersubjective opposition.

Being both the cause and consequence of violence, the opposition at its core is never resolved, but is only framed, by various social norms, laws or customs, which cannot resist all circumstances and do not unify all views. The impossibility to exercise total control over the domain of violence is perhaps related to the fact that it is not an entirely social construction. Indeed, while the contours of violence are collectively defined, hence the extreme variety of its forms in space and time, its core is occupied by an invariant, one which is unique and universal – the act of 'taking life' itself, which forms the primary definition of *hiṃsā*. As the maximum damage it is possible to inflict on a person, damage which leads to his or her total and definitive destruction as a living being, 'taking life' is the absolute of violence, the horizon towards which it inexorably steers, and the standard by which it is measured.

Killing is also the stumbling block for any social construction of violence. It is through killing that the so-called legitimate violence (this 'violence which is not violence' because it is socially defined as such) is revealed as the most instructive example, in that, despite our awareness of its existence, 'legitimate violence' nonetheless remains the most vertiginous paradox at the heart of societies – an enemy is eliminated, a condemned person is executed, *not* killed, in much the same way that a sacrifier deploys a violence that is not violence. There is therefore a line which divides the absolute of killing into two fields, that of transgressive violence and that of legitimate violence, as represented in the lexical categories which are attributed to each opposite category, in order to qualify and take sides. For the protagonists involved in this game, the line comes to separate visions of the world in an endless hall of mirrors. In a situation of conflict, one man's act of resistance is the act of terrorism of another, and vice versa.

The opposition between legitimate and transgressive violence makes it possible to confer different meanings on each death inflicted, thereby contributing to the importance of some and to the insignificance of others, and to normalise the right to kill, which is not the sole prerogative of power and justice but can also be expressed in the settling of scores, for instance, as well as in sacrifice. An object of incessant conflict, the limit that separates legitimate violence and transgressive violence is an active fault line at the heart of violence. On both sides, its various forms reflect and determine each other, like identical twins who deny their identity and compete in ways to differentiate themselves. This is because the absoluteness of killing resists any definitive interpretation, even that of the justice system. Any 'legitimate' killing can be perceived as illegitimate violence by someone, by the brother of the condemned or the cousin of the victim, or even by entire neighbouring nations, or those same parties who may develop a different point of view a few years later. Indeed, when the justifications that initially made the killing legitimate have been disqualified or forgotten, the facts of violence remain, and are thus just as easily requalified as they were qualified in the first place.

Examples of this mutability abound in Nepal. Perhaps most notable is that of Lakhan Thapa, a Magar soldier who, in the nineteenth century, deserted to form a utopian kingdom and raise an army to overthrow the prime minister who had usurped royal power. This same prime minister ordered his execution by hanging in 1876, in front of his own 'palace'. For a long time, Lakhan Thapa was an object of widespread ridicule. His name, used as a term of contempt to designate a good-for-nothing, even appeared in a dictionary with this definition.[12] This colloquial usage lasted until the end of the 1980s, when there was a sudden revision of history stemming in part from a new awareness of ethnic identities, one which cast him in an entirely new light, as someone whose memory could not be reappropriated by official history. From a figure of ridicule and a good-for-nothing, Lakhan was transformed into a hero by the indigenous Magar people. Under pressure from their associations, the Nepalese government swiftly granted him the highly honorary status of the country's 'First Martyr', and many Magars presented their active participation in the Maoist revolution as the realisation of Lakhan Thapa's dream.[13]

From these contrasted readings, placed into opposition by the dividing line that exists between legitimate and transgressive violence, an awareness of a form of violence bubbling up from this division, one which seeks to posit as legitimate what is de facto violence, is made possible. Its consequences are so impactful that the entirety of Nepalese history has been recast in the light of this self-legitimising violence, thus abruptly shifting the balance between the legitimate and the illegitimate. Shortly after a previously despised indigenous man became a national hero, repeated attacks on the nation's founding monarch, Prithvi Narayan Shah, have begun to spread through press and social media alike. Led by Newar intellectuals and activists, this new struggle aims to bring down from his pedestal – literally and figuratively – the king who had the noses of all the men of the Newar town of Kirtipur cut off for resisting his assaults in the eighteenth century. Each of his statues must now be protected by a policeman.

The anger expressed by the Newars more than two centuries after these events is surprisingly vivid. Has it remained dormant all this time and is only now finding an outlet? Does this reaction reveal a different sensitivity? These questions are difficult to answer, given that the written word in Nepal has long been appropriated for its own ends by an elite which has always been closely associated with power and its military activities. In the chronicles that relate the formation of the kingdom in the late eighteenth century, the sheer aggression of the kings is glorified as a sign of their divine power, *śakti*. The will of the gods is said to shape the course of events, particularly the outcome of battle, and the celebration of the main victor seems to take precedence over any sense of loyalty to a side. Thus, one can read, as written by a Newar author at the beginning of the nineteenth century, an account of the conquest of the Newar kingdoms which takes the side of the aggressor (Vajracarya 1963). The native Newar population is dehumanised, transformed into mere game for the conquering king. The king is then even consecrated by the protective god of the Newars, with all of this happening during a particularly gruesome episode of history, that of the bloody capture of Kirtipur, which is the root of much of the Newars' anger today. Was it more important for this writer to please the newly crowned princes, a decision which caused him to completely silence his own feelings on the matter? Was there simply very little ethnic solidarity at this time? Or did the worship of the power of *śakti* trump everything else? There are a few clues within the chronicle which might lead us to follow this last hypothesis, such as the report of the cheers for the conquering king by the conquered population upon his entry into the defeated capital.

The mechanism by which the ultimate sacrilege – the destruction of life – is turned into an act sanctified by the gods, one which contributes to the accumulation of *śakti* while offering the demonstration of one's strength, forms a loop analogous to that found in the sacrifice, when it is similarly presented as an offering of strength in order to obtain power. In war, as in sacrifice, the same game is played, wherein the strong, by demonstrating their strength, emerge even stronger. A post in Nepali that circulated in the summer of 2019 on social media explained this in a clear-cut way: 'Violence, *hiṃsā*, is not about dispute, *vivād*, but about power, *śakti*.'

Couched in this way, to sacrifice is to acquire a force which is superior in nature to that which is offered – this force is power, or the capacity to act and make others act. Force becomes an exchange with the divine, one which is activated by sacrificial violence. However, this violence evades characterisation even more so than in ordinary contexts, as the definition of sacrificial violence as a 'violence that is not violence' suggests.

'Vedic' violence

The Sanskrit formula *vaidikī hiṃsā hiṃsā na bhavati*, translated into Nepali as *vaidik hiṃsā hiṃsā hūdeina*, means 'Vedic violence/killing is not violence/killing'.[14] Its origin is not known. According to the Nepalese historian Mahes Raj Pant (2016: *ka*), it may have been inspired by the Laws of Manu, even if it is not found in this exact form in that particular collection of precepts. The formula presents two floating meanings: the first term *hiṃsā*, the primary meaning of which we have already noted to be killing, with its broader semantic field corresponding to that of violence. *Hiṃsā* is here identified in two contexts: one carries a more general sense, the other relates to the Veda, which cancels its identity.

The repetition of the term *hiṃsā* simultaneously makes clear while denying it that we are dealing with the same thing in both cases: killing or violence. Its translation by Georges Bataille's formula (1973: 66), 'to sacrifice is not to kill', therefore does not restore its precise meaning, nor its content. Indeed, contrary to Bataille, who suggests that sacrifice is not necessarily bloody,[15] the term 'sacrifice' is not under scrutiny in the Sanskrit formula, which instead focuses on the nature of the violence which unfolds therein, at least, if we agree that it is indeed sacrifice that is being referred to here, by the least determined term of the formula, *vaidikī*, 'relating to the Veda', *vaidik* in Nepali, which covers a broad spectrum. The Vedas are the bedrock of the Hindu religious tradition, and the formula may indeed refer to sacrifice insofar as it is the only religious practice which uses killing. In this case, the phrase would then mean 'sacrificial killing is not killing' or 'sacrificial violence is not violence'.[16] This assertion, which is reminiscent of Magritte's 'Ceci n'est pas une pipe', since it denies the identity of two things which have the same appearance,[17] could then mean that sacrifice is, much like painting, a *representation* of another form of violence. One can also see within this phrase, more literally, the assertion that sacrifice belongs to a plane of reality different from the ordinary, one where violence and death do not exist. The formula posits, in any case, the existence of two distinct fields, the 'Vedic' and that which does not pertain to it.

In Nepal today, the notion of 'Vedic violence' is not restricted to the ritual context. It designates a violence exerted in response to another violence. In this sense, it is reminiscent of what we understand by self-defence, but it is different in the sense that it is defined exclusively as an action exercised by men whose profession is weapons, in response to violence, not as a direct relationship between aggressor and aggressed. 'Vedic violence' is thus a category of violence located somewhere between self-defence and legitimate violence. Immediate and without arbitration, it is reserved for the Kshatriyas only, as they belong to the only caste who can use it without committing 'moral fault'. It may even have been created 'for them', according to the explanation given by the Nepalese Brahmin Bhimabhakta Man Simha Varma (n.d.: 58–59, my translation) in his exposé on 'Vedic violence', which provides us with more details:

> [F]or the Kshatriyas, a kind of violence has been fabricated (*banāyako cha*), and the moral fault (*pāp*) of this violence does not reach them. It has an inverse merit (*ulṭo puṇya*). Protecting the people is a supreme duty. For this, if violent beings like the lion or the tiger come out of the forest towards dwellings and cause nuisance there, or if they attack people in the forest, doing violence to them is accepted in the Veda, just as if a murderous person harms people, he too must be killed immediately.... He who sets fire to rice straw in another's house, he who makes another eat poison, he who seeks to kill someone with a weapon, he who attacks someone's prosperity by stealing, he who seizes the harvest from another's fields and he who take away another's wife, these six people are criminals. These, and others whose actions are violent, must be killed, without further consideration.... There is no moral fault in killing them because, in the grip of anger, they too kill people. *Vedic violence is the act of killing one person to save many others from violence. Vedic violence is not violence.* (Emphasis mine)

This traditional vision of Vedic violence defines it as a reciprocal relationship – the violent perpetrator becoming himself the object of violence – but not symmetrical, since it cannot be returned by the victim himself. Initially presented as proportional, when it comes to killing killers, this type of violence takes on a punitive tone when it comes to eliminating pests and thieves.[18] Despite its ambiguities, Vedic violence is clear on one point: it does not apply to categories of beings, but to individuals who have personally committed violence. Thus, there is no question of killing tigers or lions in general because of their dangerousness, but only those specific individuals who have attacked humans.

The act of sacrifice clearly fulfils the dual character attributed to Vedic violence by Bhimabhakta Man Simha Varma, as it is a domain reserved for the Kshatriyas as well as an act of violence for the benefit of all. However, the principle of reciprocity that frames it does not apply in sacrifice. Vedic violence, which strikes guilty parties in an ordinary context, in sacrifice targets a being who is not considered guilty or personally responsible for violence. In the case of the buffalo, however, the animal is associated with the buffalo-demon Mahiṣāsura because they look the same. In the same way, a warrior (Kshatriya) sacrificator takes the place of the warlike goddess. This same principle of similarity also determines the temporal framework of the buffalo sacrifice, with the four months of the monsoon acting as a period of chaos and the reign of demonic forces. Thus, as the Nepalis commonly say, the buffalo sacrifice 'puts an end' to the monsoon and to 'the reign of evil forces', in one and the same movement. Sacrificial killing therefore takes the place of another violence by repeating the fatal blow dealt by the Goddess to the buffalo-demon at the request of the gods. In this sense, the formula 'the violence of sacrifice is not violence' could be indicative of the sacrificial replication of the divine violence committed by the Goddess for the sake of the universe by human perpetrators.

However, the buffalo sacrifice is not an exact repetition of the myth – its temporal framework, sacrificator and victim are all more akin to approximate substitutes. It is only in the act of killing that representation in its literal meaning of presentification becomes manifest. Given the absolute nature of death, there can be no question of it being approximated. And further, as if to fully detach this most supreme act from its imperfect human setting, the killing is only made possible by the approval of the manifested presence of the invisible force. In this sense, sacrifice is the combination of real violence and the real presence of the divine (see Figure 1.1 for an example of a more tangible act of divine presence, tempered by an act of divine absence).

The repetition of the myth by the enactment of the rite makes sacrifice a device which is both abstract and concrete, of the past and the present, carried out by human and divine actors, violent and non-violent. The transposition of both the invisible and anterior planes brought about by the myth to the present real world in fact opens up a multitude of possible iterations in whichever socio-political context it is carried out. It also makes possible the idea that the myth could itself be born of a transposition from a historical reality, sketching the outline of a unique *mise en abyme* between myth, rite and reality.

Figure 1.1 Incarnation of Kumāri, a form of the goddess Durgā, Patan, 2019

Source: Author.

The work of the Nepalese Brahmin S. A. Dikshit (1958) offers such a rewriting of the myth of the slaying of the buffalo-demon, which illustrates the point of view of the sacrificers quite well. It should be noted that this booklet was published in Nepali long before the wider awakening to indigenous identities that put a stop to such discourses. S. A. Dikshit paints a picture of the fight of the Goddess against the demon-buffalo as a war of emancipation waged by the Aryas, who were enslaved by the emperor of the demons, named Mahiṣ, the infamous Buffalo. Repeatedly referred to as an outsider, Buffalo oppresses the Aryas and attempts to annihilate their culture and *dharma*. The mistreated Aryas unite after an agreement between their three main 'political leaders', who are none other than the gods of the Hindu Trinity: Brahmā, Viṣṇu and Śiva. All three put aside their differences in the face of this common threat, and their alliance causes first a general rallying of the leaders of lesser rank, then of the whole Arya people. Their combined forces come together to form a mighty army uniting all men and their weapons, from which the

Supreme Śakti is born. They finally overcome the Buffalo Emperor, notably without the Goddess appearing in this particular story.

On closer examination, Dikshit's rewriting of the myth reifies the two main characteristics of its specific Nepalese sacrificial traits – the gods are substituted by politicians and the active role of the Goddess disappears. More importantly, it posits the existence of a historical reality feeding into the myth, which would have then been distorted by it, thus making the narrative of the Goddess's mythical fight against the buffalo-demon an allegory of a real political conflict between Aryas and non-Aryas.

The idea of an interplay between the mythic and the real is now commonplace in Nepal, especially among Indigenous peoples, who have expressed this view after the political liberalisation of 1990, although they view it differently. For them, as for the Brahmin author, the buffalo sacrifice depicts the victory of the Aryas over non-Aryas, but while the author sees these 'non-Aryas' as foreign forces, without giving further precision, the Indigenous peoples see them as their ancestors. Similarly, where the Aryas are oppressed in the Brahmin writer's account, for the Indigenous peoples, they are actually the aggressors, who put an end to the peaceful reign of their ancestors, invaded their territories and introduced a political regime, thereby ensuring their domination.

The opposition between gods and demons depicted by this myth thus constitutes a basic framework onto which the antagonisms that run through society and the history that each group constructs for itself can be projected. This means that the image of sacrifice as a unifying force, where a crowd comes together as a single body against an isolated victim, falls short of the complexity of its true nature, despite initial appearances. If we look more closely, we see that a part of the crowd actually recognises itself in the subjugated camp and expresses solidarity with the decapitated buffaloes. For these people, the violence of sacrifice is painful. This is the case of the Indigenous peoples, for instance, who see it as the massacre of their ancestors. In the crowd of sacrificial spectators there are also those who are associated with the victim because they receive and ingest its flesh, the Dalits or Untouchables, who themselves display a great variety of responses to the killing of the victim. They may see reflected in the rite their defeat and domination, much like the Indigenous peoples. However, they simultaneously watch carefully over the execution, as they wish to see it accomplished without 'fault', *pāp*, something which would ultimately affect the meat of the animal and, by extension, those who consume it (that is to say, themselves). Alternatively, in some localities, they may seek to emancipate themselves from the stigma associated with consuming such degrading sacrificial remains (the impure buffalo meat) or, in the case of the Untouchable Damāī musicians, from being systematically offered the tail of the animal, which again humiliates them.

We are far from a 'world of harmonious and organic division of labour', as Jean Levi (2007: 23) describes the 'space of sacrifice' in ancient China, even if the division of labour is also essential during the buffalo sacrifice in Nepal. Indeed, the ceremony is the only occasion when one can see the priests officiating, the Kshatriyas killing, the blacksmiths sharpening weapons and the Damāī playing music, not to mention the many duties that fall to each group, such as bringing wood, oil, milk or flowers and cleaning the temple. Yet the division is far from harmonious, as some of these obligations are experienced as honours, while others are perceived as constraints or even public humiliations. In many places, Untouchables no longer want to play music at the temple, clean its surroundings or bring wood; elsewhere, young Brahmins are abandoning the profession of priest, which is poorly paid and less and less valued. However, there is still an abundance of sacrificators willing to partake in the ceremonies. The role does not require any particular training and costs little or nothing, in terms of time or money, but above all it remains an honour to fulfil such a position, attesting to both the physical and moral strength of the person who performs it.

These transformations reflect the weakening of caste society, which was suddenly declared illegal and immoral by the law in 1963 after the fall of the autocratic Rana regime. Shortly after, the conception of Vedic violence, which was remarkably similar to the Laws of Manu until the political liberalisation of the 1990s, was also modified.

Today, Vedic violence qualifies social violence as it is sanctioned by Hindu texts and it is denounced as a form of Hindu 'negationism', in the words of the (Dalit) author Sarita Pariyar (2018), who states that if an act of violence is committed in accordance with the scriptures, it is not considered violence at all, quoting the formula – *vaidiki himsa himsa na bhavati*. This ultimately means, says Pariyar, that caste-related violence is widely viewed as not being violence at all.

The disqualification of Vedic violence as a justification for the unjustifiable by an urban educated elite is clearly some way away from transforming practices on a large scale. To take the measure of this, we can cite the results of a study recently carried out on 42,000 households in northern India, indicating that 89 per cent of those who took part in the study still practise untouchability; we might adduce that the ratio would certainly be of the same order or even higher in Nepal if we consider the correlations of the practice with poverty, the degree of education and the numbers of those living in rural areas, as noted in the study (Thorat and Joshi 2020).

In the rural milieu in particular, beyond those groups who feel directly targeted by the killing of the victim, stigmatised by the distribution of its flesh or by the tasks assigned to them during the ritual, the violence of the sacrifice is also keenly felt by those who are excluded from the functions of sacrificator and the power of death, that is, women and to a lesser degree the Brahmins. The distance kept by these groups represents not so much an identification with the victim but more a generalised disapproval of the violence involved in blood sacrifice manifested by its required or imposed avoidance. This last point is especially true for women, who are often prohibited from approaching a sacrifice, either because their presence is considered polluting or because men consider that the sight of blood must be unbearable for them.

One could therefore speak of a 'categorical' perception of sacrificial violence, inasmuch as it seems to oppose groups of individuals according to the relationship that each of them maintains with the victim and its representation, or with the act of killing itself. It should be added that for some, the victim does not avoid the violence either, as when the animal is brought forward, it is very common to hear some female voice in the crowd who has chosen to interpret its bellows with the words *thāhā cha*, 'he knows'. The foreknowledge of death is most intense in the great sacrificial celebrations, where 'chain beheadings' are carried out one after the other. Thus, for any person participating in the sacrifice, whether she or he perceives it or hears it said, it is not the destruction of a *thing*, as Georges Bataille says (1973: 59–60), but of a *being* who apprehends its fate and thus transmits the anguish of death, at least to those who are receptive to it. There are others, however, who put forward opposite arguments, claiming that the animal is well aware of the fate that awaits him but consents to it, using the fact that the animal does not seem to try to flee as proof of their logic. 'He stays beside us when we pour flowers, leaves and lustral water over him, *phul pāti ra jal parchin*, even though we should not hold him at that time,' a Magar friend pointed out to me.

An old cobbler would even go so far as to say that his goat expressed joy at being able to please the deity through his body language between his consecration and execution, and for Chitra Bahadur, a former military man, the animal simply offers himself in sacrifice, *bali dān*, as he offers his life for the good of all. This did not prevent him from pointing out in the same conversation that animal sacrifice, *paśu bali*, differs from human sacrifice insofar as the animal has no consciousness, *cetanā*. All thus reformulate their ideas so that the animal is aware of the sacrifice while simultaneously negating the violence of that same sacrifice, choosing to view it as a choice made by the animal, who has been made temporarily conscious by the divine presence.

I continued my exchanges with the ex-soldier until I asked him what the audience feels during animal sacrifice. He first specified that the execution is something which women cannot perform. But then he added: 'As for the feelings of those who watch the sacrifice, you must know this, since you attended it', thereby excluding any possibility of watching violence without being affected by it, and throwing its universality right back to me.

Indeed, the effects of blood sacrifice spare no one and are not merely limited to those who witness an execution. In this respect, sacrificial violence has the same propensity as ordinary violence to divide beyond those parties directly involved. It sparks a struggle between the 'anti' and the 'pro' camps, a division which is also expressed through social networks, in Nepal as in India. Beyond the context of those directly concerned by the practice, such as Nepalese or Hindu participants, the tremors created by sacrificial violence are even felt at the furthest reaches of the subject, including by anthropologists. This is illustrated in the writings of Luc de Heusch, among other examples. From the very first pages of his comparative work on sacrifice in Africa, the author is indignant that René Girard could consider sacrifice as a violent act and, invoking the work of Evans-Pritchard, replies curtly (1986: 35):

> Violence never appears ... as such in the sacrifice [of the ox that the Nuer offer as individual offerings]. It appears even less in collective sacrifices whose main function is to confirm, establish or reinforce a change in social status, ... a new relationship between social groups, ... or the end of a vendetta.

We have here a prioritising of the ends, to the detriment of the means, a perspective which is typical of a teleological approach to sacrifice. The matter seems settled, and Luc de Heusch continues his examination of sacrifice in various African contexts, giving detailed descriptions without making further remarks on the implications of violence. We learn, for example, that in Rwanda, single mothers or even pubescent girls whose breasts have not fully grown are considered to be 'monsters' and are immolated, an information which is recounted without the author apparently being moved by this in any way (Heusch 1986: 174). It is noteworthy, therefore, when suddenly we feel that de Heusch has been touched by rites of enthronement which culminate in the capture of a man, taken at random from a distant province, and his subsequent killing. 'The fate of the unfortunate man is particularly horrible,' he writes (1986: 183), specifying that the victim is sacrificed with a blow of a spear under the armpit. The authorial approach, which had until now remained distant, even in the case of the execution of very young girls, suddenly gives way to emotion, in a case where, to use the terms of analysis used by the author, one can clearly detect a 'homology' between the latter and the victim, this particular rite threatening all men indiscriminately.

Personal proximity to the sacrificial victim therefore seems to convert their killing from being perceived as merely abstract to being experienced as a real, painful event, showing that the distance is not so much created by a world made up of third persons, just as proximity is not strictly speaking the irruption of a first person, but it is more the extent to which the subject is personally implicated in a manifestation of violence.

As Vladimir Jankélévitch (1977: 12–13) puts it, mortality says nothing about personal death, and in order to move from what he calls the 'platonic danger' of death, that is, from abstract or essentialised knowledge, to existence, one must 'feel concerned by this threat oneself' (Jankélévitch 1977: 21).

With the sacrificial rite circumscribing and targeting violence on a specific category of beings, those who do not identify with the victim are not even aware of this platonic danger of death and simply do not perceive its violence; conversely, the rite produces a feeling of supreme violence and imminent threat in those who feel touched by it, as members of the category of possible victims, by following the tangled threads of their own identifications with them, or because their point of view chimes with the derived meaning given to the rite by its executors, as is the case in the buffalo sacrifice. This does not mean that affects are always so clear-cut, nor that they are constant, but it does mean that sacrifice disturbs the group and divides it, in a constitutive way, by the violence it exposes.

Notes

1. The verb *caḍāunu,* 'to offer', literally means 'to raise, to elevate'. It is also sometimes referred to as 'giving a *bali*', *bali dine.*

2. *Monier-Williams'* dictionary suggests that the term *bali* may derive from the root √bhṛ, 'to bear, carry, bring, cherish', the latter term and its implications we will examine in the last chapter of the book.
3. These oral traditions, heard in the region of Pyuthan, are reminiscent of the practices observed in the regions of Syangja and Palpa, where the worship of certain deities requires the digging of a small basin, fixing a sacrificial post in its centre, and filling it with the blood of the sacrificed animal.
4. A former member of the Nepalese parliament defines the rite as follows: to worship the goddess Bhagawati '*for* power' (Prasai 2008).
5. For a more precise definition of violence, we can cite Yves Michaud (1978: 20):

   > There is violence when, in a situation of interaction, one or more actors act in a direct or indirect, massed or distributed manner, by harming one or more other beings to varying degrees, either in their physical integrity, in their moral integrity, in their possessions or in their symbolic and cultural participation.

   Or we have the definition by Françoise Héritier (1996 [2005]: 17):

   > [Violence is] any constraint of a physical or psychological nature likely to cause terror, displacement, misfortune, suffering or death to an animate being; any act of intrusion that has the voluntary or involuntary effect of dispossessing others, damaging or destroying inanimate objects.

6. On this subject, see Hutt (2006).
7. The existence of multiple reference points and streams of belonging have elsewhere produced a coexistence of norms that creates a relativism in terms of conceptions of violence.
8. On the Muluki Ain, see Höfer (1979).
9. This is what Yves Michaud (1978: 97) calls 'the double-relativity of violence', even though the author, despite this, comes to the somewhat surprising conclusion that there can be unity of views on violence (1978: 101): 'The appearance of violence for what it is has more to do with the dissolution of the rules that unify the social gaze than with the reality it may have.'
10. Certainly, the conditions of consent have their rules, such as equal status, full possession of judgement, and so on. The fact remains that two boxers who confront each other are not engaging in violence but in a game. Whether the latter can be qualified as violent is secondary: the consent of the

protagonists defines their activity as a game or a sport, sending its violence into the background.

11. To borrow a Deleuzian notion.
12. *Ajanta Standard Dictionary Nepali–English*, no date.
13. On Lakhan Thapa, see Lecomte-Tilouine (2003).
14. This translation is found in Bhimabhakta Man Simha Varma (n.d.: 59). Mahes Raj Pant (2016: *ka*) suggests: *Vedavihita hiṃsā hiṃsā hũdeina*, 'Violence prescribed by the Veda is not violence'.
15. Often taken out of context and even out of the sentence in which it is used, Bataille's formula nevertheless takes on a specific meaning within it: '[T]he most solemn sacrifice may not be bloody. To sacrifice is not to kill, but to give up and give' (Bataille 1973: 66).
16. Rajendra Prasad (2008: 155) translates it as 'Violence permitted or prescribed in a Vedic ritual is not real violence.'
17. See Foucault (1973).
18. In Nepal, punishment has long been carried out in the name of the king, at least for the most serious crimes that directly affected him and polluted the kingdom. In the period before the establishment of the code in the early nineteenth century, the king was liable to be polluted by any inter-caste marriage and had to undergo costly rites of expiation. The abolition of the death penalty by law dates from 1946, but offences against national security, or against the king, gave rise to executions until 1979.

2

Theories of sacrifice, with or without violence

The milestones of the anthropological approach to sacrifice have drawn a dead-end trajectory. Initially inspired by a desire to construct a unique and universal model of sacrifice through the identification of its scheme, to which Hubert and Mauss attached themselves, within a matter of decades the idea that the infinite variation of sacrifice eluded any attempts to conclusively define it imposed itself. It even led to the term 'sacrifice' being denounced entirely, on the grounds that it would artificially unify an enormous diversity of practices across the globe, as well as being too connected to a Christian heritage. Such a definitive denunciation of sacrifice was formulated by Marcel Detienne (1979: 34–35):

> [T]he notion of 'sacrifice' is indeed a category of yesterday's thought, conceived as arbitrarily as that of totemism – once denounced by Lévi-Strauss – both to gather elements taken here and there in the symbolic fabric of societies to form an artificial template, and to confess the astonishing empire that an all-encompassing Christianity has never ceased to exert secretly on the thinking of all those historians and sociologists who were persuaded that they were inventing a new science.

A few decades later, it appears that, unlike the notion of totemism, which effectively fell into disuse after its deconstruction by Claude Lévi-Strauss (1962), sacrifice is far from weakened by these remarks, nor has it even ceased to be used as a category of analysis by its author and those working in the field. Briefly put, the political history of the last three decades in particular has dramatically reintroduced sacrifice to modern anthropological thought.

As Ivan Strenski (2003) points out, the science of religions was initially uninterested in sacrifice, which was seen as an amoral and primitive practice.

Following the first works of the English school, an essay on sacrifice by Henri Hubert and Marcel Mauss appeared in 1899, when its two authors were both 27 years old. The former was a history graduate, the second a philosophy graduate, and both shared a passion for ancient languages, notably Hebrew and Sanskrit, as well as for religious trivia. Their joint essay on sacrifice, published in the journal *L'année sociologique*, moves away from the theories of their predecessors. Tylor had envisaged sacrifice as a form of gift, and sought to trace the evolution of the gift of an object or asset to that of a living being. Hubert and Mauss criticised him for having treated sacrifice as if it were merely an ordinary transaction, without fully considering that the destruction of the thing offered was a central part of the sacrificial process. Robertson Smith had focused his analysis on sacrificial communion and its role in the establishment and maintenance of a community, considering sacrifice as a form of totemism where the gods take a secondary role. The example sacrifice studied by Hubert and Mauss has no community dimension, but instead describes an individual relationship with the deity. Finally, Frazer had examined the ritual of regicide, which he compared with the agricultural cycle and associated rites of the spirit of vegetation and the alternation of life and death, drawing from a wide range of examples to support his theory. By contrast, Hubert and Mauss limited themselves to the detailed study of two historical contexts: Brahmanic (or Late Vedic) India and, to a lesser extent, the world depicted by the Old Testament, in the hope of demonstrating the fundamental unity of the 'sacrificial system' and establishing its 'scheme'.

Before examining this scheme more closely, it is tempting to look at work done by theologians prior to this period, a time which represents the very earliest period of anthropological reflection on sacrifice, from a modern perspective. By way of example, we can consider how sacrifice was presented by François-Philippe Mésenguy (1677–1763) in a work published in 1758, *L'Exposition de la doctrine chrétienne* (*The Exposition of the Christian Doctrine*). This author, who was the abbot of Beauvais, offers an analytical approach to sacrifice that examines its constituent parts separately and then questions the types of relationships created by them. Though the vocabulary is outdated, his definition of sacrifice is all-encompassing: 'The offering of an external and sensible thing, made to God by a legitimate minister, with some destruction or change of the thing offered.' Mésenguy then clarifies his terms, specifying that by 'minister' he means a person separated from other humans, a theme that would be central in Hubert and Mauss's work, and that the 'destruction or the change of the thing offered' distinguishes sacrifice from other types of offering, prefiguring the criticism addressed to Tylor by Hubert and Mauss. Finally, he emphasises that sacrifice should be considered an offering, which therefore distinguishes it from ritualised murder, for example. The abbot then sets out to answer four questions: to whom is the sacrifice offered, by whom, for whom and for what purpose? His answers are only concerned with the 'Christian doctrine'. The analysis of this author, and more generally any analysis carried out within the framework of the Church, is by nature comparative, since it is about defining Christian sacrifice in relation to the forms which existed before it, the so-called Ancient sacrifice. This exercise is reminiscent of Hubert and Mauss's two main analytical pillars, except that their comparison with India represents an innovative shift to a more global perspective. In Mésenguy's description, ancient sacrifice as described in the Bible is characterised by substitution, and its archetypes are, on the one hand, the sacrifice of Abraham, where a ram is sent by God in place of his son Isaac, and, on the other, the episode of the plagues of Egypt, where the smearing of the blood of a sacrificed lamb on houses spares the life of the firstborn. This principle of substitution that Mésenguy emphasised in the context of ancient sacrifice is, however, never used by him with regard to the sacrifice of Christ. Here he isolates three components: offering, immolation and communion. Instead of substitution, this sacrifice introduces the idea of communion, defined as a confusion of the human and the divine, which is brought about by the sacrifice. It is not, therefore, the Durkheimian 'communion' that strengthens the group, but an act that brings the human and the divine closer together, or, more precisely, one which bridges the divide which normally exists between these domains. This is why, adds the abbot, sacrifice should be considered as either a redemption or a ransom, that is, as a debt to be paid, analogous to the sacrifice of the lamb for the Ancients. This notion of sacrificial debt is thus a shared trait between 'Ancient' and Christian sacrifice.

Here we have the three pillars of the anthropological analysis of sacrifice: the principle of substitution, the notion of communion and the notion of sacrificial debt. However, there is no explicit mention of violence or of sacrificial killing as such.

The void in the Maussian scheme of sacrifice

Hubert and Mauss's essay on sacrifice (1899) also seems to hesitate about what to do with the killing which takes place in the act of sacrifice. We see it appearing and disappearing, sometimes highlighted in the definition of the act itself; at other times, it is entirely obscured by the importance the authors give to the consecration, that is, communion as defined by Mésenguy, or that bridge which brings the human and the divine closer together. The problem posed by the reality of killing in Hubert and Mauss's essay is notable in the strange structure of the 'scheme of sacrifice' that they propose. This scheme obviously reflects their embarrassment about the subject, given its somewhat shaky categorisation into three parts respectively entitled: the entry, the victim and the exit. While the names of the first and last parts describe the stages of a process, the name chosen for the central part of the sacrificial scheme, 'the victim', has no discernible action associated with it, like a void in the centre of the ritual device, even if the term 'victim' does implicitly refer to killing.

Such a structure gives the impression that sacrifice is a dynamic process, the key part of which is not qualified, other than the fact that the offered being's destiny is somehow involved in it. The obliteration of the core of sacrifice can also be seen throughout the text by the sparing use of action verbs which refer to the execution of the victim.

Hubert and Mauss nevertheless emphasise from the outset the essential character of the destruction of the 'thing' presented as a sacrifice, a key difference in their eyes, understanding it as the very act that distinguishes sacrifice from a simple offering. There is an 'unequal gravity' and an 'unequal effectiveness' at play between the two, with 'stronger religious energies' at play in the former (Hubert and Mauss 1994 [1899]: 13), we are told, without the cause of this intensification ever being made explicit.

The authors then shift from considering observable actions – 'the destruction of the thing offered' – to presenting an interpretation that focuses on an invisible process of transformation involving 'religious energies'. The shift is expressed in the two contrasting definitions of sacrifice they propose within the same paragraph, which goes from 'any oblation [wherein] the offering is destroyed' to a 'religious act which, by the consecration of a victim, modifies the status of the moral person who performs it' (Hubert and Mauss 1994 [1899]: 13). In the space of these two definitions, the element of destruction has disappeared completely, and while the first is factual – to sacrifice is indeed to give while destroying that which is offered – the second is a theory based on a religious explanation, one which goes on to constitute the thesis of the rest of the essay, that is, to sacrifice is to transform oneself through consecration. By following this movement which encourages the authors to move away from the process in which man is the sacrifier, sacrifice is soon presented as a 'curve' or a 'movement', between the profane and the sacred. The removal of the act of killing is completed, and sacrifice is transformed into a 'continuous movement which, from entry to exit, continues on two opposite slopes' (Hubert and Mauss 1994 [1899]: 51). Whereas the part of the scheme entitled 'victim' or even the mention of the 'consecration of a victim' remained indicative of this most central destruction, all trace of it has disappeared in this last formula. Furthermore, while the text specifies the nature of these two slopes, namely sacralisation and desacralisation, nothing now indicates what happens at the point which forms its apex, even though it would have the capability of reversing its inclination.

However, in the section of the scheme consecrated to the 'victim', killing remains a central feature, described alternately as a 'supreme operation', a 'solemn moment', a 'murder' or a 'crime', thereby underlining its importance and revealing something about its nature. However, this key point is almost immediately eclipsed by the desired end point, which reduces killing to a simple operation of separation from what has been conferred upon the victim by its consecration: 'the *divine principle* ... is still engaged in its body.... Death will *release* it' (Hubert and Mauss 1994 [1899]: 35, italics added). Yet the action of killing itself, much like the invisible entity upon which it acts, is not well defined – there are mentions of 'releasing', 'making escape' or 'liberating', but also of 'eliminating', a thing sometimes called 'force', sometimes 'energies' (Hubert and Mauss 1994 [1899]: 48), sometimes 'spirit' (Hubert and Mauss 1994 [1899]: 33), which is sometimes presented as something to be feared and eliminated, sometimes as actively dangerous when liberated.[1] One catches glimpses of the idea that killing might play a role in what may emerge from it, at the beginning of the formula (here noted in italics): '*by murder, an ambiguous, or rather blind, force was released,* fearsome simply because it was a force'. Despite this, the authors deem it better to swiftly repress this idea and reaffirm the autonomous existence of the force in question, which, strictly speaking, justifies the thesis of the primacy of the rite of consecration over sacrifice itself. Even the apologies made prior to the killing are not addressed to the victim, according to Hubert and Mauss, but rather to the sacred entity that has entered it, so as to attenuate the danger of its imminent release (1994 [1899]: 33). The term 'violence' (or its adjective 'violent') does not appear at any point in the essay, even though its authors, having arrived at the very moment of the killing of the ox, underline its pathos by the use of facts that are lacking in their analysis material and which are in fact borrowed from Greek and Roman antiquity, with quotes such as: 'It is a crime that is beginning, a kind of sacrilege', 'one moaned at the death of the beast, wept for it like a relative. One would ask it for forgiveness before striking it'.

After the publication of this foundational text, the anthropological study of sacrifice was not revisited until the 1970s from two fields of research: the ethnology of Sub-Saharan Africa, around the work started in 1975 by Michel Cartry and his colleagues, including studies by Luc de Heusch, whose text, *Le sacrifice dans les religions africaines* (Sacrifice in African Religions), appeared in 1986; and the historical anthropology of ancient Greece conducted by Jean-Pierre Vernant and Marcel Detienne, who published *La Cuisine du sacrifice en Grèce ancienne* in 1979.[2] These new investigations followed the publication in 1972 of the seminal *La violence et le sacré* (Violence and the Sacred) by René Girard, which left its mark on an entire generation.

Contrary to Hubert and Mauss, who posited the existence of a sacrificial system with a variable scheme of practice, Luc de Heusch (1986) introduced the idea of sacrificial systems in the plural, which are ordered either around a mythology or by the gathering together of heterogeneous elements which, taken together, form a coherent whole. Whereas Hubert and Mauss granted a central place to the sacrifier – the individual who offers the sacrifice – de Heusch uproots the investigation by focusing on the victim and the importance of its domestication. He distinguishes two main sacrificial models: one related to the sacred king and the god, based on the renewal of the cosmic order, and the other being a domestic sacrifice, whose function is to help determine the boundaries of the community from both the rest of the social and supernatural worlds. Finally, Luc de Heusch proposes replacing the variants of sacrifice, defined by Hubert and Mauss according to their relationship to the profane and the sacred – sacrifices of sacralisation and desacralisation – by a typology which opposes 'conjunctive sacrifices' to 'disjunctive sacrifices', or those which either connect or keep apart two spaces, the human and non-human. Luc de Heusch considers that Hubert and Mauss's opposition between the profane and the sacred is not relevant in African religions, and proposes replacing it with the dichotomies of domestic and wild spaces and the human/non-human.

It can nevertheless be said that these apparently more neutral oppositions are not suited to all contexts. In the Himalayan region, the human and the non-human are often confused, not only in the practices of possession but also among certain categories of people, such as the Brahmins, traditionally considered 'gods on earth', or the king and the queen, avatars of Viṣṇu and her consort, and the virgin girls, venerated as deities. Similarly, the *topos* of the domestic and the wild interpenetrate at many points, as is the case with paths and streams, for instance, nor is it always easy to set a limit between domestic and wild animals: domestic pigs or chickens are little differentiated from wild boars and wild chickens, because these are often captured in the forest and then raised at the homestead either for economic reasons or in order to have 'pure' meat at home – wild animals being considered purer than their domestic counterparts. Similarly, in mountainous areas of Nepal, buffaloes are not fully domesticated and are so unpredictable that it is impossible to use them for any menial task. Indeed, until recently, only lactating females were kept near human dwellings, while the others were released back into the forest, where they were simply given salt once every fortnight. On the other hand, L. de Heusch's focus on the victim and its domestication shed an interesting light on the buffalo sacrifice in Nepal by linking the demonic aspect of this animal with its lack of domestication. Yet the buffalo is not the only animal to hold such a position: the cat is also considered a wild domestic animal and by certain aspects even the dog is still akin to his 'cousin' the jackal, the former often leaving poultry for the latter to eat due to their kinship.

The work by Jean-Pierre Vernant on the historical anthropology of ancient Greece stands out for the relevance of its formulations, as precise as they are inclusive. In his inaugural lecture at the Collège de France, Vernant (1976: 6) defines sacrifice as a 'putting in place of a correlation between a human subject and a divine absolute', populated by 'powers' which translate a form of action or a type of power and which maintain a relation with the world which is neither entirely transcendent nor entirely immanent, but rather of varying degrees. Vernant does not believe in a general theory of sacrifice and objects to Hubert and Mauss that among the ancient Greeks, 'ritual gestures do not uproot the sacrificer or the participants from their civic or family groups, nor from ordinary activities' but, on the contrary, 'integrate the actors into the groups to which they normally belong and prepare them for their private or public activities'.

If he highlights such differences between the scheme presented in the essay and the practices of ancient Greece, Vernant does nevertheless recognise that there is some type of unity of sacrifice, since he states that he studies one 'particular configuration' of it. Vernant (1979) sees in sacrifice a practice which establishes a distance between men and other categories of beings: the gods, who are fed on perfumes and ambrosia, and the animals, who devour each other raw. The Promethean trick which is conducted during a sacrifice, as described by Hesiod, is the foundation of the separation between men and gods, who consume different parts of the sacrificed animal. In this context, there is no confusion between the varying roles to be played by the sacrificer, the victim or the god, and those whose practices are different are not considered part of the *polis*. The organisation of sacrifice is thus superimposed onto the socio-political organisation: the sacrificial practice, open to all the men of the *polis* – that is to say, the Hellene, free, male and adult – reflects not only the Greeks' egalitarian organisation in the sharing of equal parts of the victim but also the exclusion of barbarians, whose sacrifices are depicted as burlesque, and of women, who perform terrifying and transgressive sacrificial rituals associated with savagery.

Despite its ostensibly key role in the distribution of the various attributions associated with each category of the population in the *polis* and the wider world around it, sacrifice was in fact subject to denial and concealment during the Buphonia ceremonies that took place on the acropolis in honour of Zeus (Durand 1986). The myth behind the origin of this ritual features a population of vegetarians performing bloodless sacrifices until an ox approaches the sacrificial cakes and eats them. In anger, the sacrificer, a Cretan foreigner, kills the animal. A terrible drought ensues, and the Pythia oracle is duly consulted. She declares that it is necessary to reinstate the victim and put it 'back on its feet' during a new sacrifice, and also to punish the murderer. The Cretan is found, who agrees to take part in the ceremony on the condition that the murder be undertaken communally. A procession is thus formed to bring the ingredients and utensils needed for the sacrifice, in particular the knife, hidden in a basket, to the sanctuary.

Then, after asking the ox for its consent, a 'relay' killing takes place, where some provide water to sharpen the weapons, others sharpen them, one takes them and hands them to two others, one takes the axe and stuns the animal and another takes the knife and slits its throat. Still others skin it and, finally, all taste its meat. The skin of the animal is sewn up and stuffed with hay to 'put the animal back on its feet' and it is tied to a plough. At the end of this ceremony, the murder is judged and the blame is passed from person to person until finally the knife itself is accused.

Such a dilution of responsibility through collective organisation, which may have been considered a central feature of ancient Greek sacrificial practices, has been relativised in recent studies, which consider the description of the Buphonia as biased, given that it comes from a Pythagorean, that is, a vegetarian, by nature opposed to blood sacrifices (Jacquemin 2014). It also seems that the sources merely mention the goodwill of the animals during the sacrifices, with no mention of their actual consent and thus the relief from guilt for the human sacrificers (Jacquemin 2014). The reality of the concealment of the sacrificial knife in the basket during the procession has been the subject of careful questioning by Pierre Bonnechere (1999: 35), who warns against the danger of elaborating theories based on source material that does not provide 'the exact course of the ritual operations of the sacrifice' and of which one does not know 'the precise meaning of the vocabulary used'.

Vedic sacrifice, the organising principle and its violence

This was already the conclusion reached by Hubert and Mauss, who, for this reason, chose to base their analysis of sacrifice on the Brahmanic (that is, Late Vedic) texts, which offer particularly detailed descriptions. Their choice may appear surprising, however, given that these are complex rites, where even the identity of the central element – namely the *soma*, or vegetable 'king', in whose honour an animal is strangled before being itself 'put to death' by pressing its stems – remains shrouded in mystery. In this context, each libation, each formula, each measure, each artefact or substance used in the rite all are explicitly presented as a sacrifice in and of itself. Such a proliferation of sacrifices, accompanied by often obscure explanations and rules as to how to proceed and what practices to avoid, means that any path to investigation into such ceremonies must be trodden very carefully. We have a clearer vision today, thanks to the investigations by a number of scholars. Among the most remarkable, the work of Charles Malamoud holds especial interest for our purposes because it explicitly addresses the question of violence and the effects of sacrifice.

In the Late Vedic texts, the rite is primary and takes on a hypertrophied form.[3] The myth provides the reason for the rite's existence or its genesis. As for the gods, they have no temple or fixed sanctuary and only exist 'through the words addressed to them and the offerings made to them' (Malamoud 2005a: 242). Created by sacrifice, they are devalued, whereas Sacrifice is endowed with autonomy and personality. Sacrifice itself is a god who gives the measure of, organises and incorporates all things.[4] Sacrifice couples with Speech (or Remuneration), making of the rite a world 'closed in on itself, autonomous, perfect, fruitful', from which the gods are evicted. It is only through a kind of rape that Indra manages to break into their union (Malamoud 2005b: 58).[5]

The Sanskrit term, which is generally translated as 'sacrifice' (although not all modern-day Hindus agree on this translation), has two meanings: 'Strictly speaking, the *yajña* is the essential part of the sacrificial ceremony, this culminating point which is the killing of the victim', while in a broader sense, 'the *yajña* includes all the acts, the ingredients, the texts, the ways of pronouncing them, the psychic and physical forces (spirit, breaths), and the characters, both human and divine, that are involved in the ceremony' (Malamoud 2005b: 63). Finally, despite its first definition, the *yajña* does not always include killing and is characterised 'by its structure, not by the nature of what is offered to the gods' (Malamoud 2005a: 250).

Strangely enough, despite the all-encompassing nature of sacrifice and its ability to create the human world, there is no such thing as civic sacrifice in Vedic India. The sacrifier does not act on behalf of any group, but as an individual. Similarly, the consumption of the victim does not create or unite a group through communion and does not define status, but only strengthens the bonds between two individuals forming a couple, such as husband and wife, or teacher and student.[6]

The sacrifier performs the sacrifice to ensure a future place in heaven for himself and is assisted by a team of officiants and his wife. As Charles Malamoud explains, he secures this place by joining the same path the victim has been placed upon, according to ritual procedures that affirm his identity with the being to be sacrificed while simultaneously maintaining their separateness. Thus, at the final moment of the killing, the sacrifier verbally enjoins the victim to go to heaven, while the officiant who stands at his side murmurs: 'the vital breath of the victim is one thing, the breath of the sacrifier is another' (Malamoud 2005a: 256). This is a remarkable illustration of the 'game of coincidence and discrepancy between the self of the sacrifier and his substitutes' from which the whole sacrificial device and its complex procedures derive (Malamoud 2005a.: 202).

The violence of sacrifice seems to be caught on a sort of see-saw, on the one hand, by the blurring of the limits between life and death that is manipulated during the ritual – as well as the power over these states attributed to the figure of the man who sacrifices – and, on the other hand, by an acknowledgement of the existence of sacrificial violence, which is expressed by its denial.

To the well-known idea that sacrificial violence is not really violence, the Vedic texts add that sacrificial death is not really death and, less explicitly, that violence is to be found everywhere within the rite. Indeed, to carry it out is to 'execute' it: 'One kills the sacrifice even while doing it' (Malamoud 2005a: 250; 1989: 222–223).[7]

Sacrifice 'is fundamentally violent' and 'each of the gestures of sacrifice is understood as violence': putting the animal victim to death, pressing the *soma*, pouring the vegetable or offering milk into the fire, and even turning the earth over in order to prepare the sacrificial area (Malamoud 1989: 104–105). Despite all of these components of sacrifice being recognised as violent, the true core of sacrificial violence, the killing, is the object of numerous devices that aim to transform its nature, such as the use of euphemisms – the victim is not killed, it is 'appeased' – and the requirement that the animal, and even its 'family', all consent to the killing.

Much like punishment, the prerogative of the king, sacrifice implements a violence that does not defile. However, the idea also exists that the victims might take revenge, that they might eat the sacrifiers in the next world (Malamoud 1989: 204, 206). Perhaps this is why an origin myth explains how domestic animals came to accept being sacrificed following the establishment of a regime of terror.

Originally bipedal, animals would have cowed in terror at the sight of the sacrificial post being planted in the ground by the gods and would then have accepted their fate. This terrifying symbol must always be present during the sacrifice, even though it is not used for the killing, because 'to sacrifice without a post would be as if one were trying to undertake some evil deed in secret' (Malamoud 2005a: 251). The secretive atmosphere surrounding sacrificial death is expressed in other ways too. Thus, despite its apparent purity and the negation of its nature, the killing itself should not be attended by unauthorised persons. The officiants and the sacrifier do not witness the killing, for example. The victim is tied to the sacrificial post located at the edge of the ceremonial space, the sacrifier and the officiants position themselves outside of it, and death is brought at the hands of the executioner who strangles the animal (Malamoud 2005a: 251–253).[8] After that, the sacrifier's wife brings breath back to the victim through the administering of libations, so that the 'lethal fragmentation is abolished after having been carried out' (Malamoud 1989: 217–218). The victim must go to heaven 'alive', with a reunited body, to which one ritually restores 'the spirit, speech, breaths, hearing, sight' (Malamoud 1989: 256). Then, its butchering is perceived as a new violence (Malamoud 1989: 254–255), which seems coherent, if we consider that the animal has ritually come back to life as it is about to be cut up.

The sacrifier, the victim and the sacrifice are caught up in what Malamoud (2005b: 29) calls a 'tautological vortex'. The sacrifier is transformed into 'a self, made of poetic meters' based on the model of the sacrifice, a self 'that is not distinct from the very machinery that is supposed to produce it' (2005b: 24). The sacrifier is also a module of the sacrificial structures. Lastly, he himself is the victim, and his substitutes are his replicas. These two-way correspondences between sacrifier and sacrifice, between sacrifier and victim, bridge all gaps: 'The victim is the *alter ego* of the sacrifier.... *Alter*, the animal suffers the violence of death and division to the very end; but because it is also *ego*, one cannot admit that this violence is irremediable, nor even that it is real' (Malamoud 2005a: 259–260).

To Frits Staal (1979), whose thesis states that the 'how' of Vedic ritual should be explanation enough, Malamoud (2005b: 12) recalls that most of the Vedic texts are about the 'why', about 'meaning', 'purpose' and the 'justification of rites'. He concedes, however, that it is possible that the complexity of ritual procedures may have subsumed the plane of meaning for practitioners, while pointing out that the contemporary reconstructions of Vedic rituals on which Staal relies are interpretations far removed from what is actually contained in the texts. In particular, ritual killing is now forbidden in India, thereby severing sacrifice from its 'point of accomplishment: the violent act' (Malamoud 2005b: 11). For Malamoud, this evolution can be explained by a change in the Brahmins' diet, as they became vegetarian more than two thousand years ago. Sacrificial killing is inseparable from the consumption of meat, he explains, because it is impossible to offer a victim in sacrifice without then eating some of its flesh (Malamoud 2005b: 248–249). It should be noted here that the reverse situation is not envisaged by the author, namely the possibility that the Brahmins could have become vegetarians by choosing to stop conducting blood sacrifices, since conversely, the only consumable meat according to the Laws of Manu, is sacrificed meat.

Unlike Frits Staal (1979, 1990: 51), who approaches Vedic sacrifice by trying to reconstruct it from a contemporary standpoint, Charles Malamoud (2005b: 15) addresses the question of the effects of sacrifice on the sacrifier, clearly not 'in real life' since it is not possible to observe them, but from what is supposed to happen according to the Vedic texts. At the new and full moon sacrifices, the sacrifier vows to speak only the truth and, in so doing, leaves the world of humans for that of the gods. Likewise, the Kshatriya who undertakes to sacrifice obtains Brahmanhood for the time of the sacrifice. Both return to their original states at the end of the ritual, upon declaring, 'Now I am what

I am'. What happens during this 'interval of truth' and, if nothing happens, why bother sacrificing? (Malamoud 2005b.: 16–17)

The texts give two answers: the first is a simple obligation to follow what is prescribed within its pages; the second describes two specific effects of sacrifice: one which is both immediate and invisible, a journey to heaven while the rite is taking place; the other, which is deferred, the assurance of going to heaven after death, in a world that the sacrifier will have 'made for himself' (Malamoud 2005b: 17–18). To this first typology of motives, Malamoud (2005b: 48) adds the repetition of the divine gesture, since sacrificing is also about 'commemorating, confirming, symbolically redoing or updating that which the gods have done'.

These three reasons for sacrificing – to conform to what is written, to actualise what the gods have already done and to obtain a place in heaven – tell nothing about the sacrifier's affects. And yet, Malamoud adds (2005b: 32), the Vedic texts show the anguish of loneliness and the terror of death of the first sacrifier, Prajāpati. All alone, Prajāpati becomes Sacrifice in order to multiply himself and, becoming simultaneously sacrifier, officiant and victim, births all the constituents of the universe (Malamoud 2005b: 76). Every sacrifier joins the continuity of this first sacrifice, as if in a sacrificial loop.[9] However, considering the complexity of the ritual procedures of the Vedic sacrifice, Charles Malamoud considers that for the sacrificing man, 'anguish fades before the concentration that the execution of the rite requires' (2005b: 32).

The fact remains that Vedic sacrifice displaces the death of the *ego* onto the *alter* and that its violence is presented as a dramatisation of the sacrifier's own mortal fate, one which summons the myth of the first sacrifice of Prajāpati (or Puruṣa), the primordial man, the idea of the journey into an afterlife, as well as an absolute power over the life of the *alter*. As Georges Bataille (1988 [1955]: 336) said: 'In sacrifice, the sacrifier identifies himself with the animal struck down by death. Thus he dies by seeing himself die, and even in a way, by his own will, at one with the weapon of the sacrifice. But it is a comedy!' The sudden reality check to which Bataille subjects the reader seems to be expressed in the Vedic texts in the constant back-and-forth between denial and recognition of the violence of sacrifice, which evades and opposes both views.

The Late Vedic texts, on which Hubert and Mauss's essay on sacrifice, as well as the work of Charles Malamoud, are based, are themselves the heirs of an earlier period, documented by obscure texts, where sacrifice forms the framework for a real unleashing of violence between sacrifiers and non-sacrifiers, or even between 'good and bad' sacrifiers (Oguibénine 1994). The 'arena of sacrifice' of the Vedic period, as described by Jan Heesterman (1993, 1995: 647), is where warriors struggle for power. Power relations are put to the test there, pitted against unknown combatants, to emerge either reinvigorated or torn apart. This very ancient relationship between sacrifice and warlike violence, which had disappeared by the time of the Late Vedic texts, is central to the practices that can be observed today in Nepal.

Sacrifice is thus caught in the motion of a pendulum which swings between the unleashing and denial of violence, a fact which is manifested within the same tradition, from one era to the next, from one context to another, and even, as Charles Malamoud shows with finesse, from one paragraph of a text to another.

Sacrificial violence and the decline of meaning

The interpretation of sacrifice seems to follow this movement between two extremes, which is specific to the perception of violence. A large lacuna seems to separate those scholars who do not see it, such as Luc de Heusch (1986), those who view it as a lure, like Claude Rivière (2003),[10] those who found new denials of the sacrificial violence and, for instance, consider that sacrifice is not violent because violence does not exist in the absence of guilt[11] and, finally, those who, conversely, see in sacrifice a disguised form of collective violence, following René Girard (1972).

The literary critic René Girard developed a thesis wherein the lynching of the scapegoat is the origin of sacrifice, based on the study of numerous texts, and this for a reason that would be specific to collective violence (Girard 1972: 437). Indeed, the author holds that the act of narrating is forced to adopt a single point of view, one that masks the totality of the processes at play in the collective violence that befalls a victim. To capture its nature, one needs to examine it from a diversity of points of view.

Girard identified this collective violence against a scapegoat in many contexts, which he considers the ultimate principle of regulation of social life, in that it aims to safeguard society from the permanent danger of the war of all against all. In theory, such a generalised violence would threaten humans insofar as they are driven by desire, which is itself mimetic by nature: if A takes an object, B wants it, leading to general violence. This type of situation cannot be resolved by a contract, as Hobbes held it, but rather, according to Girard, by pitting evil against evil, that is, by using violence to combat violence. In his view, in a situation of pure rivalry, all social differences are erased, so all bets are off, but if A sees B kicking C, he will imitate him, leading to a convergence of violence upon a single being. These 'mimetic rivals' would thus attack a single individual who would also be held responsible for the violence that befell them, creating a movement which, on the one hand, sanctifies violence because it cannot be traced to one source in particular and which, on the other hand, appeases the crowd by the death of the victim. The violence of the group initially projected onto this scapegoat later coalesces to focus on a ritual victim as a surrogate. Therefore, sacrifice can be considered a concealment of the original mimetic violence of all against one, which, 'as soon as it is spotted as such', becomes ritualised, almost as if the rite were a mask hiding what cannot be shown.

One important critique which could be levelled at Girard's model is that it reduces the variety of social constructions of violence to a single scenario and the wide range of possible human actions to mere instinct. Even from a simple, logical point of view, the pattern of mimetic violence derived from mimetic desire is flawed, given that it is then difficult to explain how person A could desire an object that person B does not possess in the first place, let alone how this might initiate the cycle of violence.

The author is more convincing when discussing how individuals band together against a person who occupies an exceptional position in society, who forms a unique 'model-obstacle' to the desires of all, and must thus be eliminated. Transformed into a scapegoat, this figure becomes a source of social cohesion, in that even the most disadvantaged members of the group take part in the violence and are therefore integrated into a society which would otherwise exclude them, through the rite of collective violence. This scenario can be seen, according to Girard, in the rite of elimination of the sacred king, a rite which reveals, reciprocally, that the ritualisation of the 'victim mechanism' is not always complete. Much like the scapegoat, the king is in opposition to a crowd. He maintains a double relationship with the group, ranging from adulation to execration, which Girard (1985) attributes to the 'capital function of a perverse man' that the king fulfils, either in a ritualised or institutionalised way – a thesis later developed by Luc de Heusch (2000) on the basis of African materials.

But Girard goes further. For him, the figure of the sovereign scapegoat can 'resurface' with revolutions and totalitarian regimes, and this idea allows him to extend his model into the political domain to suggest that it is possible to define a society by how it treats its victims: 'Any society in which the scapegoat reassumes its immemorial role of establishing and restoring transcendence ... is totalitarian' (Girard 1985: 140).

The sequences laid out in the Girardian theory of the genetic link between collective violence and the constitution of the sacred are often questionable because much of the data used has been cherry-picked in order to support the demonstration, while any discrepancies have been pointedly left out of the analysis. A striking example of such a selective reading is his analysis of the Book of Job, where Girard (1985) strives to paint Job not as the victim of God's trials but as a scapegoat of the society in which he lived and the object of mimetic violence. To achieve this, he is forced to first disregard the prologues and then postulate that the anonymous collective moved to act by the same hunger for violence is in fact only represented by the three friends of Job, these influential men whom the author introduces as simple spokespeople for the larger crowd.

Throughout the text, however, Girard assigns them an active role in the convergence of violence: '[T]he community therefore has great need of trustworthy men who will seek not to nip violence in the bud, but to prevent it from randomly spreading through the community, channelling it towards the best victim, the one most likely to unite the crowd against them,' he writes (Girard 1985: 90). Thus 'mimetic' violence nonetheless remains socialised, controllable by certain individuals who, we must understand, are driven by forces other than 'mob' mimicry. These remarkable characters do have an effect on violence in Girard's interpretation, since they can either stifle or focus it, but strangely, the author does not envisage that they may also play a role in its emergence.

If the mimetic theory does not provide a sufficiently robust interpretive framework from which to deal with collective violence and sacrifice, this does not mean that we must dismiss mimicry entirely because, as many works have shown, it does play a part in the construction of collective violence. Thus, in the tortures inflicted by colonists on Indians, Michael Taussig (1987) sees a reflection of the very savagery the invaders feared, condemned and invented, a sort of 'colonial mirror'. This theme is dear to post-modern approaches, which have used it to shed light on many different aspects of the colonial period, but it cannot be applied to the history of Nepal because the country was never formally colonised. It is, however, possible to use this mirror to examine the relations between 'Aryas' (or Hindus) and Indigenous peoples, as well as, to a lesser extent, the Untouchables, as suggested by the readings of the myth of the buffalo-demon already mentioned, where the violence of the sacrifice is seen as a legitimate response to the mythical violence of the demonic, impure or tribal Buffalo against the Aryas and their gods.

Likewise, the cathartic role that Girard attributes to the sacrifice of the victim, whose death puts an end to collective violence and strengthens the whole of society, is not absent in Nepal, even if it cannot summarise the total effects of sacrifice. It is true that in the village environment, the opposition to blood sacrifice that can often be heard during the ceremony falls silent once the executions are over and that everyone participates in the banquets that follow them. Nevertheless, the ceremony is as divisive as it is cohesive, as it makes use of the internal oppositions specific to the social structure in order to reaffirm it as a composite whole. The *dhunī jāgar* spirit possession ceremonies of western Nepal and Kumaon provide a setting where ritual violence explicitly deals with social violence. The rite achieves this by transposition. It moves the village community by night into the forest and turns it into an assembly of ascetics gathered around a *dhunī* fire. All participants mark themselves with the ashes of this fire of renunciation and some of them subsequently become possessed by invisible entities. The *dhunī jāgar* thus takes place in a space of uncertainty created by the ritual, at the intersection between the human and the invisible worlds, between social identity and the otherworldly identity conferred by the ritual setting.

Any disputes between villagers are then expressed through circumstantial conflicts which take place between the deities who have taken possession of the participants. Violence thus takes place at a distance from the ordinary world. It is then literally torn to pieces by third parties who constantly intervene in the altercations between the possessed so as to divert the violence by multiplying its objects, an act which is akin to splitting it. Finally, the initiator of the ritual violence is violently punished, thereby putting an end to the *jāgar*, the final point of which is sealed by an animal sacrifice offered to the deities who have manifested themselves during the ritual (Lecomte-Tilouine 2009c). Here, violence is translated into a parallel universe to be dealt with by ritual violence. Yet we might be mistaken for thinking that the ceremony is cathartic and resolves problems within the community. Indeed, to hear the participants talk about it, it appears instead that a dispute which has been exposed in a state of possession is now made real. And while the apparently cathartic rite does indeed make the violent expression disappear, it does not offer a definitive resolution. The conflict, now official, is not over. As for the rite which exposes it, a multitude of wildly differing interpretations are proposed by those taking part in it. I was able to film one such rite and discuss it with several of its protagonists during its viewing. For some, people who are victims of injustice are inhabited by evil spirits, *bhūt*, who also cause demonic possession of other participants. They jump into the fire, fight and swear as demons do. In this way the rite can be compared to a kind of exorcism of the occult forces born of injustice (locally called *nimun*, from 'nemesis'?). For other participants, on the contrary, the violence that can be attributed to the possessed is a false reading, an illusion. They are inhabited by gods who come to care for humans out of love, *prem*, and all their gestures, including the most terrifying, such as tearing a child from his mother's arms to throw him above the fire, are an expression of this love.

The myriad interpretations of this rite diverge from its original source in a process that is both divisive and unifying. It evades concrete definitions, with some considering it an arena of violence and others a therapy, which emphasises the importance of taking parallel perspectives on violence into consideration, not so much because its true meaning is hidden in the stories or rituals which surround it, as Girard says, but because the rite exposes the cleavage at the heart of the field of violence and its shifting fault line between the legitimate and the transgressive.

Violence is missing from Hubert and Mauss's analysis of sacrifice, who abandoned the primacy of the destruction of the thing offered to turn sacrifice into a process which transforms the sacrifier, where the victim only plays the role of 'body double', onto which the sacredness accumulated by the sacrifier is transferred, which is discharged by the killing of the victim. Charles Malamoud, who looked at sacrifice within the same tradition, gives a more central place to the animal victim, which, duly transformed into a psychopomp by the ritual, opens a path to heaven for the sacrifier after his death. There is indeed violence in both of these cases, but the intention is not to destroy the victim, but rather to initiate a process which requires its destruction.

In ancient India, *soma* stalks were crushed and 'killed' to extract their ambrosia. Today, when Brahmins offer grains and butter in the sacrificial fire, it is to produce an aroma which nourishes the gods, or even, in the words of a Nepalese Brahmin who insisted that I organise such a ceremony with him at the foot of the Eiffel Tower, an effective treatment against holes in the ozone layer. The destruction which constitutes the sacrifice is thus absorbed by the ritual, which does not focus on it, forcing us to go further and consider sacrificial violence as part of a larger process, to put ourselves in the shoes of those who offer the sacrifice or, alternatively, to dismiss them as fools.

From the point of view of the sacrificers, the benefits of executing the victim far outweigh its loss. Beyond any measurable properties that can be attributed to it, killing is not simply the destruction of the thing or being offered, or, according to Jankélévitch (1977: 7), the passage from 'the existing to the non-being', but must be understood as the transformation of the living being into an entirely new form of existence. It is true that the flesh of the victim goes on to rot, but it is far from being seen as a 'residue without stable form in the process of decomposition' (Jankélévitch 1977: 401). By its death, the body of the living being releases its precious blood, which, in Nepal, nourishes the gods and is rightfully returned to them. Immediately collected in pure receptacles, made of cow dung or leaf, the victim's blood is offered to them until the very last drop by dragging the carcass in a circle on the ground, using the last dregs of blood to trace an enclosure around the sanctuary. Simultaneously, the sacrificator seizes the victim's head, which, now separated from the body, can be manipulated like a ritual object. He hands it to the priest, who places it solemnly into the sanctuary as close as possible to the divinity, facing it. The appearance of life is maintained, with the head left with mouth agape and eyes wide open, unlike humans, whose eyes and mouth are closed once death has been pronounced.

The life that manifests itself after sacrificial death is sometimes staged, as in the sanctuaries of the goddess Barāhī, where the decapitated bodies of goats and pigeons are thrown into the water. The devotees watch them spin in concentric circles or flap their wings as if making their last flight. These untheorised practices echo the ritual procedures of Brahmanic India, where the animal is 'brought back to life' after having been executed. The carcass is then dealt with, with the entrails being extracted, above all the liver, from which a specialist reads the omens contained within aloud, before cooking and consuming them at the sacrificial site itself. Finally, the body is cut up and divided according to fixed rules.

The body of the executed victim thus lives a brief but intense existence, whose particular temporality mobilises all the attention and energy of the participants in the sacrifice. Dazzled by the initial spurting of blood and the cutting of the head, followed by an immediate gutting, then a cutting up and sharing of the body on the site of the sacrifice, all these tasks consume the men and make them feverish. The haste with which the living being is deprived of its vital breath transforms the animal into a foodstuff, which must be consumed as soon as it is prepared, lest it go bad. Like any food, it cannot be consumed reheated, and this even less so the day after it has been cooked – except by those who are not sensitive to defilement, such as the Untouchables or young children.

The link between sacrifice and the transformation into consumable matter is so essential that this religious practice is very closely correlated with diet, even if, as mentioned earlier, no one can say whether the Indian Brahmins stopped sacrificing by becoming vegetarians or whether they became vegetarians by ceasing blood sacrifice.[12] In Nepal, the Brahmins, who are strictly forbidden to kill any living being with their hands, commonly offer animal sacrifices to their lineage deity, which they have executed by Kshatriya sacrificators. They are also the priests who officiate the collective blood sacrifices, for which they ensure that the correct purification procedures have taken place, in particular that of the arena, the sacrificial post and the victim itself. In addition, most of them do consume 'pure' meat, such as goat and sheep. However, it is the rule that the eldest member of the lineage or family becomes a vegetarian (and shaves his moustache) upon the death of his father. He thus carries the values of renunciation on behalf of the rest of his family, lending a certain freedom to his younger siblings.

Alongside these traditional uses, vegetarianism is spreading all across Nepal, especially in urban areas, through religious currents of Indian origin which advocate non-violence, which have often joined forces with organisations fighting for animal welfare, and a 'charismatic' movement characterised by possessed individuals who exhort the virtues of puritanism. In line with their militant vegetarianism, the followers of these currents advocate for the end of sacrifice. Each group is so closely linked to the other that only a vegetarian can risk publicly opposing sacrifice, as illustrated by the incident that occurred on 27 November 2019 in a town located in the district of Bara, near the Gaḍhī Māī sanctuary. The cult of the 'Mother of the Fort', which brings together several million devotees every five years and carries out hundreds of thousands of sacrifices, had begun, attracting many 'antis', as opponents of animal sacrifice are called locally. Some of these activists, who had come specially to advocate for the end of sacrificial practices at the Gaḍhī Māī sanctuary, had sat down to lunch in a restaurant, several kilometres away from the sacred site. They had ordered a meal there that included meat when they were recognised as anti-sacrifice activists by someone in the room. They were immediately attacked, reviled and eventually beaten by a growing angry mob, one which both a nearby policeman and soldier struggled to contain. The idea that one could eat meat and demand the end of blood sacrifice was unbearable to the crowd.

The incident invites us to consider the growth of the animal rights movement and the direction the approach to sacrifice has taken in its wake, which is diametrically opposed to the original anthropological approach to the subject. The writings of Florence Burgat (2017) will serve here as an illustration. The author brushes aside the logic behind sacrifice, which she sees as a false justification for violence, refusing to acknowledge its meaning at all, on the grounds that such an approach results from a 'ritualistic creed' (Burgat 2017: 232). Indeed, the author considers that 'the rite is the place where meaning is emptied out' (Burgat 2017: 234), even if she also asserts that 'the rite makes those who need to believe, believe at little cost' (Burgat 2017: 235), two propositions that are difficult to reconcile. The idea of the absence of meaning of the ritual, which is coupled here with an absence of meaning of the belief, has been widely disseminated in the vein of the work of Frits Staal (1979). Breaking radically with the symbolic current that dominated religious anthropology at the time, which proposed to view ritual as a sort of code to be deciphered, Staal (1979: 3–4) substituted the idea that the rite is an activity both contained within itself and absorbed by itself. The rite is 'above all an activity', because 'what is important is what you do, not what you think, believe or say', so it would be a mistake to consider that it consists of 'symbolic activities that relate to something else'.

It is true that, much like the Brahmins interviewed by Frits Staal (1979: 4), most Nepalis responded to questions about ritual practice with a dismissal, the classic form of which is: 'it is our tradition, *paramparā*'. Despite this, it was always possible to continue the dialogue on the content of this tradition and the details of the practices it encompasses. Is this insistence forcing the meaning of things, as suggested by Jean Bazin (1998)? Perhaps, but this attitude is not unfamiliar to the group practising the ritual. In Nepal, the interviewer is considered to be like a child who asks incessant questions about what the adults are doing. Let us add that the example of Christian baptism cited by Jean Bazin (1998: 38) to support his thesis that one attends a ritual mechanically, without thinking about it, is rather poorly chosen, since its liturgy, more than that of any other sacrament, includes numerous explanations – on the meaning of light, of the white garment, of the sacramental oil, of the holy water – as well as a series of questions from the officiating priest to which the audience must respond, thereby guiding their attention in a prescribed manner.

More profoundly, the theory of the inherent meaninglessness of rituals is contradicted by the instructions found in the Nepalese ritual manuals, which, like the Vedic texts, are filled with exegesis on the meaning of the ingredients to be used and the gestures to be performed. Any householder ritually assisted by a Brahmin is thus infantilised by the priest, who corrects his gestures and specifies the precise meaning of each thing used in the rite.

This may be illustrated by an excerpt from a manual for the cult of Durgā, whose popularity can be measured by its first print run of 10,000 copies (Subedi 1988: ii, my translation):

> On the first day, smear a pot with cow dung. What is the reason for smearing the pot with cow dung? Cow dung has many qualities: it is pure ..., evil spirits (*bhūt pret*) cannot go to places smeared with cow dung. Dung is one of five sacred products of the cow. Even doctors use it against cholera. In dung there is a power (*śakti*) that destroys all microbes. This is why cow dung is smeared. As much as possible, it is desirable to smear an earthen pot with dung, because mud is a part of the Earth and there is a power (*śakti*) and a quality in Her that ensures the remission of faults, and She is the bride of Viṣṇu. Similarly, there is a power in the mud that erases faults. Dung easily attaches to mud and barley germinates well in it. Why do we plant barley seeds in it and germinate them? Barley is a great remedy, barley gives as many qualities as milk. Barley is the king of cereals. Barley is dear to Viṣṇu.

The text goes on to explain why this pot must be filled with water and then who the goddess Durgā is who is to be invoked within it, so that each constituent of the representation, as well as its whole, is duly explained. Many of the qualities attributed to the elements of the rite are used in everyday life and are part of a shared knowledge: houses are smeared with cow dung every morning to clean them and bandages are made from it to prevent wounds from infection, just as barley porridge is offered to oxen at ploughing time in order to strengthen them. Here, the rite concentrates powers and knowledge in one object, in superabundance.

The idea that the rite is meaningless or performed mechanically, which is today often endorsed without further questioning, is especially problematic when applied to sacrifice. Removed of meaning, sacrifice is indeed nothing more than gratuitous violence, and this new way of denouncing the practice reconnects with the old position taken by the science of religions, well before the development of anthropology. The decline of meaning, which gives way in Girard to a primacy of (mimetic) instincts – that the sacrificial rite masks – and in other scholars to a morality which condemns sacrifice, brings us back to a debate whose terms have been masterfully posed by Kierkegaard in his essay on the sacrifice of Abraham (or Isaac, depending on the perspective adopted). From an ethical point of view, says Kierkegaard, Abraham wants to kill his son; from a religious point of view, he wants to sacrifice him. From this latter point of view, Abraham, unlike Agamemnon, does not act for the general good. Contrary to the tragic hero, who is made great by dint of his moral virtue, who sacrifices himself to the collective, like Agamemnon offering his daughter in sacrifice for the good of his people, Abraham places himself above others, in an absolute relationship with the Absolute, thereby rendering ethics entirely relative and, conversely, making his deed utterly senseless[13] Hence his silence, his absolute isolation. So, Kierkegaard argues, one can only approach it with a type of religious dread: 'Where is the soul so gone astray that it has the audacity to weep for Abraham?' he asks (1983 [1843]: 61).

One could argue that Abraham's sacrifice is in no way comparable to the buffalo sacrifice in Nepal. However, if one accepts the idea of sacrificial systems of Luc de Heusch (1986), or only the idea that the notion of sacrifice is not expressed in the unfolding of a single type of ceremony but in the whole ritual setting that the participants in the sacrifice of the buffalo, for example, are led to perform, then one is struck by the presence of this absolute power which is unbound by ethics. This power is expressed in the buffalo sacrifice, which requires that 'impure' people be constrained to receive the consecrated remains, but it appears in a much more obvious manner in the injunction formulated by some deity speaking through the mouth of a medium, or in a dream, to offer a transgressive sacrifice. It is also expressed in the recourse to extreme sacrificial practices in desperate situations, such as illness, for example. Once a Newar woman, whose child suffered from epilepsy, told me that she had tried to cure him by feeding him a powder, bought at a high price, which she explained was brain tissue, and more precisely from the brain of a man who had been captured, chained and fattened by 'tantriks', and then trepanned while still alive. It is likely that she had been duped by those who sold the powder to her, but the important thing here is her faith, which trumped her ethical compass, until she stopped herself abruptly at the sight of my widened eyes, and it was then impossible to return to the matter.

The double constraint of sacrifice, expressed in a dilemma between faith (or necessity) and ethics (or law), is also encountered in a more ordinary context, in the cult worship addressed to the tutelary deities of the patrilineages, the *kul devatā*. The lineage group worships its own deities in this context, according to its own modalities, the most common of which is the phenomenon of men becoming possessed by the family gods, followed by the sacrifice of he-goats or rams to the deities that have manifested themselves in the lineage, in that unique combination of real presence and real violence.

Each householder of the bloodline must offer an animal that he himself has raised for the occasion. But baby lambs and kid-goats are particularly cherished by women and children, who take them in their arms and sometimes also sleep with them. Their sacrifice by men causes much screaming and crying, which leads many fathers to sell their animal to a neighbour and buy another one from him in return, some time before the ritual, so as not to sadden their family by putting the animal they so fondly cherish to death.

Often, however, the rite is cruel, because the rule of lineage requires that the animal must have resided long enough in the house for the gods to accept it, or even that it must have been born there. This places the householder in a situation which is reminiscent, *mutatis mutandis*, of Abraham's position vis-à-vis his wife Sarah, to whom Kierkegaard gave full prominence in *Fear and Trembling*. Interestingly, the ten-day long Dasaĩ ritual combines the painful sacrifice of the young goat in each household, on the eighth day of the ceremony, prior to the 'royal' ceremony of the buffalo sacrifice which takes place the next day. Sacrifice here violates all family groups indiscriminately, before targeting certain categories.

Certain patrilineages have even more contradictory ethical obligations when they worship their tutelary god, such as making an offering consisting of a sacrilegious sacrifice, of a man or a bull, two beings whose killing is strictly prohibited. They are thus forced to find alternatives, such as offering a few drops of their own blood to substitute for the human victim, as certain clans of Brahmins or the Tharu priests of the sanctuary of Gaḍhī Māī do, or to cut an effigy of a bull, as do the blacksmiths in the village of Darling. Others prefer to be imprisoned than risk disobeying the gods. During a stopover in Baglung, an old man told me how he had spent time in prison for having sacrificed a bull to his lineage deity, as requested, and how this deity became his saviour: 'He opened the door of my cell,' he confessed.

The requirements of tutelary deities are not limited to unethical demands but also include tasks which are impossible for humans to perform, such as making offering cups out of tiny leaves, instead of the large ones generally used.

We see, through these requests, that sacrificial necessity is regularly pushed to the limits of what is feasible, both morally and technically, placing humans in a double bind. Are these disruptions of the correct order of sacrifice, given that the buffalo, the royal sacrificial animal, is itself a borderline case because of its polluting nature? Or are they a constitutive feature of sacrifice, which enables the buffalo sacrifice to consecrate the organisation of society, because this caste-based organisation is the only one capable of resolving the double constraint of the buffalo sacrifice, its required purity and the constitutive impurity its remains generate, a problem which an individual or a group of the same status cannot resolve?

If, as Girard says, violence appears and disappears depending on the perspective considered, and if, as Malamoud points out, the violence of sacrifice is highlighted by its negation, or if the same act is a murder or a sacrifice depending on whether it is considered from an ethical or religious point of view, as Kierkegaard shows us, how can we account for it other than by a multi-centred description, which posits violence as a singularity, that is to say, an object which escapes analysis and which can only be approached by considering the entirety of the relations which are tied up in it?

Notes

1. See Hubert and Mauss (1994 [1899]: 33, 47–48).
2. *The Cuisine of Sacrifice among the Greeks* (Chicago: The University of Chicago Press, 1989).
3. The myth teaches that 'the paradigm of the rite is there in advance' (Malamoud 2005b: 51) and that, by means of the rite, time itself is constructed (Malamoud 2005b: 43).
4. 'Sacrifice, the organizing principle of all that is, tends to include within itself that all which it organizes' (Malamoud 2005b: 64).
5. Sacrifice is thus a rival of the gods, whom Indra seeks to subordinate. The risk for the gods is that humans discover that the rite is effective in and of itself and that they can do without the gods who are its recipients (Malamoud 2005b: 37).
6. The destination of the parts of the sacrificed animal is evoked 'in a vague and elusive way'. The common consumption of the same sacrificial material creates or confirms a link between two people, not the establishment of a larger social group. There is also no indication of the social rank or function of the eater by the share attributed to him (Malamoud 1989: 213–214).
7. So personified, sacrifice also inhabits a world apart, one which is different from 'ordinary life' (Malamoud 2005a: 54). In this world, 'the staging of the

act is part of the act itself and the boundary that separates the two planes is at the same time the seam that holds them together' (2005b: 40).

8. The decapitation of the victim is forbidden, as is the offering of its head: for this reason Charles Malamoud (2005b: 39) considers that the five heads placed in the structure of the fire altar should not be seen as offerings.
9. 'The story of the reconstitution of Prajāpati by the gods ... merges ... with the description of the Fire Stacking ritual' (Malamoud, 2005 b: 77).
10. Rivière's arguments are based on a particular conception of violence, which he associates with cruelty and hatred, not with killing.
11. On this question and, more generally, on the Christian influence that informs the notion of sacrifice, see Lemardelé (2016).
12. On this topic, see the discussion by Tull (1996).
13. Kierkegaard (1983 [1843]: 59–61).

3

Sacrificial violence in narrative forms

The buffalo sacrifice is closely related to myth. It brings into being the Goddess's combat as described in her *Celebration*, the *Caṇḍī pāṭh*, and a recitation of the text is incorporated into the liturgy of the ritual. In its dual role as both a model for and an integral part of the sacrificial rite, the myth is doubly brought to life. Does it narrate the unfolding of the action? Or is it simply enough to read its contents in order to shed light on all the different aspects of the ritual? The answers to these questions will be proffered in the next chapter, which is devoted to a detailed description of the ten days of Dasaĩ, where the *Celebration of the Goddess* is conducted, as both a narrative and a sacrifice, during a holistic rite in which the organisational structure of society and the power of the chiefs are renewed. The rite therefore goes beyond the combat that it plays out, and summons other mythical models, models which present caste society and royalty as being the products of sacrifice.[1] This broader framework must first be sketched out, without undertaking a textual analysis, but by considering how the myth manifests itself in everyday life in Nepal, in allusions or short stories, which form so many threads in the tapestry of the world which makes up 'Brahmanic teaching'.

The recitation of the text by the Brahmin carries the same term, *pāṭh*, as that used for pedagogical teaching. In Nepal, this 'teaching' has long passed for a child's basic education, as these words of an old Rai make clear: 'We did not know as much as today about the outside world. We had heard of Sri Lanka, Ayodhya, Benares and Badrinath from the Puranas. We believed the earth was flat and resting on water, held to the surface by the serpent Shesh Nag.'[2] In rural areas, it was not until the 1990s that a rationalist movement emerged among the Indigenous peoples, which targeted some of the contradictions and fantasies to be found in Hindu mythology. The movement then turned against the specialists of the myths, the Brahmins, recasting them as educated liars. And the Indigenous peoples reformulated Paul Veyne's famous question[3] to ask: 'Why did the Brahmins make us believe in their myths?'

Despite the recent erosion of Brahmanical discourse, the sacrificial shaping of the social and political organisation that it simultaneously affirms and negates has nevertheless deeply infused society.

Sacrifice and organisation: model myths

Puruṣa and the birth of a sacrificial society

The myth of the Sacrifice god, Puruṣa or Prajāpati, is the subject of the first chapter of Sylvain Lévi's work devoted to the doctrine of sacrifice in the Brahmanas, which inspired the essay by Hubert and Mauss explored in Chapter 2. For Lévi, the sacrifice of the primordial man forms the 'unique reality' from which everything which follows borrows the 'semblance of existence'.[4] For Lévi, its strength is such that man is 'the victim par excellence' and that the only authentic sacrifice is suicide (Lévi 1898: 133). In the wake of this study, reflection on Hindu sacrifice has since largely relied on this myth of primordial self-sacrifice, while the sacrificial nature of both the society and the sacrificial figures to which it gives rise have not received as much attention. For the Nepalis, the focus is reversed.

In the oral versions of the myth told in Nepal, there is barely any mention of the circumstances or of the manner in which Puruṣa died. The only thing that matters is the creative force that emanates from different parts of his body. In a village in northern Gulmi one afternoon, Burmali Bahun told me the story as he was arranging strips of felted wool to make a blanket.

> In the beginning, there was only Puruṣa, and he was alone. Having sacrificed himself, everything came out of his body: the sky was created from his skull, the sun and the moon from his eyes, everything was created. Then the different species (*jāt*) came out of his body, one by one, from his mouth to his feet. The Brahmins, who perform the rite, came out of his mouth; the Kshatriyas, who provide protection, from his arms. These two species wear the sacred thread and are called *dvijā*, Twice-born.

In the texts, these classes are set in opposition to the Vaiśya farmers, but since this specific group does not exist in Nepal, Burmali explained at this point in the story that the 'alcohol drinkers', *matwāli*, that is, Indigenous peoples, are considered their substitute. 'In our Nepal, those who are called Vaiśya, there are none: they are called *matwāli*.' He then specified that these first three species (the Brahmins, the Kshatriyas and the Matwālis) are 'pure' and that between them 'water was to circulate', *pāni calna bhayo*. 'Lastly, the Śudra came out of Puruṣa's feet, and their occupations were arts and crafts, *kalā*, and water did not work with them. And if you are asking why they were born from the feet,' he added, 'it is because in their occupation, *peśā*, they touch impurity. This causes them to lose status (*jāt jāncha*).'

There is only one other account of the creation of society to compete with the myth of Puruṣa in western Nepal. Told by the Indigenous peoples, the story also speaks of a division into four groups, but these are born of four distinct deities, who in turn were born of a cow, their mother. As recounted to me by a Magar, the story presents the Brahmins as being the descendants of Brahmā, the Kshatriyas of Viṣṇu, the Matwālis of Maheśwar (or Śiva) and the Śudra of Viśwakarma. Brahmā and Viṣṇu, the elder deities, cause their younger brothers to lose their status by inciting them to kill their mother, simply telling them, 'Come on, the cow must be sacrificed.' She is put to death by Maheśwar, then Viśwakarma eats her flesh. Both are then summarily rejected by their elder brothers as wrongdoers, *pāpi*, and the four groups of humans born from the four gods retain the statuses determined by the story from then on.

In both narratives, we are told of the emergence of a society which is structured and hierarchised according to the body from which it is issued, and to the sacrifice, or more precisely to the sacrifice of the body which has birthed them. These stories attract attention for their ability to attribute the act of dividing and differentiating humans to sacrifice itself, an operation which is re-enacted during the execution of the buffalo sacrifice, where each caste group fulfils its own established function.[5] The myth of Puruṣa thus exposes how sacrifice is a divisive force, ordering human beings through the establishment of a 'sacrificial' social organisation. We may consider it as such not only because it was born of a primordial sacrifice, but also because it is maintained by the presence of victimised groups in charge of taking impurity upon themselves for the entire society and more especially by eating the impure victims. A caste organisation can be deemed yet more sacrificial in its Nepalese reality because it is reordered and renewed annually through a holistic sacrificial ceremony. As a counterpoint to the cosmic order set out in the Brahmanic narrative, the Indigenous myth introduces a political dimension to this sacrificial division by attributing it to a conspiracy, a frequent theme in the origin stories of both the Untouchables and Indigenous groups in Nepal, many of whom tell of how they were tricked into their current social positions.

Far from the Girardian vision of a victim chosen at random at a time of social crisis, the scapegoat here is institutionalised and as such is born without the possibility of escaping its condition. It is not a case of an isolated individual who is opposed to a crowd, but rather an entire group which is set in opposition to the larger group. This opposition forms the fundamental dichotomy on which caste society is based, as suggested by its many 'regional *facies*',[6] where it is not uncommon that one or more of the three pure castes is missing, as in Nepal, but the opposition between pure and impure groups nevertheless remains constant.

The social dimension of the myth is so important in Nepal that the story of the sacrifice of Puruṣa tends to take a back seat, so that some beings are said to be 'born from the mouth' or 'born from the feet', without the owner of this body being named specifically. I once asked a woman who she was in passing, and she showed me her mouth by way of answer. I did not initially understand that she meant that she was 'born from the mouth', that is, a Brahmin, until she began to recount the myth with the help of large gestures. Placing her hand above her head, she said, 'The gods are there,', then added, pointing to her face, 'Under the gods, there are us [the Brahmins],' then placed her hand at chest height for the Kshatriyas and finally pointed to her feet in the direction of the Śudras. Her own body represented an image of her society's organisation, for this woman who had in fact substituted her person for that of Puruṣa without explicitly referring to him, thereby suggesting that the myth is embodied in each of the members of the very organisation it created.

This very ancient narrative still circulates to this day, and the specifically Vedic understanding of sacrifice that it establishes has informed Hindu sacrifice to a large extent, as Madeleine Biardeau explains (Biardeau and Malamoud 1976). She specifies that with the rise of the devotional movement, sacrifice was recast as a way to renunciate the mundane life for the divinity. Similarly, the organisation of the exchange of services between caste groups is inspired by the remuneration of the officiants by the sacrifier in the Vedic period, with it being the price which was to be paid so that the profane body of the sacrifier, abandoned in the sacrifice, would return to its possessor at the end of the ritual. As Charles Malamoud states, this price is part of the general economy of debt which, in Brahmanism, governs not only sacrifice but also the organisation of the entire world (Biardeau and Malamoud 1976).

Indeed, in India, the patron of an artisan is called his *jajmān*, a term which in the Vedic period originally designated the sacrifier who paid a Brahmin priest for his role in the sacrificial rite, and this type of transactional relationship is called the 'jajmāni system'. This situation is different in Nepal, however, as I unfortunately learned the hard way. Thinking that I had done ample reading on the subject, during my first period of fieldwork I asked a Nepalese blacksmith how many *jajmān* he had, a question which elicited much laughter from the men present. Through continued fits of giggles they told me that the patron of a craftsman is known locally as his *biṣṭa*, whereas *jajmān* designates the householder who remunerates a Brahmin for conducting the rites on his behalf – or the patron of a Brahmin priest only, as was the case in ancient India. I had inadvertently equated the Untouchable blacksmith with a Brahmin priest. In this regard, as in terms of blood sacrifice, in which the Brahmins still officiate, Nepal does indeed represent a closer version of ancient India, as Sylvain Lévi (1905) noted over a century ago. As such, it is important to emphasise the place occupied by royal sacrifice within this context.

In the myth, earthly kingship itself is a sacrificial institution, created by sacrifice and for the purpose of sacrifice. I heard the story of its creation in Dullu, the old imperial capital of the Khas Malla rulers, located in the midst of a religious complex of natural gas flames. The servants of these extraordinary temples are ascetics of the Nāth sect. Passing through the temple of Padukā, I learned from the ascetic officiant that he was in charge of the *śraddhā* of Dharmarāja, that is the ritual of ancestor worship addressed to the King of Death. Curious to know more about this custom, I questioned him further, and he thus explained that Yamarāja (another name for Dharmarāja, the King of Death), having had no son, is 'without descendants', *nirsantān*. Therefore, it is they, the Nāth ascetics, who celebrate the god's ancestor worship, in the absence of any male heirs. He added that through his daughter, however, Yamarāja had had an offspring, who gave birth to the first earthly king, then to the kings of Dullu, his descendants, in the following circumstances.

The King of Death's offspring

Yamarāja's daughter was married to a childless king, at whose sacrificial ceremony the gods refused to appear. The king then organised a fire sacrifice, during which a creature came out of the flames and handed food to his wife. Yamarāja's daughter ate it and gave birth to a son. He became King Bena (Vena in Sanskrit), who possessed the qualities of his grandfather, Yamarāja. Bena was a terrifying king who hunted men as if they were gazelles. He aroused the anger of the Brahmins, by saying: 'I am king, I am the *yagya puruṣa* (the man of sacrifice), in me are all the gods, you should no longer offer sacrifices to any other gods than me.' Upon hearing these words, the Brahmins decided to kill Bena. Convening at the place of the sacrifice, they began to strike him with *kuś* grass[7] and killed him.

As a consequence, finding themselves in a world with no king, the poor began to attack the rich. To put an end to this, the Brahmins 'churned'[8] the thigh of King Bena's corpse, and brought forth a little black man who bore all the faults of the dead king. They chased him into the forest. Then they proceeded to 'churn' the right hand of the royal corpse, and this time brought out King Pṛthu, bright as the sun, who gave his name to the land, Pṛthvī.[9]

The killing of Vena by the Brahmins in the sacrificial arena results from a conflict between the divine king with delusions of ultimate power and the sacrificial elite. Its bloody resolution in turn provokes another conflict, which, this time, is generalised. Here again, it is from the pure and impure parts of the sacrificed body that the social order is established: from its lower part, the Brahmins expunge the faults of the dead king, embodied in a tribal king who, as scapegoat, is sent far from the civilised world. From the right hand of his corpse, they produce a king who will maintain order, one who knows his place. This new king will no longer oppose the theoreticians and practitioners of the rite, the myth tells us, and will guarantee social peace, which includes keeping 'the poor' where they are.

Much like caste society, royalty is thus split in two by means of sacrifice, a theme that is found in historicised form in the chronicles of the royal families of Nepal.[10] Among these tales, of particular note is the case of the Shāh of Gorkhā, who were to become the sovereigns of the unified Kingdom of Nepal at the end of the eighteenth century, or the Malla dynasty, who reigned over the Kathmandu Valley until their defeat by the king of Gorkhā. The story of the establishment of these two dynasties, originally from India, is preceded by the splitting of the royal family, with the degradation of one member of the family, following an impure sacrifice in both cases, an event which was necessary for the king's progress towards his future kingdom and marked a degradation to the tribal rank in the former case and the rank of Untouchable in the latter.

The fact that both the mythical and so-called historical origin stories match up in this way presents an irresistible narrative to the people of Nepal, one which presents social exclusion as the consequence of a founding sacrifice which establishes order. The authority figures that these stories present – the primordial man, the first human king, the first king of a dynasty – all draw inspiration from each other. Prefiguring the tale of King Vena, the earliest hymn dedicated to Puruṣa relates his collective killing by the gods. Vena, in turn, describes himself as the 'Puruṣa of sacrifice', with both of their bodies being transformed by sacrificial death into a life-giving entity, evoking the 'tautological vortex' of sacrifice described by Charles Malamoud.

From the time of the Brahmanas onwards, Puruṣa takes on the form of a troubled paternal figure, that of Prajāpati, the father of all the goddesses – who is therefore forced into incest, and then of Dakṣa-Prajāpati, the organiser of a famous sacrifice that went catastrophically awry and whose story is one of the best known in Nepal. The text is indeed included in the *Svasthānī vrat kathā*, which is read aloud each year during the month of Māgh (February–March) in Brahmin families, often in the presence of neighbours, or in public places. With Dakṣa, the sacrificial machine veers sharply off course.

The sacrifice of Dakṣa

In the Nepalese version of the myth, Dakṣa is the father of thirty-three million goddesses, each married to a god. One day he invites all of his daughters and sons-in-law to a great sacrifice, except for Satī, who is married to Śiva, a god whom Dakṣa dislikes. Satī hears the news and becomes very upset. She decides to go to her father's ceremony and accuses him in front of his guests, reproaching him for not treating her like a daughter and for organising a sacrifice in their absence, one which, without the presence of her husband, will not be complete. Dakṣa tries to pacify her, assuring her that he has nothing against her but that he does have an aversion for her husband, who goes dancing around naked, his body covered with ashes and his eyes reddened by cannabis. Upon hearing these words, Satī flies into a rage, strikes the ground with her heel, hisses like a snake and, while exclaiming 'Śiva, Śiva' and beating her chest, throws herself into the fire of her father's sacrificial pyre, to the shock of the assembled guests.

Śiva immediately has knowledge of what has happened and the resultant anger which pours forth from his third eye causes the monster Vīrabhadra to be created. The monster takes charge of Śiva's demonic horde and marches towards the place of Dakṣa's sacrifice. A terrible storm accompanies their arrival, destroying all the trappings of the ceremony. Vīrabhadra then cuts off

Dakṣa's head and then proceeds to decapitate the billy-goat that the latter was preparing to offer in sacrifice. The monster seizes the body of the goat and the head of Dakṣa and throws them both into the sacrificial fire, in front of the terrified gods.

Śiva finally makes his appearance. At the request of the gods, he brings Dakṣa back to life, placing the head of the sacrificed goat onto his beheaded body, to mark him as a villain. He then takes up the remains of his wife, places them on his shoulders and goes out into the world, overcome with pain. To put an end to his incessant wandering, the gods end up causing Satī's body to decompose, with each part which falls onto the ground giving birth to a 'seat of power', *śakti pīṭh*. Later, the Goddess will be reborn secretly in the form of Pārvatī, the daughter of King Himālaya, and will devote herself to asceticism in order to regain the love of her husband in her previous existence, thereby giving rise to a new myth.

For Brian K. Smith and Wendy Doniger (1989), the story of Dakṣa's sacrifice is a demystification of the sacrificial liturgy based on substitution, in that it highlights the difference between the sacrifier and the real victim. The myth therefore reveals the essential illusory nature of the rites that actually take place.

It is true that the myth of Dakṣa may seem bleakly comic, but its very literal presentation of the identification between sacrifier and victim both reinforces the logic of substitution at work in sacrifice and demystifies it, by showing how much real danger the sacrifier, as the 'head of the sacrifice', faces in terms of suffering the same fate as the victim.

Whatever its purpose, the myth of Dakṣa explores the possibility of catastrophe at the heart of sacrifice, and the chain reactions it may trigger. Within its flawed, incomplete framework, the sacrifier's offspring is sacrificed, before fusing with his victim, in two monstrous hybrids, where the *alters* (sacrifier and victim) go from being substitutes to each forming one half of the totality of the offering and of the sacrifier. The first transgression, Satī's immolation, repeats Puruṣa's sacrifice by its reflexivity but violates its constitutive masculinity. The sacrifice, in the first instance the action of the 'male' – the meaning of the name Puruṣa – is carried out by a pair of male *alters*, the sacrifier and the animal victim, but here takes on a feminine and filial form. This shift destabilises the place of the father and the sacrificial ceremony that consecrates his position, leading to the savage destruction of both, whereas the myth of Puruṣa institutes the organisation of the world through his sacrifice.

Dakṣa's sacrifice, the moral of which is that no one should have been excluded from it in order for the ceremony to be 'complete', recalls the civic sacrifice of Dasaī in Nepal, in which the entire population must participate. The mythical ceremony further evokes the rituals of Dasaī through the transformation of the sacrificial scene into a fighting arena, pitting two sections of society – parties associated with Śiva and Dakṣa – against one another. Moreover, the fusion of the *alters* (the goat and Dakṣa), through their warlike decapitation, contrasts with the Brahmanical methods of killing by suffocation or fire but is characteristic of royal sacrifice in Nepal. The connection between Dakṣa's sacrifice and Dasaī finally becomes explicit during the ritual itself, on the 'dark night' of the eighth day of the festival, which is often presented as that of Satī's self-immolation, which took place amid her father's sacrificial ceremony.[11]

With the sacrifice of Dakṣa, which depicts a fundamental disruption, the various ritual ways by which the myth is actualised take different directions. Notably, two different forms of sacrificial practice are situated at opposite ends of the spectrum. *Satī jāne*, 'to go away as Satī', the cremation of widows on their husbands' funeral pyres, was practised in Nepal as late as 1920.[12] The practice refers to Satī's fidelity to her husband, which marks the gruesome fulfilment of the initial 'gift of the virgin' made by the father at the time of his daughter's marriage. However, the real-life practice moved away from the original mythical narrative, where Satī chooses death and therefore separation from her husband, in response to her father's slight. On the other hand, it does restore a more acceptable meaning to the sacrifice of the daughter, by transforming the opposition against the father presented in the myth into the ultimate declaration of attachment to the husband. At the same time that *satī jāne* was abolished in Nepal, the myth of Satī took on a new life, as more and more women began to self-immolate in protest from the 1920s onwards.[13] This pseudo-sacrificial practice, aimed at denouncing institutional violence through self-inflicted violence, mobilised the ancient heritage of mythology and, in turn, started to reflect back onto the myths. Thus, in modern images depicting the sacrifice of Satī, we no longer see the sacrificial pyre of Dakṣa into which the goddess throws herself, as written in the story, but the flames directly coming out of her body, as if it were a self-immolation started with flammable liquid.

These mythic realities of sacrifice are sometimes depicted as forces of world-creation or world-ordering, as in the story of Puruṣa, but sometimes as forces which bring disorder and destruction, as in Dakṣa's story. This duality very much corresponds to two visions of the same society that produced these tales. On the one hand, it was depicted as a stable and orderly system where competition is prevented by a hierarchy rooted in shared values, notably by Louis Dumont (1966); on the other, as proposed by André Béteille (1992) in opposition to Dumont's theory, the different castes are antagonistic groups that depend on the struggle to define themselves. These two opposing effects of sacrifice on the order of things are brought to bear during the rite of Dasaĩ, where both order and disorder manifest themselves at the end of the reading of the *Celebration of the Goddess*, the *Caṇḍī pāṭh*, which is performed daily during the first eight days of the rite.

The *Celebration of the Goddess*

The *Caṇḍī pāṭh*, also called *Saptaśatī*, 'Seven Hundreds', from the number of verses it contains, or *Devī māhātmya*, the 'Celebration of the Goddess', is a well-known narrative in Nepal, where it is widely considered to be an independent text.[14] To corroborate this idea, Jean Varenne (1975: XVII) highlights that the text has been inserted by 'unconvincing' artifices into the *Mārkaṇḍeya Purāṇa* (chapters 81–93), which was composed in the fourth to sixth centuries, and Manmatha Nath Dutt (1896: iii) calls it its 'most important episode'.

The *Caṇḍī pāṭh* opens and closes with a framework narrative describing the circumstances and effects of its first narration. It is therefore a text which consists of repeating what has already been said, in this case to a defeated king who is still worried about his kingdom and to a Vaiśya driven from his home by his family who is still concerned about his household. Both ask the hermit they have found refuge with what the cause of their persistent attachment might be. The ascetic replies that they are under the influence of the goddess Maya (Illusion), who created the world and governs it. At the request of the king, he then describes the various ways in which the Goddess manifests herself.

In the first canto we hear of two demons, born of Viṣṇu's ear while he is resting in cosmic sleep, who wish to kill Brahmā. In a display of sheer power, Brahmā invokes the appearance of the Goddess and lavishes her with praise, glorifying her double character as the source of both life and destruction, of goddess and demoness, 'Nature by which the elements are ordered' and 'Night of terrible bewilderment'.[15] Then he implores her to 'manifest her energies' against the demons so that Viṣṇu awakens and kills them.

This brief episode fits rather poorly with the rest of the text, which describes the creation of the Goddess and her warlike nature. Here the text has her existing even before her creation and intervening so that another deity can take action. By awakening Viṣṇu from his cosmic sleep which separates the eras, the Goddess initiates a new temporal cycle but does not herself fight.

The second episode, which the rite actualises and has thus kept the text alive, begins as a battle is raging between the gods and the demon armies commanded by the Buffalo. The demons beat the gods, who announce their defeat to Brahmā, Viṣṇu and Śiva. When they learn of this, the deities' faces burst into flames of anger, and then from all the assembled gods. These emanations of divine anger merge into a fiery mass that sets the universe ablaze and then transforms itself into a woman. Despite being born from this shapeless mass, the Goddess reveals herself as a fully composite body, in which the glow of fury of each individual god remains identifiable and localisable.[16] Next, each of the gods duplicates their specific weapon, attribute or adornment and offers it to the Goddess. Thus adorned, she bursts into peals of laughter, causing the earth to sway and the mountains to crumble.

The buffalo-demon, intrigued, approaches and catches sight of her terrifying form. He immediately launches a myriad of armed demons, chariots and elephants to attack her, which she repels without emotion. Suddenly, her breath as she fights turns into thousands of troops, who, 'raised by the energy of the Goddess', slaughter the enemies, while others beat the drum or blow into conches, so that 'the battle became a feast' (vv. 2, 55). The story then becomes 'enthusiastic', as the Nepalis say: some demons are cut in two, others, crushed, vomit blood; some fall with their chests burst, others, riddled with arrows, are transformed into porcupines; heads roll, headless bodies get up and dance, excited by the music, still brandishing their weapons against the Goddess. Soon the battlefield is littered with corpses to the point that no further progress is possible, and the land courses with rivers of blood.

The *Celebration of the Goddess* here combines the most abject violence with pleasure, in a macabre feast where even the beheaded enemies are seized with a frenetic dance. The scene is observed from the heavens by the gods, who sing the praises of the Goddess and rain flowers down upon her, bringing a celestial touch to the carnage. The fight continues with duels between mighty demons and the Goddess herself, who shape shifts and shatters weapons in the form of Bhadrakālī the Blazing, then strips herself of all lustre and strikes down the Buffalo's lieutenant with a single syllable – 'hum'. Lastly, the Goddess enters into a rage and goes berserk, killing a demon with rocks and tree trunks, another with her teeth. Her fury sets the brute force of the Buffalo in motion, who rushes into the ranks of the gods and sows death in all directions. He uses no weapon, but his size is such that he crushes the surface of the earth with his hooves, bursts the clouds with his horns, crumbles the mountains with his flanks and causes the oceans to overflow with his tail. The Goddess captures him like common cattle with a lasso, from which the demon tries to free himself by successive transformations: he changes into a lion, she cuts off his head; he becomes an armed man, she tears him to pieces; he transforms himself into an elephant, she splits him in two. Resuming his buffalo form, he turns to face the Goddess. Her eyes red with anger, she is inebriated, bursts into laughter, then juggles him with her feet and kills him as he tries one last time to change his buffalo form into that of a man. Immediately the demonic hordes flee, while the gods sing out in joy.

The canto which follows is a hymn of praise addressed to the Goddess by the gods. It contrasts with the intense action that precedes it and adds an unexpected dimension to the text, namely the compassion (*dayā*) of the Goddess who, according to the words of the gods, purifies the enemy by the contact of her weapons, so that they ascend to heaven by dying in battle (vv. 4, 19–20). There was no indication of this happy fate of the slaughtered beings in the description of the battle, and compassion in the form of supreme violence is an oxymoron which is rather difficult for many Nepalis to accept, who do not believe that the victim of the sacrifice benefits from being killed. The text of the *Caṇḍī pāṭh* itself does not attempt to convince the reader of this in any real way, since it specifies in the next episode that the demons Sumbha and Nisumbha, killed by the Goddess, end up in hell (vv. 12, 33). This last episode of the *Celebration* begins as these two demon chiefs both decide to take the Goddess as their wife and send increasingly strong warriors to bring her back to them. They are each slaughtered in turn, but the intensification of the assault angers the Goddess. Her body turns black and from her forehead emerges Kālī, a horribly emaciated form of herself, with red eyes and a hanging tongue, who swallows men, chariots, elephants and horses in her gaping mouth, then tears them apart with her teeth. Kālī beheads two generals, turns to the Goddess, her *alter*, and offers her their heads as a sacrificial offering. Already duplicated, the Goddess then further multiplies herself into an army of Mothers, manifestations of the energies of each god, in order to fight Raktabīja, an invincible demon every drop of whose blood which touches the ground transforms into another form of himself. The duel thus takes the form of a gigantic confrontation between *alters* who are constantly multiplying on both sides. The intervention of Kālī, who laps up the blood of the monster to the last drop, puts an end to the fight, leaving the Mothers, drunk with blood, to perform their victory dance. The Goddess finally reabsorbs all her forms into herself to deliver the fatal blow to Sumbha and Nisumbha.

Her new victory is once again lauded by the gods. In return, the Goddess assures them of her protection and then addresses the humans: 'In autumn, a great ritual should be celebrated every year, where my Celebration will be recited' (vv. 12, 12), she tells them, adding that hearing her tale 'makes a man a hero' (vv. 12, 14), annihilates enemies, dispels misfortune, casts away children's fear and reconciles estranged friends.

The framework narrative comes full circle by way of conclusion: edified, the king and the Vaiśya devote themselves to the veneration of the Goddess, for three years presenting to her 'offerings moistened with their own blood'. They then obtain the realisation of their wish from her: an invincible kingdom for the king, and for the Vaiśya the knowledge that allows him to free himself from the misconception that had caused him to say: 'I have, I am.'

The primary effect of the *Celebration*, as the Goddess says, is to embolden men. And, to further enhance its effects, it is the only text that certain Nepalese Brahmins learn by heart in order to increase its beneficial effects, *phāl*. Its reading during the eight days which precede the buffalo sacrifice acts to fortify the bravest men of the community for the execution of the most vigorous of animals, a veritable mass of muscles, in a meeting of extreme forces reminiscent of the duels described in the *Celebration*. The fortification is continued in a more intense manner in the ritual killing of the buffalo, which habituates the men to the sight of blood and renders them able 'to wage war'.

While the recitation of the *Celebration* forms the heart of the rite demanded of humans by the Goddess, and constitutes the main thread of Dasaĩ, this does not mean that it is listened to religiously or acted out to the letter. Only a few people, mostly the elderly, go to the palace or temple to hear it read out, and the rite follows the main thread of the story at only two points, the awakening of the Goddess in the form of Durgā and the killing of the buffalo-demon.[17] Kālī's fight against the demon Raktabīja is also often mentioned without being acted out, even though this demon is only an underling of Sumbha and Nisumbha, the supreme demonic figures who have nevertheless not made their mark on the imaginations of the audience and largely go unnoticed in the rite.

The in-between-ness of the epic

Between the *Celebration of the Goddess* and the sacrifice that brings it to life, there is a historical weight which takes root in the epic, born of that in-betweenness between myth and history. Dasaĩ, it is said, was instituted by Rām (Rāma in Sanskrit), the ideal king of the *Rāmāyaṇa* epic, when he celebrated this rite in autumn instead of spring, in order to gain the support of the Goddess in his warlike expedition against the demon Rāvaṇ (Rāvaṇa in Sanskrit). Rām thus duplicated the rite, which is still celebrated in Nepal on two twin occasions: the Great Dasaĩ of autumn, where the buffalo is sacrificed, and the Little Dasaĩ of spring, its somewhat diminished counterpart, where usually only chickens or goats are offered.[18]

Sacrificial ruptures

People say that the rite was originally instituted by Rāvaṇ in the spring, but Rām's devotion was so extreme that he proposed to offer his own eye in place of a missing ingredient for the ceremony in autumn, a gesture which won him the favour of the Goddess despite its inappropriate timing. By the sheer force of his sacrifice, Rām therefore superseded Rāvaṇ's sacrifice, which made it all the easier to overthrow him.

Sacrifice here enters the realm of history by the means of a more extreme form of itself, which has transformed its timing.[19] Every year, the local newspapers recount the episode of Rām and Rāvaṇ, as if it were breaking news. All of these exceptional circumstances make the buffalo sacrifice a uniquely twisted rite, one which was originally demonic, designed to obtain power in the epic, but which is also used as a tool in the competition between those seeking power.

Indirectly, Rām's story also sheds light on the relationships at play within the sacrifice. According to Smith and Doniger (1989), between man – the prototype of the victim – and his surrogates, there are differences of degree found in different ancient Indian texts, and the sacrificial quality of the beings can take different directions. Sometimes it is man, the prototype, who possesses the most qualities; sometimes, it is at the other end of the chain, the sacrificial goat, who is seen as a chimera of all living beings who may be sacrificed. The substitution of the human *ego* by his goat-shaped *alter* thus replaces the 'most' by the 'whole'.

In Nepal, the two main sacrificial *alters* are the buffalo, an impure and wild animal, which takes the place of the demon, the enemy, the foreigner, the Indigenous or the Untouchable, concentrating in it all the attributes of Otherness. On the other hand, there is also the billy-goat, a docile animal that is often invited inside the houses and pampered like a child of the family, whose pure flesh is consumed by those who have raised it. In polar opposition to each other, the buffalo is an *alter* of the Other, the billy-goat an *alter* of *ego*.[20] The alterity of the buffalo is in stark contrast to the familiarity of the goat, representing an affective relationship expressed in opposition, characterised by distance or proximity. However, while the images of the distant *alter* are numerous, nothing is said of the closer one, just as there is a complete silence surrounding the sacrifice of the closest person to the (male) *ego*, that is, his eldest son. The sacrifice of a son by his mother forms a figure monstrous to be sure but not unheard of within the community. It is by such an act, say the villagers, that a woman becomes a witch, and the myth of Sati depicts the sacrifice of a daughter caused by her father's actions. The pampered goat, whose sacrifice breaks the hearts of the family, seems to be a silent stand-in for man's most precious *alter*, his son, who alone can conduct his funeral rites to ensure him an enviable place in the afterlife.

The epic also sheds light on the tug-of-war between identity and difference that is expressed in sacrifice in Nepal, much as it was in ancient India. Systematically questioned about my family in Nepal, when I replied that I am the mother of twin boys, I was often met with the exclamation: 'Ah, you have Rām and Lakṣmaṇ!' These inseparable heroes of the *Rāmāyaṇa* are indeed regularly used to name twins, sometimes in a specific way, but also generically. On the other hand, whereas Westerners inquire whether my sons are identical or not, I am asked in Nepal which of them is taller. The fundamental difference between twins is therefore taken for granted – one must necessarily be taller than the other, and Nepalese curiosity centres around how this difference fits in with birth order – the idea being that the second-born is generally the taller.

Interestingly, this most famous heroic pair are not twins, but half-brothers, born to the same father and his two most distant wives, the eldest and the youngest. The matter is complicated by the fact that Rām and Lakṣmaṇ have other siblings, and among these brothers, there is in fact a pair of twins, with Lakṣmaṇ being one of them. However, his relationship with his twin brother is conspicuously absent from the *Rāmāyaṇa* and has not given rise to any important figure. Lakṣmaṇ, the twin, is on the other hand vitally attached to Rām, his half-brother, whom he cherishes to the point of following him into exile and assisting him in his most perilous adventures. He behaves much more like a twin towards him, going so far as to marry the younger sister of Rām's wife.

Natural proximity is thus denied in favour of an affective construction, so much so that the real twins are named with the names of distant half-brothers, whose union ruptures the true genetic bond that one of them shares with his twin brother. This strange situation is likely a model, since it is found, in an attenuated version, in the other great Hindu epic, the *Mahābhārata*, in an episode where Yudhiṣṭhira, the elder Pāṇḍava brother, finds his four younger brothers dead and has the possibility of reviving only one of them: he chooses the one he loves best, one of his two youngest brothers, who are also twins. The epic not only constructs affective relationships as taking precedence over relationships based on identity but also violates them, since they are achieved at the cost of a rupture. The *alter* of the ideal king is thus torn from his natural *alter*, in a rupture that is reminiscent of the sacrifice of Isaac and his severance from his mother, which Kierkegaard often evokes, or even of the suffering of women and children in Nepal when their kid-goat is led to sacrifice by the father.[21]

The vernacular epics of Nepal and the effects of violence

The vernacular epics of western Nepal relate the violence of war, injustice, infidelity and revenge, and are specifically designed to produce emotions. It is for this reason that they are of interest to us, as a sort of guide to help us understand the effects of sacrificial violence. In this region, such a bleak history is not exclusive to the epic tales but can also be found in informal accounts of the past. People speak, for example, of King Khem Cand of Saḍaur who, spurned by his minister's wife, took revenge by killing his son and then invited him and his other ministers to a dinner where the child's flesh was served to them as a stew.[22] His plot having been revealed by a little finger floating in the dish, the king was then hunted by his ministers and put to death; or of Megjyu Ṭhakurī who, unable to offer his ritual friend the impossible gifts he demanded, ended up offering himself as a sacrifice, by throwing his own flesh piece by piece into the sacrificial fire.[23] The memory of the past is thus anchored in acts of violence, with the epic constituting a most exemplary form of it, one that is both qualified as history, *itihās*, and as 'words of truth', *satya kurā*, while its performance aims at producing codified emotions.

The Nepali epic repertoire, which developed in the mediaeval period (twelfth to seventeenth centuries), judging by its content, has remained entirely oral until today and is transmitted within bardic Untouchable families.[24] Performances are commissioned on the occasion of life cycle rituals, especially the marriage of Kshatriyas of royal rank, known as Ṭhakurī.[25] It is then the bard's task to increase, *baḍhāi*, the prestige of his patron and to 'make him a name', *nāu banāuna*, as if the ordinarily despised speech of this Untouchable man was suddenly imbued with authority. This sudden change in status occurs when the bard delivers a 'word of truth', in a situation which is similar to the transformation of the sacrifier who left the human world to join that of the gods, by swearing to tell the truth, in Vedic times (see Chapter 2).

The bard is as much a dancer, an actor and a storyteller as he is a musician and a singer. He arms himself with a variety of tools to bring the text to life on an emotional level, on the one hand, and an intellectual one, on the other, flitting between what can be sensed and what can be understood. The session is opened by the recitation of the patron's genealogy,[26] then two or three choristers take their place at a specific point in the imaginary circle where the bard will weave his yarn, to accompany him with their voices, according to different prescribed procedures. They sometimes repeat the second part of the verse sung by the bard, like an echo, or sometimes sing it in unison with him, but often they complete the second part of the stanza on their own, making the bardic session a collective art, one which is entirely dependent on a shared knowledge (see Figure 3.1).

The first song is always an address to the gods, inviting them to 'come and sit'. Then the story begins, performed alternately as song and spoken declamation. The text of the song, in an archaic, verse form, transports the listeners to the past and creates emotion in a variety of ways, by the obscurity of the language, the melody, the dialogue between the main performer and the choristers, as well as the bard's acting and dancing talents. When this first part ends, the bard takes up the text of the song and recites it in a more modern language, during which time he paces around, his index finger pointing to the sky, as if he were delivering a lecture. The narrative then progresses to a new episode which is sung and danced, so that the epic constantly moves back and forth, building up its structure in a sort of herringbone pattern.

The performance of the epic therefore makes use of a multiplicity of effects to transmit its messages: the story is told with several voices, sometimes in

Figure 3.1 Bards of Achham district performing an epic, 2009
Source: Author.

chorus or echo, sometimes in stereo, jumping from past to present, alternating between poetry and prose, and switching between song and spoken recital.

All of these narrative strategies are applied to stories which are full of unexpected twists and turns, sudden reversals of situation and unexpected behaviours. Added to this there are a variety of formulas at the storyteller's disposal, in the form of interjections, questions, swear words and bawdy formulas which cut into the story and blur its intelligibility, and thus have nothing in common with the Homeric epithets which are designed to bring regularity to the story. These disorientating effects are further accentuated when the formula itself is cut into two parts that are recounted at different moments during the narrative, or when there is a sudden shift in the register used, one which is in sharp contrast to the content of the story – for example, a bawdy tone used at the most tragic moment or a more regal register being adopted in the midst of an otherwise zany scene.

The bards of western Nepal say that their artform was born of war, that they once accompanied their master to the battlefield, singing of the victory to come and the events which took place upon their return. They even play this role within the epics they recite, where they teach their master the cunning that will ensure their victory. We could qualify them, like the Welsh bards, as warrior-poets (Markale 1956: 19), but the epic in Nepal differs in that it often sings of very bitter victories and of the most abject violence, or even ends in the most tragic way, with the death of the hero. Such is the case of Kaśirām.[27]

The child-king Kaśirām learns from his ritual father that King Hindupati of Morang killed his grandfather Candraman Mal, his father Kālīman Mal and his paternal uncle Asubasu Mal and kept their heads in his kingdom. Filled with fury, he does not listen to his mother, who implores him to be careful, nor to the dark omens seen by the astrologer, and sets off.

From the roof of the palace, the youngest wife of King Hindupati sees the drums, the glittering swords and the standards led by Kaśirām, who is mounted on his black horse. A flame of fury comes out of the child-king's mouth. She runs to warn her husband, who sends messengers, and then goes in person to Kaśirām, accompanied by his whole army.

> – 'How is your kingdom, O child-king? How is your family, young Kaśirām? How are your seven queens? How is your reign? How is your palace?'
> – 'All will be well when I kill you,' Kaśirām replies.
> – 'What are you saying, Kaśirām? You are breaking my heart! It is not our fault, it was a bandit, it was a brigand, it was an enemy, it was an Untouchable. Appease your anger, Kaśirām.'

King Hindupati fills a pipe with a drug and hands it to the child-king, who smokes it and falls unconscious. He has him locked in a cage while a battle ensues between Kaśirām's army and Hindupati's. Kaśirām wakes up and curses, 'Son of a whore, horse of an Untouchable, he drugged me on Bhaumari Ridge.' In his golden cage in Hindupati's palace, Kaśirām promises a black goat to Kālīkā, a golden umbrella to Mālīkā and implores them, 'Have mercy on me, open my cage, have mercy on me.' By the effect of his prayer, the padlocks of his cage break one by one and Kaśirām emerges, drunk with revenge.

> He kills a hundred men, he kills two hundred men....
> he kills two hundred men, he kills three hundred men,
> he kills four hundred men, he kills five hundred men...
> Kaśirām goes mad, Kaśirām goes mad,
> O Great King, what will be the fate of the hero?

The soldiers regain courage upon seeing Kaśirām, then decimate the enemy army to only three hundred soldiers and surround the palace. Hindupati then faces the child-king and asks for mercy. In response, Kaśirām chops off his head. The enemy soldiers flee in all directions and Kaśirām's army massacres the people, disembowelling pregnant women, cutting off the tongues of any who speak. Lastly, Kaśirām and his men confer about which road to take back, and the child-king decides not to take the one he came by, but to follow the Trisuli River. There, on a bridge, two of King Hindupati's men show him where the heads of his father and grandfather are buried. The child-king duly hastens to this place, grabs one head and, as he grabs the second, receives an arrow fired by these men, which splits his skull in two. Kaśirām unties his belt, ties it around his head to join the two parts together and, carrying the head of his forefathers in each hand, heads for his palace. On the way, on the bank of the Trisuli, he cuts down a juniper tree, makes a pyre of it, places the heads of his ancestors on it, then addresses them: 'If you are the heads of my father and my grandfather, may you burn by yourselves.' Immediately, the heads ignite. The child-king writes a missive to his mother and has it delivered to her, then jumps into the pyre.

Kaśirām forms what the bards call a 'saddening', *runuwā*, or 'compassion-inducing', *dayālu*, epic.[28] This particular register, defined by a decrease in vitality and a desire to weep, constitutes one of the polarities of the epic. It is opposed to 'enthusiasm', *jos*́, which is associated with pleasure and laughter. *Jos*́, said Gome, bard of Dhami gaon, causes one to leap; *dayā*, on the other hand, causes one's body to slump. Each epic is assigned one of these overall emotional registers, somewhat reminiscent of a musical mode, that is, in a major or minor key. Specifically, as in European classical music, the overall tone of the piece is characterised by the beginning and the end of the epic. Discussing Kaśirām in particular, Gome saw it as having a sad beginning and end but a rousing middle section, especially the battle scenes, which generate more pleasurable feelings. What is more, the rise of 'enthusiasm' in the narrative is specifically initiated by a comic line delivered by the hero, in the warlike laconism of Kaśirām, who, in response to the courteous questions posed to him by Hindupati, curtly declares that all will be well once he has killed him, a retort which makes the assembly laugh. The hundreds of deaths, the disembowelled women and those with their tongues cut out are placed in this register of enthusiasm, akin to warlike fury, which is expressed in the text by the flame emerging from the mouth of the angry hero.

The epic of Rani Rāwat is considered, by contrast, to be an 'enthusiastic' story. It begins in a palace which has been deserted by its king in favour of another of his residences but which is still inhabited by its seven queens and his elderly mother. A low-caste shepherd takes advantage of the situation to break into the palace and take the place of the king. Until then, the story, interspersed with comical scenes, is entirely 'enthusiastic', but the shepherd ends up locking the queen mother, who is utterly indignant at the turn of the events, in a dark room, which sets the scene for a 'touching' episode. She laments and writes a missive to her son Rani Rāwat, which she ties to his parrot's leg, to let him know that she is being mistreated and that he has been cuckolded. The king, duly warned, gets on his horse, returns to his palace and subjects the shepherd to cruel ordeals, having him burned and then dunked in water by his queens, under the pretext of appeasing the gods of his dwelling. This violence is cheered on by the laughter of the audience. In the end, Rani Rāwat is killed by an enemy king, but in a way that is not entirely saddening, since he dies from an arrow that pierces both him and the shepherd who had cuckolded him, uniting them in death.

As is often the case, the story continues into the next generation: the newborn son of King Rani Rāwat, deprived of his father, and of his mothers who have been abducted by the enemy, is raised in a cave in the forest by the old queen mother, whose surge of compassion has brought milk back to her breasts. With the child's explosive growth, the tale becomes 'enthusiastic', and so, when he finally comes out into the world, as a twelve-year-old giant, his violence is terrible, but still childlike. Sobhā, the child's name, eats all the herdsmen's food and forces them to carry stones all day long, only to return them by evening. Growing tired of petty punishments, the boy finally reveals his princely nature by an act of pure cruelty: after having made a herdsman dig his own grave, he cuts off the man's tongue and buries him alive. It is then that the villagers understand who he is, and the orphan sets forth to the palace, puts on golden clothes, takes up a sword and goes to fight the enemy king who killed his father. He avenges him with the help of his family bard, who has recognised the boy as his rightful master and teaches him how to kill his father's murderer by disguising himself as a bard.

This 'enthusiastic' epic nevertheless also contains many episodes of the opposite emotion and this mixture is the most characteristic feature of the genre. Its power to draw a crowd lies in the double polarity of the epic, as the bards themselves say, claiming that their art consists in 'making people laugh and making people cry'. In the same manner, a dictionary of Dotyali (the local dialect of Nepali) defines the oral epic as both 'attractive' (*ākarshak*) and 'poignant' (*hṛdayasparśī*),[29] which is to say it exerts a force which sometimes 'pulls the other to oneself' and sometimes 'touches the heart, affects it, melts it, liquefies it' as per the definitions of these terms by Parajuli et al. (1983: 101, 1426, my translation).

Of these two polarities, the one that brings together poignancy, sadness and compassion is familiar to us, but the association of violence, enthusiasm, attraction and delight is more perturbing. Several commentators on mediaeval tales, where the same mixture is found, have endeavoured to find suitable moral meaning underlying this association, suggesting that the text somehow neutralises the violence it describes, either by an effect of catharsis, that is to say, by conjuring up violence with a surfeit of horror, or by concealing violence through the use of humour (Vinot 2004: 79). For others, this mixture merely serves to legitimise violence by essentially making genocide seem pleasant, as Jean-Charles Payen has written (1979) about the *Chanson de Roland*. These views are reminiscent of those who try to find a unique, determining meaning in sacrificial violence, regardless of the complex reality.

The epic of Chiyā Bhiyā, the full text of which can be found online, in audio, transcription and translation, allows us to examine this dichotomy more closely.[30] The text begins abruptly, with a presentation of the hero, Chiyā, whom the bard addresses as if he were present:

Get out of the way, Chiyā, get out of their way!

The second verse slides into narrative reality, with a change of speaker, who presents himself by his geographical origin, without giving his name, and forcefully takes up the bard's initial exhortation to Chiyā.

Here I am, Kumaoni of Kumaon, get out of the way!

We are here placed in a scene of a verbal jousting match, the violence of which we can grasp, without yet understanding the reason for it. The answer to these injunctions, however, reveals that we are in the presence of a fiercely oppositional will:

> *'And what kind of hero would leave the passage? And what kind of ascetic would abandon the sacred fire? And what kind of Brahmin would leave the altar? What kind of hero would leave the way? If my torso is sliced up, I would offer my head. If my torso is sliced off, I would offer my body. I will not give way. Get out of here yourself, Kumaoni warrior.'*
> *He did not leave the path.*

The scene closes with a short sentence in the third person which acts as a transition, allowing the bard to now 'explain' what has just been said in these preceding verses sung in part by the bard, in part by his assistants. He then addresses the audience, as if it were the king himself:

> *O, Sire, at that time, Sire, Bikrām Cand, the deceitful king of Kumaon of the Twenty-Two Kingdoms, had set out, at the head of his army, exclaiming: 'Let us go to Sātsāri Katyur!' Sire.*
> *And, for his part, Chiyā Kathāyat, younger brother of Bhiyā Kathāyat of Sātsāri Katyur, had also set out, saying: 'Let us go to Kumaon of the Twenty-Two Kingdoms!'*
> *Sire, they met halfway, Sire, at the top of Pattharlek, Sire. And then, and then, Sire, the deceitful king of Kumaon, Bikrām Cand, spoke thus: 'Get out of the way, Chiyā warrior, get out of the way! Here I am, Kumaoni from Kumaon, get out of my way!' He spoke these words.*

The entire dialogue, which was initially sung, is thus taken up in spoken word form, which provides additional details, and then moves the action one step further:

> *While, Sire, the king of Kumaon of the Twenty-Two Kingdoms, Sire, was leading his army toward Sātsāri Katyur, Sire, in Pattharlek, Sire, moving upwards, a terrible battle was waged, Sire, in what manner?*

This new outcome gives rise to a new enactment, in a sequence of sung verses that forms the 'how' of the narrative, opposed to its 'why' contained in the recitative.

> *Sire, from below, from above, a terrible fight began, terrible, from above to below (c) Sire, hand-to-hand fight, bone-breaking, bone-breaking,*
> *Sire, it was a fight to heat the gauntlets, to heat the gauntlets,*
> *Sire, it was a fight to be grabbed by the forelock, to be grabbed by the forelock,*
> *Sire, it was a fight to kneel, to kneel,*
> *Sire, rivers of blood began to flow, O king, of blood, king. (b)*
> *Sire, there was the sound of gunfire, O king, of guns, king*
> *Sire, there was a shower of arrows, O king, arrows, king*
> *Sire, as the lightning sparkles in the sky, the lightning of the sky*
> *Sire, so fell the sword held by Chiyā, held by Chiyā (c)*
> *Sire, he slayed ten enemies, destroyed twenty enemies, ten enemies he slayed, (b)*
> *Sire, he slayed twenty enemies, destroyed ten enemies, twenty enemies he slayed,*
> *Sire, he struck down thirty enemies, destroyed forty enemies, thirty enemies he struck down,*
> ...
> *Sire, he slayed ten enemies, offered them to Kālīkā, ten enemies he slayed,*
> *Sire, he slayed ten enemies, offered them to Mālīkā, ten enemies he slayed,*
> *Sire, he slayed thirty enemies, offered them to Bhairava, thirty enemies he slayed. (c)*

The description of this bloody battle strives to highlight its density through an effect of repetition and parallelism. Its descriptions grow progressively more expansive, from the fighting bodies, the sound and visual effects of the weapons to end with an evocation of the battlefield, dripping with blood, where corpses and the wounded accumulate in increasing numbers over the course of the verses. These bodies are immediately offered by the hero to the goddesses Mālīkā and Kālīkā, as well as to the wrathful form of Śiva. These offerings thus equate combat with sacrifice, but more than representing a sacralisation of the enemy, the swift dispatch and large number of these bodies deny them any individual dignity, reducing their personal warrior sacrifice into a vast sacrificial butchery, orchestrated by Chiyā.

The bard repeats the whole episode in the recited part which follows, all the while keeping the suspense going as to the outcome of the battle which, when it comes, is as sudden as it is surprising:

> *And as [Chiyā] was about to annihilate the whole army, the deceitful King Bikrām Chand said to himself: 'I will finally kill this one by trickery.' And King Bikrām Chand shot Chiyā Kathāyat with his double-barrelled shotgun and killed him. After killing him, the deceitful King Bikrām Chand of Kumaon of the Twenty-Two Kingdoms made his own army with those who remained of Sātsāri Katyur's army and marched on Sātsāri Katyur to sack it.*

At this point in the story, leaving the fate of the royal capital in suspense, the scene suddenly changes, much like in a film, taking us to a jail in Kumaon where Bhiyā, the brother of Chiyā who has just been killed in the most cowardly fashion, is being detained.

Bhiyā is asleep and Chiyā (or rather his spirit) 'breaks into Bhiyā's dream' to address him:

> *'O elder brother Bhiyā Kathāyat, may you die eating your offspring in sauce, I had set out from Sātsāri Katyur, at the head of the army, saying to myself that my elder brother was here in Kumaon of the Twenty-Two Kingdoms.'*

Chiyā then tells his brother of the battle, how he was killed, and warns Bhiyā that their kingdom is about to be annihilated. At these words Bhiyā wakes up and lets out a curse, then laments his fate and appeals to the gods. The Goddess hears him, takes pity on him and breaks his chains, then seizes him and causes his body to tremble with spirit possession.

> *And as Mother Gureli took possession of him, everything trembled, Sire, and the foundations of the fort of the deceitful King Bikrām Chand split into four parts, and his 99 kilo iron chains broke.*

A maid goes to warn the queen, who manages to stop Bhiyā just as he was about to leave the fort, and forces him to swear an oath to spare her husband's life. Bhiyā cannot refuse, but the oath causes his ire to rise again. On his way to save his kingdom, he raises all the men he meets along the path to make an army with him, and goes to find his king who has taken fright and hidden himself in the forest. Bhiyā enjoins him to return to his fort, then send his men to lie in wait, ready to ambush the enemy army upon his order. He then goes in person to beg for alms from them, dressed as an ascetic wanderer. He finds the enemy soldiers starving, having not eaten for seven days for fear of being attacked at this ritual moment when the soldiers have to take off their clothes and lay down their weapons. Bhiyā offers to watch over their equipment while they prepare a meal for themselves. The soldiers accept and Bhiyā takes the opportunity to tie up their clothes into tight knots and place their weapons in their fires. He then he raises the call to battle. Here are the last verses which describe what happens next:

> *There were blasts, Sire, of guns, showers, Sire, of arrows.*
> *Of blood, Sire, rivers flowed.*
> *He slayed ten enemies, Sire, annihilated twenty, He slayed twenty enemies, annihilated thirty, He slayed thirty enemies, Sire, annihilated twenty.*
> *Like lightning flashing in the sky, Sire, fell the sword that Bhiyā wielded.*
> *'I have annihilated the army of Kumaon of the Twenty-Two Kingdoms.*
> *At last, only the deceitful King Bikrām Cand remains, Sire.'*

Just like the battle waged by Chiyā, Bhiyā's battle ends in a head-to-head confrontation between the hero and the enemy king. In both cases it is hardly a fair duel: Chiyā had been brought down by a rifle shot, and the fate of the king, at Bhiyā's mercy, is particularly gruesome:

> *'By Nārāyaṇ, may you die eating your offspring in sauce, I would gladly have annihilated your existence,*
> *but as I was about to leave, your queen addressed a request to me, he said, Sire, and it was granted.*
> *However, I must only spare your life,*
> *he said, Sire. And he broke one of his arms and turned it over on his back.*
> *And he broke his other arm, Sire, and turned it over in his back, Sire, and amputated his ears,*

gouged out his eyes, and cut out his tongue.
So he left him only breath to speak, and thus led him, Sire, to Sātsāri Katyur.
As he led him, he made the tiger-king Bikrām deva put on his finery, Sire, and put him in the saddle.
As for the deceitful King Bikrām Cand, Sire, he made him a horse, and, in Sātsāri Katyur, having placed seven buffalo skins on his back, Sire, he made him turn around, and then finally [said to him], Sire, 'Go, go, now, to your Kumaon, deceitful King Bikrām Cand, go to your Kumaon of the Twenty-Two Kingdoms.'
He said, Sire, and after he had said this, Sire, throughout the land, Sire, vast as the ocean, Sire, Bhiyā Kathāyat was mourned, in what manner?
O yes, let the memory of the brave warrior endure, his name remains through the Four Ages.
He complied with the request of [Queen] Phulhari, Sire, for 100,000 years,
O yes, in what era did the battle take place, O king, in what era is his fame?
O yes, the battle took place in the Age of Truth, O king, its fame endures through the Four Ages.

The powerful foreign enemy king is thus fashioned into a fearsome pack animal and paraded before the king in the heart of the capital. Then, having literally been turned into a buffalo, he is mocked and chased out of the kingdom. Barely has his revenge been consummated, the hero becomes nothing more than a memory, one which both closes the story and secures his lasting place in history, in two ways. The first way is explicit, and is marked by the shift from the narrative past to the optative tense, expressing the bard's wish for immortality, which opens onto the future to come, until the end of time. The reference to the time in which the events take place, the Age of Truth, reminds us that the bard's words, themselves words of truth, are impervious to the passing of time, much like the hero's renown, which will endure 'through the Four Ages'.

The bard also ensures the lasting effect of his art by making sure to disturb the audience far beyond the performance of the narrative itself. Who, upon hearing this story of a queen's promise kept so cruelly, would not be plunged into a lasting malaise, into a profound rumination on the morality of the hero?

This final effect of the epic, on top of those more explicit effects we have already mentioned, is a kind of brutalisation of the audience, who have been subjected to situations that are alternately 'poignant and attractive' and 'enthusiastic and saddening'. This switching technique of this double effect of making 'laugh and cry' which, according to the bards, forms the heart of their art, is maintained long after the performance has ended.

The use of opposing emotions in the oral epic mirrors the alternating form which we have seen in the text of the *Celebration of the Goddess* and in its recitation. The recounting of her deeds does indeed alternate between the violence seen in combat and the compassion shown in the praise of the gods, while its recitation shifts from hand gestures and prosodic rhythms taken from an obscure language, Sanskrit, to a flatter reading in ordinary Nepali. The co-existence of these opposite feelings is also made manifest in the sacrifice itself, without it being formally codified, but we can observe in this context the transition from laughter to terror on the faces of the participants during the ceremony or, even more pronounced, we see a mix of these emotions play out at the moment of sacrifice itself. Such an opposition of affects also inspired the leader of the revolution in Nepal to create his most popular motto, one which was constantly repeated by the Maoist warriors engaged in the sacrificial combat of the People's War: 'We cry while laughing, we laugh while crying.'

The similarity of the emotions generated by the narrative of violence and by the participation in violent action invites us to take the context into consideration. The epics of western Nepal developed in a society which was organised for war, where every man was required to take up arms, in order to follow his clan elder or king in whatever enterprise he saw fit. The epic describes the existence of massive levies of men, clan by clan, at the time of the Khas Malla empire (Lecomte-Tilouine 2004). Revealingly, while we know of no example of epic composition referring to characters or events after the seventeenth century, the tradition was reborn in a similar modern situation, with the Maoist movement. Some bards indeed composed new epics recounting the People's War (Lecomte-Tilouine 2016), a context in which there were once again massive levies of fighters by the Maoist party, sometimes even with the same one-man-per-house rule, especially in the remotest region of western Nepal, where the epic tradition is still alive and well. If, as Jankélévitch (1977: 185) says, from birth to death, 'life is an adventure' in the sense of what happens (the series of advents) between life and death, war represents a condensed form of such an adventure, one which brings together two distinct states of being in the process. Sacrifice represents a snapshot of this process.

Conversely, war, and even more so sacrificial rite, which concentrates within itself the deadly violence of war and implicates the whole community in murderous violence, at least as spectators, cannot do without a narrative, which ensures its inscription in time.

Notes

1. These stories are strongly associated with the Brahmin class in Nepal, where in 1950 the literacy rate did not exceed 5 per cent, a number which most likely corresponded to male Brahmins, and the small political and economic elite of Kathmandu.
2. Quoted in Anonymous (1993), 'A Study of Para village', *Himalaya* 8 (2): 14–19. The Puranas, 'Ancient [texts]', are anonymous religious texts, composed during the second half of the first millennium. Śeṣanāga is the name of the serpent upon which the Earth rests in Hindu mythology.
3. Did the Greeks believe in their myths? (Veyne 1988).
4. The publication in 1898 of *La doctrine du sacrifice dans les Brâhmanas* by Sylvain Lévi preceded the *Essai sur le sacrifice* by Hubert and Mauss (who were his students), which was published the following year. The work, published hastily by Lévi's own admission, brings together his lectures of the previous few years. Its aim was to sketch out a unified doctrine of sacrifice from the enigmatic and scattered formulas contained in the Brahmanas. For Lévi, this doctrine leaves no room for morality, but instead presents sacrifice as a 'magical operation' by which the sacrifier rises to the divine.
5. The narrative can sometimes provide a retroactive explanation for the state of affairs, as in Burmali Bahun's account, where an individual's occupation determines their place of exit from the status-defining body, not the other way around.
6. Expression used by Louis Dumont to designate the variety of caste organisations found in the different regions of India.
7. *Kuś* is a sharp grass used by Brahmins to purify the sacrificial area and the various ingredients needed for sacrifice as well as their own persons. In Nepal, the officiants make a ring of it, which they wear on their finger for the duration of the rite.
8. The verb used, *pārna*, means to produce by rotation or friction. It translates the action of churning when applied to milk, but is also used for the production of fire by friction of two pieces of wood.
9. This account can be compared with the different versions of the myth presented by W. Doniger O'Flaherty (1988: 321–368). The main features

of the myth are more or less the same in all of them, but Vena's violence is often more extensively described, as well as his verbal exchanges with the sages. The latter sometimes put him to death with sound, not grass, and after his death, it is sometimes brigands, not poor people, who attack. Pṛthu is sometimes created from the dead king's thigh, and in some versions, a twin sister of Pṛthu comes from his other thigh and marries her brother.

10. The motif of the perdition of the king with divine claims is also widely historicised in Nepal. The case of the king of Iḍākoṭ in Baitadi can be cited here. The Brahmin priests of the temple of Nīgālā Sāinī, which will be discussed in the following chapters, relate that this king had compelled their ancestor to worship him before the Goddess. The terrified priest complied, but one day he forgot to erase the sandalwood powder that marked his forehead and presented himself before the Goddess. Surprised, she asked him whom he had worshipped before her, and the Brahmin revealed the king's demand. Nīgālā Sāinī became angry and that very night caused such a cataclysmic storm that it submerged the valley of the kingdom of Iḍākoṭ, razed the king's palace to the ground and annihilated him.
11. In Bengal, the relationship between the myth of Dakṣa and the celebration of the Durgā pūjā takes on a pacified form, since the rite commemorates the reconciliation of father and daughter, who on this occasion comes to visit him, accompanied by her four children.
12. The practice, limited by a set of rules in the 1854 code of law, was finally prohibited in 1920 (Michaels 1994).
13. The first known case, with significant consequences, took place in 1914. In Calcutta, Snehalatā, a fourteen-year-old Brahmin girl, seeing her father ready to sell his property to offer her a dowry, dressed in white, climbed onto the roof of her house, poured kerosene over herself and set herself on fire in order to be seen by as many people as possible. Her gesture was followed by a wave of self-immolations of young girls and gave rise to ritualised practices of commitment against the dowry. Today, self-immolation by fire accounts for more than 10 per cent of all suicides in India, with two-thirds of those who use this method being women, the majority of whom are under the age of thirty. We do not have such statistics for Nepal, but the figures are likely in the same range (Lecomte-Tilouine 2012).
14. It was translated by the pandit Shriyukta B. P. Padhyaya into the 'Gorkha language', an ancient name for Nepali, in 1904 (1961 VS).
15. The passages in quotation marks are taken from the translation by Jean Varenne (1975).

16. From her mouth emanates the ardour of Śiva, from her hair that of Yama, from her arms that of Viṣṇu, from her chest that of the Moon, from her belly that of Indra, from her legs that of Varuṇa, from her buttocks that of the Earth, from her feet that of Brahmā, from her toes that of the Sun, from her fingers that of Vasu, from her nose that of Kubera, from her teeth that of Prajāpati, from her three eyes that of Agni, from her eyebrows that of the two twilights, from her ears that of Vāyu.
17. While Dasaī is also known as the cult of Durgā, the Goddess is not often referred to by this epithet in the *Caṇḍī pāṭh*. Thomas Coburn (1984: 115) notes that it appears only seven times, compared to twenty-nine for Caṇḍikā, twenty-five for Ambikā, fifteen for Nārāyaṇī and fourteen for Kālī.
18. On the opposition between Great and Little Dasaī, see Satyamohan Joshi (1982: 34).
19. The *Rāmāyaṇa* and *Mahābhārata* epics are rarely performed in oral form in Nepal, unlike in neighbouring Uttarakhand, India. Bhanubhakta's translation of Valmiki's *Rāmāyaṇa* into Nepali, published in 1887, is believed to be the first literary text written in this language, which was previously reserved for administrative use only.
20. The qualities of sacrificial beings are not discussed in Nepal. Instead, there is much discussion of the defects that would make the sacrifice of a particular animal unsuitable.
21. Symmetrically, the fate of the symbiotic twins is fateful in the epic tales of western Nepal, which often make reference to them. Sijā and Bhijā are considered bastards by their maternal uncle. He takes them away from their mother, his sister, before the twins even get to see their father. He then leads them through mountains and forests on a journey full of hardships to the place of their torment, where he kills them in a particularly cruel way, by impaling them. Another local epic describes the sad fate of twin sisters, caught up in an irrepressible desire to return to their parents, who together find death on their journey to their native home. There is thus a multitude of tales which make the fusion of the similar into something utterly mortifying.
22. A former kingdom located in the district of Baitadi, in far Western Nepal, which will be discussed later in the book.
23. These two stories, which are very popular in Baitadi, appear in written form in Bhandari (2003: 190, 205).
24. The bards of Western Nepal are members of the Damāī caste. Unlike the other Untouchable castes, whose occupation is handicrafts or music, the Damāī have a double specialisation, combining tailoring with their

practice of music. They thus occupy an intermediate position within the Untouchable castes, who are now referred to as the Dalit: like artisans, they are bound by contract to high-caste patrons, but when they play music, they are more akin to itinerant musicians, who are said to 'beg' when they ask to be paid for their artistic performances. The bardic session, like any musical performance, is 'priceless', and there is no limit to what the bard might expect by way of payment. The patron of the session, in fact, sets the measure of his own prestige on this occasion.

25. On the epic tradition in Nepal, see Gaborieau (1974), Bordes (2005) and Lecomte-Tilouine (2016).
26. On the genealogical knowledge of bards, see Lecomte-Tilouine (2009d).
27. A twenty-minute montage of the performance can be seen on the DVD attached to the book *Bards and Mediums* (Lecomte-Tilouine 2009a).
28. On the display of emotions generated by the bardic performance by a Nepalese bard, see Lecomte-Tilouine (2017).
29. 'For those who understand the meaning of the bardic session (*huḍkeli*), it is an attractive (*ākarshak*) and poignant (*hridayasparśī*) genre ..., it exerts great subjugation on the spectators' (Chataut 2001: 936–937).
30. This version was recorded in 1969 by Marc Gaborieau and Mireille Helffer. It was transcribed by Jaya Raj Pant, translated into French (by myself), then synchronised and translated into English by Boyd Michailovsky, as part of the ANR program: *Epopées Népal*. The oral text, its transcription and its synchronised translations are available at the following link: http://epopee.huma-num.fr/corpus.php. It should be noted that this is an out-of-context recording and is an abridged form of the epic.

4

Sacrificial practices and partitions

The rules which govern sacrifice and killing, their associated groups and inter-relations on a daily basis in Nepal are an extension of a larger socio-sacrificial cosmogony, one which exposes the causal relationship between blood sacrifice and socio-political organisation, in much the same way as they did in ancient Greece (Vernant 1979).

Two main principles emerge from the ethnography of sacrificial practices in western Nepal: first, that whosoever is entitled to kill is also entitled to sacrifice (with the result that killing and sacrificing are little differentiated in practice) and, second, that only those who are entitled to kill can themselves be killed. The right to kill thus traces lines of partition within society, lines which trace out a social structure which is parallel to that of the castes.

Whosoever can kill can sacrifice

In the region formerly occupied by the Twenty-Four and the Twenty-Two Kingdoms, apart from the Brahmins, who are forbidden to kill any animal whatsoever, any man can be a sacrificator or butcher, in the absence of caste-based specialisation in these roles, as is seen in the Kathmandu Valley.[1] Killing is thus strongly associated with masculinity and takes on an initiatory character. Since childhood, boys aspire to be entrusted with this responsibility and it is not uncommon to see them insisting on the right to kill their first chicken. Permission is granted to them by their parents only once they are old enough not to cause the animal undue harm. Indeed, causing the victim to suffer is a fault, *pāp*, one which brings harmful consequences to the one who causes it. If a young boy kills a chicken in the wrong way, a member of his family rushes to blow *phuphu* on the sickle used in order to 'drop the blame'.

Sometimes even in a ritual context, a botched sacrifice must be repaired by another small sacrifice, of a baby chick.

Anyone who is entitled to kill can also sacrifice, at least for themselves. There are some Nepalis who have never killed an animal nor consumed meat outside of a sacrificial framework, like a Sārkī family I met in Dullu in 2012, for instance. These shoemakers were so poor that the husband, who is the 'incarnation' of Bhurulle Bhairav, could not even afford the luxury of drinking milk with the single daily meal of bread allowed during the first eight days of Dasaī̃, when he must fast in his temple. On the eighth day, the sacrifice of both a goat and a rooster is offered by all the houses of the Sārkī lineage, who share the meat equally, reserving only the head and a thigh for the priest and the medium. This particular medium told us that 'castrated goat (*khasi*) is tastier, but the gods do not eat it, so the meat smells a little'.[2] These Sārkīs the next day again receive a share of the buffalo offered to the Goddess of Victory by their patrons, then six months later, another share of goat meat during the second annual sacrifice offered to their Bhairav.

Apart from these occasions which occur two or three times a year, sometimes a *bhākal* sacrifice also allows them a hearty meal of meat. Otherwise deprived of milk and butter, lacking the means to raise a cow or a buffalo, each haul of animal meat is for these people a source of vigour, *tāgat*, as the cobbler pointed out to me. The scarcity of meat consumption and its close correlation to sacrifice here confer a literal meaning on the conception of sacrifice as a circulation of force, in a local context where the everyday diet is highly deficient in important nutrients. The need for sacrifice is thus alike to a vital one,[3] which justifies even the most prohibited practices. It was thus that one of my friends, who often spoke to me of the time he had spent in Nagaland as a porter when he was only fifteen years old, and of the 'savages' he had seen there, told me one day that 'they even ate their enemies' in sacrifice. 'Have you seen them do it?' I asked him. 'Yes, I have seen them,' he replied, adding at once, 'it's because they don't have salt there.' I did not see the connection and replied, 'So what? —So, human meat is the saltiest of all, it contains more salt than that of the animals. They want to eat salt,' he replied simply.

The consumption of animal meat is not always as rare as among the Untouchables of western Nepal, whose poverty is extreme, but all over rural areas, it is occasional and strongly correlated with sacrificial rites. In the early 1990s, this same Magar friend who had stayed in Nagaland hoped that his son could join the army, and mentioned not the amount of pay, but the fact that the military received one meal of meat per week. The correlation between sacrifice and meat consumption is even stronger, in that the limit separating slaughter and sacrifice is not well defined. Thus, among wealthy families, it is customary to kill a rooster or a kid-goat when a guest arrives. One evening, I arrived unannounced at the village of Darling after a long absence, and a kid-goat was killed and, just like in sacrificial rites, they first roasted its liver. I received a portion with these words, 'take your *prasad*' or sacrificial remains. Had the animal been adequately sprayed with pure water in the yard? Did the neighbour who had beheaded the kid have time to perform any ablutions? It is unlikely. However, the liver of the animal retained its ritual place, regardless of the conditions of slaughter. Omens were divined from it and it was grilled separately. In addition, this house was inhabited by two spirits of evil death, *bayu,* which meant that the householder was obliged to offer them two portions of the food first. The *bayu* of his first wife, who died in childbirth, and that of his stillborn child come to feast at each meal with the family. In the absence of such directly present spirits, there are the ancestors who expect a share of the animal, or even the 'masters of the game' spirits, if the animal is killed while hunting. Any killing is thus more or less a sacrifice, in the sense that a part of the animal is offered to the invisibles and thus establishes a communion with them.

Even a human death is often interpreted as a sacrifice, especially when it is sudden. One hears that so-and-so has had his 'heart eaten' by such-and-such a spirit in such-and-such place, or that the Goddess took her meal, *bhog*.[4] Beyond the circumstances of death, the suddenness of which may recall sacrificial execution, all humans who die are said to be consumed by the invisibles on the cremation ground, where the *masān*, *bhūt* and other *rākṣa*s spirits feast on their flesh.

Nepal also abounds with rumours of human sacrifice, especially in regions under the influence of Tantrism, such as the Kathmandu Valley (Michaels 1984), where transgressive practices are reported with grisly regularity. At the Varāhī shrine in Tistung, where I was lucky enough to observe the festival which takes place there only once every five years in 1997, the Newars say that they used to sacrifice a pregnant woman in ancient times. Today, the goddess Varāhī is embodied in the body of an Untouchable Poḍe, who is carried from neighbourhood to neighbourhood to drink the blood of the victims presented to him, by sucking it directly from their jugular veins. Their meat, cut into pieces, is then laid out in the enclosure of the sanctuary for several days before finally the celebrants throw the pieces, at this stage already starting to smell rather gamey, into the crowd who fight to catch it. Similarly, at the temple of Ugra Tārā in Daḍeldhurā, in far western Nepal, I was led by a group of children to a blood-stained statue of the Goddess, near which they drew my attention to a small stone portico. They stood there, arms outstretched, to show me how young boys were sacrificed there. Even their act of mere mimicry was enough to convey the sheer power at play in such practices, and led me to feel discomfort by this statue (see Figure 4.1). Certain deaths, such as that of a

Figure 4.1 Bloodied Kālī statue, Ugra Tārā temple, Dadeldhura, 2017
Source: Author.

male child, whether intra utero, at birth, or by infanticide, or even the suicide of the husband, are still today often interpreted as sacrifices which women commit in order to acquire the powers of witchcraft. The murders of children commonly attributed to Yogis by villagers in Nepal are also described as sacrifices aimed at acquiring magical powers. Even the Government of Nepal itself treated criminals in a sacrificial way, at least in the nineteenth century, by having the condemned executed at Dasaī, along with the sacrifices of goats and buffaloes, and by leading the suspects in front of the royal statue of Kāl Bhairav for the ordeal – if they trembled, like animal victims, they were found guilty and condemned to death.[5] In contrast to this dark domain where crime and sacrifice are intertwined, the arena of war creates a magnified setting for the 'great sacrifice', *mahāyagya*, where soldiers offer themselves in combat for a cause beyond themselves and meet a pure, glorious death, one which does not defile their relatives as other forms of death do.

These bridges between the different ways of dying and sacrifice do not mean that there is complete confusion between them. Thus, hunting and sacrifice are distinguished by significant details: the hunter offers neither the blood nor the head of the game, but he does make an offering of the ergot (a small horny protuberance situated on the back of an animal's fetlocks), feathers, fur and sometimes even the ears and the tail, explaining that by restoring these parts of the animal, he prevents the anger of the masters of the game, by offering just enough parts of the animal to make them believe it is still alive.

Similarly, sacrificial uses vary greatly from one region to another, as can be judged from two villages inhabited by the same caste groups and the same Magar ethnic group, located some 50 kilometres from each other in the Kālī Gaṇḍakī region. In the first, a 'fountain of blood' is first offered, followed by the animal's head. However, this latter appendage is presented as a token diversion to keep the divinity waiting for what she or he desires more than anything: the liver, the part of the living being considered to be the purest, *śuddha*. It is extracted and cooked separately, or along with the heart. In the second village, however, neither the liver nor the heart is offered to the deity, and only the head of the victim is placed near to where they are purported to be. Sometimes a small piece of the animal's flesh is also sliced off by the priest to be presented to the god or goddess. The blood is not only poured like 'a fountain', into a pure receptacle, but is also smeared on the top of the sacrificial post, and bloody palmprints are made on the wall and the door of the temple. These palmprints are themselves subject to different interpretations: some see them as a 'joyous celebration', while others consider them to be an obligation, intended to prove that the sacrifice of the animal was indeed executed as a sign of loyalty to the king, adding that officials used to come from village to village to verify it.

Apart from the Brahmins, individual men of all ranks take it upon themselves to execute the animals sacrificed in the name of their families, but as soon as the animal is offered by any collective larger than the household, restrictions relating to caste purity are applicable. The Untouchables cannot sacrifice an animal intended for consumption by pure castes (apart from in Tantric contexts, where inversion prevails),[6] as they would defile even a cucumber by cutting it. If these rules have somewhat faded today in secular contexts, all of their value is retained in a religious ceremony. Since every Untouchable caste considers any castes lower than its own to be Untouchable in turn, the sacrifices they perform generally only bring together one singular lineage group, as collective consumers of the animal offered.[7]

In terms of the village community and the ranks within it, extra purity is expected of the man who performs the sacrifice. It is true that a certain morality is required of the sacrificator, with those who drink or who lead an otherwise depraved lifestyle being excluded from this role. In certain places, such as the second village of the Kālī Gaṇḍakī mentioned earlier, virginity and even a purity of descent are required of the sacrificator, whether for a collective or even just a lineage sacrifice. He must not only be 'unmarried', *abibāhit*, but also be *vyāite*, that is, born of a father and a mother who were never part of another marriage before their union. Of these two criteria, purity of ancestry takes precedence , since in the event that only a boy who is too young to execute the animal meets these requirements to be the sacrificator, it is possible that a married man who is *vyāite* can replace the child, while an unmarried man who is not *vyaite* can not.

The men of Nepal, then, each with their own 'clientele' and their own origins and particularities, form an array of butchers and sacrificators, which reflects different facets of the same reality, where sacrifice is synonymous with mastery and virility. When you ask Nepali men about how they feel when they perform a sacrifice, it is these two aspects that stand out most of all. Many declare that they feel charged with a 'responsibility' and that they apply themselves to fulfilling it as best they can, with concentration and pride, and even with joy, thinking of the festive meals that the sacrifice foreshadows. Others speak of a real sexual excitement: 'When you've never offered a blood sacrifice, it's like when you've never had sex with a girl, you're curious about how it feels. And when you've done it, you feel the same way as when you've had sex. It makes me feel ashamed to talk about sexual things, but you have to say it, it feels the same,' a villager in his fifties told me.

Whether it is a new responsibility or an unimaginable experience for those who have not yet experienced it, which may be considered analogous to the sexual act, the passage of men to adulthood is accompanied by the exercise of supreme violence.

This important initiatory act is only authorised on the condition that the young man is able to accomplish it in a 'non-violent' way, that is, without causing pain. We find here a combination which dissociates the two definitions of *hiṃsā* – first, as the act of taking life and, second, as the action of causing suffering – and it is almost as if the 'responsible' killing of sacrifice, one which causes the least amount of suffering, was an alternative incarnation of the formula 'sacrificial violence is not violence', a sort of popular *vaidik hiṃsā*. Of those I asked if they thought it was better for the animal to be killed or sacrificed, nobody chose the first answer. While for many there is no discernible difference between the two ways of dying, others say that at least in sacrifice the animal is informed of its death and accepts it, which is proven by the fact that it does not try to run away, so that they might even say it is happy to be offered to the gods, but above all, they say that the animal then dies without suffering, which they hold is even the case in sacrificial contexts where it is attacked from all sides by men bearing weapons. Outside a sacrificial context, a resident of Dullu told me, some people have fun killing animals in a barbaric way, starting by cutting off their legs, then committing all sorts of horrors upon them. The rules of sacrifice would therefore prevent the savagery of men towards animals.

Killing not only makes boys into men but also makes princes into kings, because its sovereign dimension naturally extends into the political sphere. Sacrificial decapitation at one time thus represented a kind of initiation for young princes (Baral 1964: 44n70) and the sacrificial sword was paraded during state celebrations. The value of the royal weapon was such that it represented not only royalty, in an abstracted sense, but also the king himself. For instance, until the end of the monarchy in the years 2006–2008, any time His Majesty could not attend a religious ceremony, he would send his sword in his place.

It is in this way, then, that the symbol of power around which the kingdom gathered was uniquely mobile, giving the king a form of ubiquity, not only to 'attend' ceremonies without actually being present but also to entrust his power to emissaries in order to participate as directly as possible in various important events, such as the killing of a traitor.[8] In the region of the Twenty-Four Kingdoms, the royal sword is often seen as the main tutelary deity of the kingdom. It is possible that its deification was accentuated with the disappearance of the local kings, but it certainly existed before they were overthrown at the end of the eighteenth century, as there still exist traces of their power in another ceremonial use of the sword. Many former village chiefs wield swords which they claim to have received as a sign of investiture by the local king. These swords are revered by each member of their lineage group as their tutelary deity. Through this 'sword cult', a rather striking image emerges, of a vast family of holders of royal power, all related by their connection to this same instrument of death. The strength of such a network has not prevented the occasional confiscation of the royal sword, as it has sometimes been decommissioned in a process of Brahmanic divinisation, as in Ismā (see the next chapter), or, more commonly, it has been captured and brought back as a trophy by the enemy, especially during the 'unification' campaign led by the Gorkhālis. This is evidenced by the collection of weapons in the National Museum of Nepal, where these trophies are displayed. With Nepalese royalty being represented in this way, we understand that the supposition was that for each new generation, the sovereign would be able to keep his sword, thus creating a close association between the exercise of power and competition and/or war.

In accordance with the importance of the sword for the smooth functioning of the kingdom, the only acceptable form of killing is decapitation, either in sacrifice or traditional methods of slaughter. Any other killing method requires explanation, be it moral or technical.[9] Within this shared act, however, difference in rank is expressed through the type of weapon used – the sword is reserved for the king or the chief, the curved *kukhuri* cutlass is generally used during collective village sacrifices, and the sickle in a lineage or domestic context.

Only those who can kill can be killed

The right of death spares three distinct categories of beings, each of which includes humans and animals: those who have just been born, that is, children and young animals, those who give life, women and female animals, and those who are associated with the priesthood, Brahmins and cows. The killings of these beings constitute major crimes for Hindus.

Conversely, from among these excepted groups, those who are capable of killing (that is, Brahmins, women and children) are prohibited from inflicting death on anyone, human or animal. Killing thus obeys a principle of reciprocity according to which only those who can kill can be killed, and vice versa.

For those excluded from death, there does, however, remain the possibility of them killing themselves. Their suicides have given rise to established forms, such as the ritual suicide of the Brahmins, as attested in Nepal in the territory of Dullu, where there is a 'ritual suicide cliff', or the 'custom' of Satī among women, banned in 1920. To these practices, now extinct, one may add the suicides of women, children and Brahmins who are the victims of injustice. These events give rise to particularly harmful spirits, the *bayu* and the *barmā*, who drive those who have brought them into existence to madness or even death, forcing the community to work tirelessly to pacify them through ritual practice.[10]

These three categories of beings are all united by their exclusion from the power of death, which means that they must all be protected. However, they do not all share the same relationship to sacrifice. Children and young animals are distinguished from the others by their 'sacrificial becoming', as their fate is already stretched out before them, and they will go on inexorably to participate in it, either as appointed sacrificators or as designated victims. They have the purity required for these roles, and there is no precise limit which sets out when they might become sacrificially active. Young boys are especially eager to kill an animal, to participate in the sacrifice and join in the fight. The epics encourage this fledgling bloodthirstiness, recounting that there were boys as young as twelve who took part in battles, all the while continuing to call them children, *bālā*, and historical accounts confirm this, telling us that Prithvi Narayan, the founding king of the nation, was proud of the youngest of his brothers who accompanied him on the battlefield. In his *Divine Counsels*, he recounts how the child took part in the attack on Nuwakot against the advice of his older brother, grabbed the 'elder sword' and cut off an enemy's head with it. These are not merely events of the past, as shown by the active participation of child soldiers during the People's War at the turn of the 2000s and the personal testimony of young Usha, who told me how it was (technically) difficult to decapitate a man, as she herself had experienced.

She explained that she had been helped by her young comrades who held the victim down, before adding not her regrets, but her disgust at the result: 'Men, without their head, are not pretty to see.'

Animals are also sometimes brought to sacrifice at a very young age, occasionally so young that ripples of indignation can be heard throughout the assembled crowd. This is particularly the case when the sacrifice is offered in exchange for a demand or wish addressed to the deity, since there are usually rules setting a minimum age for victims in lineage cults. As for the buffaloes, they are chosen for royal ceremonies for their size and strength, at least in the mountain region,[11] but are nowadays offered while still very young and frail, by the hundreds, at the now much maligned site of Gaḍhī Māī. In reaction to my surprise at the diminutive stature of these buffaloes during the November 2019 festival, the temple priest explained that they had been selected at such a young age to ensure their perfection. If there was even a hint of the slightest defect on a hoof, the slightest scar, then the Goddess would no longer want them. The purity and perfection required of both the sacrificator and the victim are thus in direct opposition to the nominative limits that keep young children and animals out of the sacrificial rite.

The second category of people who have neither the right to kill nor be killed, the Brahmins, are nonetheless essential actors in the sacrifice. Their presence is imperative for collective rituals such as Dasaĩ, where only they can perform the gestures that sanctify and purify the weapons, sacrificial post and the victim itself. In addition, the majority of Brahmins make sacrificial offerings of goats or rams to their own lineage gods. For their execution, they call upon a Kshatriya sacrificator. The complementarity of these dual holders of spiritual power and of temporal power respectively is brought into sharp focus during the process of sacrifice: the former, as they say of themselves, 'make the cult happen', whereas the latter actually perform it, thus forming a relationship of reciprocal exchange.

Thus, of the three categories of beings set apart from the power of death, only women are truly excluded from sacrifice. First of all, they are physically excluded from it, whereas no such prohibition prevents a Brahmin or a child from attending any ceremony whatsoever. The list of ritual occasions where the presence of women is prohibited is long: cremations, the marriage of their own son, sacrifices to the gods of the mountain summits and ridges, to the divinity of the territory and, most often, to their lineage gods. The sacrifices of Dasaĩ are thus an exception to this list, as everyone, including women, is expected to attend them. However, women have no role to play in them, other than to be spectators. Even the cooking of the *prasād* is done by men, as if to show the women, who are usually so tied to the kitchen, that they are to have nothing to do with sacrifice. On closer inspection, however, women are more involved in sacrifice than it would initially seem, but take on the role of victims.

The sacrificial gift of women

Daughters are offered as a gift, *dān*, by their father at the time of their marriage.[12] This transfer creates a specific attitude towards women from early childhood, because, as a friend's mother told me: 'The girl, we must give her, we must not get too attached to her, so as not to suffer. We don't sleep with her.' Women talk about their daughters as they do about their goats, who end up under their husband's knife. This is not a coincidence. The gift of the virgin, *kanya dān*, much like sacrifice, *bali dān*, is generally conceived of as if the girl had died. As soon as she has been 'given away', the girl is excluded from her clan and she is no longer admitted to the sanctuary of her native home, which in practical terms in rural areas means that she can no longer go to the back of her house, beyond the main pillar, or access the attic where the storerooms are located, since the ladder leading to them is located in this part. Moreover, since for her own people she is now considered an outsider, they will no longer be polluted by her actual death and will thus not take part in her funeral rites. It might be assumed that the woman simply changes her identity by marrying, and that her death to her birth family means she is reborn in her marital family, but this is not quite the case.

In western Nepal, when a married woman dies, her body is carried to the funeral pyre in a palanquin suspended to a single pole, similar to the one she was taken to her husband's house in at the time of her wedding. By contrast, the corpses of men are transported on a two-pole stretcher. To explain this difference, the Chetris (or Kshatriyas) of Jumlā interviewed by Satya Shrestha-Schipper (2003) say that the woman already used one pole when she was carried in a wedding palanquin, and that is why she is only entitled to one more when she dies. This logic that makes marriage a sort of 'pre-funeral' is not restricted to this region. It was shown with much fanfare following the assassination of the royal family in 2001, when the body of the Queen of Nepal was carried to the cremation ground in her wedding palanquin, the very same one in which she had been taken to the palace a few decades earlier for her wedding. The king, her husband, who died at the same time as her, was transported on a stretcher. The diminished status accorded to the life of the woman given in these 'funerary' nuptials also ends when her marriage does, which was ample justification in the past for the custom of Satī, and today legitimises the exclusion of widows from auspicious events, such as the naming ceremonies, or even, on rare occasion, from their own home. This custom, which persists in some Brahmin hamlets, can be imposed in a brutal manner. In the village where I lived for a long time, an old Brahmin woman, recently widowed, used to come regularly to ask for food from Magar families, explaining that her son and daughter-in-law were now throwing raw grain at her as food, to convince her to leave for the holy confluence of Ridi, where many widows of her caste await their ends, clad in white, their heads shaven, begging for food.

The ceremony of the 'gift of the virgin' itself takes place in a manner reminiscent of the sacrifice of the kid-goat, with crying and laughing being elicited in equal measure from the audience. The ritual takes place at the girl's home, and the men of her family, who form an alliance and obtain the highest levels of merit through the giving of this gift, parade around, veritably radiating joy. The women, on the contrary, cling tightly to each other and sob like mourners.[13]

Despite the suffering they express and the exclusion from the family inflicted upon the bride, it is the bride's father who gains the merit of the *kanya dān*, with it even being considered a day of his 'sacrifice'. Willing to do anything to correctly offer the 'gift of the virgin', in the person of his daughter, he covers the exorbitant costs of the wedding, as well as offering a substantial dowry, a practice which had started to take on such a grandiose dimension in certain regions of Nepal that it was prohibited by law in 2012. The sacrificial attitude of the giver of *kanya dān* can sometimes go so far as to include the sale of his goods and even of his own organs, to compensate for any expenses incurred, the obligations associated with this gift being so strong that in the absence of a daughter, a man will participate in a gift offered by one of his relatives, so as to receive its associated merit.[14]

The pseudo-sacrifice of marriage thus mobilises a vast array of registers relating to the *hiṃsā*, as that which causes death or suffering, and touches many of those who participate in the rite, not merely the one who gives (the father, in his role as the sacrifier who is sacrificed in material terms), or the one who is given (the daughter, who is ritually half-killed when offered), but also those who suffer from the gift (the mother who, since the birth of her child, must begin the process of steeling herself to endure the ordeal which one day will come). This very bleak picture must clearly be weighed against recent changes in society which allow many girls to have their say, or even to choose their husbands. Nevertheless, the fact remains that the *kanya dān* underlines a second sacrificial fault line that both divides and orders society, one which separates men and women along a vertical axis which transcends all caste statuses. Indeed, it is in this way that the 'hermaphrodite' body is represented in Hindu statuary, as a being cut vertically into two parts, one male, the other female. This vertical fault line that separates the sexes intersects with the horizontal fault line that keeps the Untouchables apart, the so-called water barrier which divides the pure castes from the impure ones.

Indeed the vertical fault line periodically bends to become horizontal and merge with that which carves out untouchability, when women are struck by impurity. Traditionally, the ideal moment for Hindu girls to be given in marriage was before their puberty, a practice which stopped when the law pushed back the age of marriage in the last decades. Prior to this change the two major transformations that affect women, puberty and marriage, were then confused. Indeed, as soon as puberty starts, a woman's life is punctuated by monthly 'degradations' lasting five days, corresponding to the time of her menstruation, during which she becomes untouchable, regardless of her caste. She can no longer enter her own house, let alone a shrine, nor engage in any activity that is sensitive to impurity, such as cooking, carrying water, or milking animals. In western Nepal, women cannot even drink milk or eat butter for fear of making the cattle sick and drying up their milk. In this region, they are confined in small huts during their periods, and the government is now working to have the police destroy these buildings, as they have received much criticism in the media, and have already carried out brutal operations, images of which were posted on social media in December 2019 and January 2020.[15]

Even if it is only periodic, the impurity affecting women is undoubtedly more extreme than that affecting the Untouchables, since it leads to their exclusion from their own homes, and even for all intents and purposes from the face of the earth for those who go so far as to follow the injunction not to defile the sun and shut themselves away. Impurity is expressed in both cases by the same deprivation of autonomy – it has made the Untouchables into 'service castes', living on the subsidies granted to them by their high-caste patrons, and women into 'dependents', *bhāryā*, who even today do not have the right to inherit their own father's property.

Thus, the terms used to describe the partitions that divide human beings and the attributions associated with them all borrow from a sacrificial language. The responsibility of men, the exclusion of women, the distance to be upheld with the Indigenous peoples, the ostracism that strikes the Untouchables, are all expressed in these terms. We must therefore try to understand precisely how the sacrificial model is able to provide so much texture to the world, and in so many registers.

Before we begin this examination with an ethnography of an holistic sacrificial ceremony, it is important to emphasise the sheer ubiquity of sacrifice in Nepal, a fact which is undoubtedly related to its fundamental indefiniteness, in its exemplary form of *bali dān*.

This undefined quality manifests itself especially in the vocabulary used, starting with the absence of a specific name designating the sacrifier. If one pushes the Nepalis to pin down a title for this person, they regularly answer that we can call him the devotee, *bhakta*, or the doer, *kartā*, but these terms are not understood as referring to the sacrifier outside of a context which has already been defined as sacrificial. Conversely, any 'devotee' or even any 'doer' can be considered a sacrifier. Similarly, the officiants who act during the sacrifice are all indifferently called *pūjāri*, the 'attendants to the cult', whether they are Brahmin priests who sanctify the victims or the sacrificators who execute them, which suggests that the sacrifice itself is not differentiated from the ritual. If it is necessary to designate them individually, they can be distinguished by their class name, while the executor can also be described by his action, as 'the one who strikes death', *mār hānne*. Finally, there is no term corresponding to 'victim' either, with the chosen animal being simply designated by its species name – buffalo, ram, goat, pig, rooster, pigeon, duck, mouse. The name of the animal may occasionally be attached to the term *bali*, as in *bali bakhro*, the kid-goat of the sacrifice, while the term *paśu*, which was used to designate the victim in ancient India, is used in the expression *paśu bali*, which means 'animal sacrifice', but is not used to designate an animal individually, nor specifically the victim.[16] The indeterminacy of the *bali dān* is also expressed in its shifting orientation, which does not necessarily follow a progressive chain of operations starting with the sacrifier and ending with the invisible recipient, passing successively through priest, sacrificator and victim. Its intention and realisation are likely to emanate from different starting points. It is in this way that a victim can offer themselves for death, or the addressee is able to make a sacrificial offering to themselves, or can even choose the sacrifier as their victim. This fluid perspective on sacrifice can also reverse the attributes of each actor, with man becoming a demon for his victim, for example. To confound matters even further, the different roles needed during the course of the sacrifice become superimposed in changing configurations as the ceremony itself proceeds. When the sacrifice is domestic, for instance, the householder offers the animal, sanctifies it and executes it, thus acting as sacrifier, priest and sacrificator. Similarly, the victim and the invisible recipient merge at the defining moment of the all-important tremble which occurs in the body of the victim, but is ultimately caused by the divinity, in a show of true consent, wherein the animal and the god display their joy, *khuśi*, together, the latter of receiving an offering that pleases them, the former of satisfying the divinity's request.

A fusion at the beginning of the chain, between the sacrifier and the animal also sometimes occurs, when the victim is refused by the deity, which demonstrates that their bond is implicit in any sacrificial ceremony. It is true that the victim is often isolated from its donor in case of refusal, carrying the blame attributed to its physical imperfections. But it is also possible that the victim is rejected due to a fault on the sacrifier's part, either because he is not in an adequate enough state of purity, for example if he 'did not wash his feet', as the Nepalis often say when asked for the reasons why a sacrifice can be refused, or else if he does not tell the truth, *satya*, This latter point is not only a matter of uttering 'lies', *jhuṭo bolne*, but also of 'not doing what one said he or she would do', *āphule bhaneko kurā purā nagarne*, as a group of devotees explained to me.[17]

The victim thus carries with it something of the sacrifier, both ritually and ethically. Reciprocally, after its death the animal carries the blessings of the divinity, *prasād* or *prasādi*, with it, as well as a message directly addressed to the sacrifier inscribed in its liver.

It is in this way that the body of the victim connects, both upstream and then downstream, the sacrifier and the deity, but the strands which connect them are so asymmetrical that it turns the giving of the gift into an ordeal, the giver a beneficiary and vice versa. This contradictory condition means that the sacrifice is constantly at odds with itself. Its paradoxical model allows for changes of perspective and roles, as we have seen in the case of marriage.

Such reversals are also commonly observed in the discourse surrounding social organisation, which is also based on a sacrificial model. Even the Untouchables can be accused of being the very source of their own discrimination which they face on a daily basis. The tape recorder cannot always be there to record these terms for posterity, but one scene recorded during a discussion with a cobbler of Dullu, the medium of Bhurulle Bhairav who was fasting in his temple, will serve here as an example:

The cobbler had explained that the temple was that of the patron deity of his lineage, and my friend asked him, 'How many temples do you Dalits have here?', using this politically correct term in place of his caste name, Sārkī, which is considered offensive. The cobbler understood the term as referring to his caste specifically, even though the term 'Dalit' also refers to the Untouchable castes as a whole, and replied: 'We Dalits, in Dullu, in Ward Two, have only two [temples], this one and another, at home. For us, brothers, there's only two places we worship.' The cobbler referred to the members of his direct patrilineage as 'brothers', as all Nepalis do. However, he triggered the anger of a Kshatriya who was listening to the conversation and hastily interjected:

> – 'But we are all brothers. And if we are affected, *lagānī* [by this god], we too can come. It's collective. Your shrine is everyone's, it's not just yours. This shrine, why do you say that it is only for Dalits by making remarks that exclude, *chutyāeko kurāharu*? It's not just the god for his own guardians, *pālī* [a term which designates the main devotees of a god].'
> – 'But I just said that it is our shrine, the shrine of the Dalits,' the cobbler said in an effort to defend himself.

The Kshatriya was not done:

> 'Do the Dalits have a *khodāī* [god of the territory]? [Here he is reminding him that the Dalits have no such gods because they have no land and no rights over the soil]. Bhurulle is also called *khodāī*. [He insists upon this point, showing him that this god cannot be the god of the Dalits, since he is recognised as a territorial deity]. You too are discriminating, *bhedbhāva*, that I know. This is another form of discrimination. Are the shrines private? They are not. We have the same rituals and the same culture. And why is it not separate? It's like the Dalits, there are the Damāī apart, the Kāmī apart, but they are Dalit.[18] The gods for me are collective. You, brothers, are its guardians, your lineage is separate, but it's not just your lineage. If tomorrow someone is affected by your god, he will come here, or he will come after having made a request that your god will have fulfilled. Today we worship Kālīkā and you too come, while we are its guardians.'

In an attempt to return to the cobbler, my friend again asked: 'Do the other castes come here to make offerings, *pūjā*?'

> – 'Some Bhaṇḍāri [the clan of Kshatriyas to which the angry man belonged] come. But they don't come to make offerings, they come to be examined when the god holds a consultation session [through his oracle],' he replied.

By mentioning him specifically among the devotees, the cobbler had succeeded in defusing the anger of the Kshatriya, who spoke again:

> 'That's what I was trying to say. We also try to bring them, the Ṭhakurī. They too must come. Why would only we go to the Ṭhakurī's? It's very well said. Thank you. We are all identical men. If we cut ourselves, we all bleed the same blood, which is why we are alike, and the world is one: there is only one woman and one man. It's very good, really very good. You said some very good things. That's what I meant, everyone must come and worship. There are differences here, the Kāmi are different, the Damāī are different, the Bādi are different, so don't be pained by my words.[19] Your lineage, *kul*, is apart and worships this god; you are apart, and you no doubt venerate him differently. Some offer lights, some do not, but what is collective, all must respect, all must respect the Goddess at her collective shrine. At home, we do it for ourselves, in our own way. That's what I was trying to say. Where is there a large private Dalit cult? That's what I meant. Here it is your tutelary god, and for you, his devotees, it is important, but it is not so eminent that everyone would come here for a big religious gathering, *melā*.'

In summary, after accusing the cobbler of discriminating by his exclusion of other castes, the Kshatriya reminds him that as an Untouchable he has no rights to the land, and then rebukes him for presenting the temple as belonging to his caste, pointing out that he does not have exclusive ownership of it, nor does he deprive himself of going to the temples of others. Once his anger has somewhat subsided, we understand that the Kshatriya is associating himself for a moment with the Dalit, because they are both inferior to the royal Ṭhakurī, in whose ceremonies both Dalits and Kshatriyas participate during Dasaī, while the Ṭhakurī do not reciprocate under any circumstances. Seemingly caught between these two polar opposites, the Kshatriya proclaims the shared identity of all men (but clearly not of man and woman, as most Nepalis do, even in their most egalitarian declarations). However, his credo immediately fades into a reaffirmation of difference between castes and patrilineages, with him eventually proclaiming the pre-eminence of the Goddess who brings everyone together, who is none other than the tutelary deity of his superiors, the Ṭhakurī kings, and he finally affirms the insignificance of the cobbler's temple. He thus deftly puts everything and everyone back in their rightful place.

The twists and turns contained within this short example of this type of discourse revolve around the exclusivity of the rite among the Untouchables, which stems from their exclusion from society, but which can also be perceived as a form of exclusion of the Other. Similarly, the inclusiveness of the worship of the Ṭhakurī appears as both a domination and also as a unifying integration. These extremes of exclusion and inclusion place the Kshatriya in an uncomfortable situation, since he cannot claim either one side or the other, his social position placing him squarely in the middle, a fact which makes him briefly consider each component and its opposite within the system. Finally, this scene illustrates, if more proof be needed, how social and religious exclusion translates into a censorship of speech and the prohibition of the right to present things simply as one sees them.

This fundamental undefined-ness of sacrifice and all the directions it spreads out in, which can be understood both lexically and socially, mirrors the great variety of forms that the same sacrificial ceremony can take, as well as the myriad meanings which we can attribute to it, as we will examine in detail in the following chapter.

Notes

1. In this context, precisely, the sacrificators of the royal palace are men from the butcher caste, Khaḍgi. On this group, in Bhaktapur, see Gutschow and Michaels (2005: 58–60).
2. By contrast, a Brahmin from the Gulmi region told me: 'We Nepalis consider that the meat of an animal that has been offered to the gods as a sacrifice is more delicious, *rasilo*.'
3. In nineteenth-century Paris, the butcher of Gentilly had written on his door: 'Hic morte vita datur [Here life is given by death]' (Delort 1821: 304).

4. In the urban parts of the Kathmandu Valley, road accidents are often presented as 'accidental sacrifices' caused by the Kumārī or other neighbourhood goddesses.
5. The last execution in Nepal took place in 1979.
6. At a number of shrines in the Kathmandu Valley, the Untouchable Poḍe perform the sacrifices. Their status is reversed during the rite. At the aforementioned Tistung temple, a Poḍe medium who has become possessed by the Goddess tastes the meat of the sacrificial victims first, right from the plate. This gesture, which in ordinary times would defile the food, transforms it into consecrated remains, *prasād*, which the Brahmin officiants consume after him, before offering some to the assembled devotees.
7. When a collective which includes members of pure castes offers impure sacrifices to certain deities, these offerings are performed by impure priests. An individual pertaining to a pure caste who is personally affected by a god also has his favourite, impure, food offered to him by the hand of an impure sacrificator, but does not consume it himself.
8. For examples, see Lecomte-Tilouine (1996).
9. Outside a sacrificial context, the explanation is technical: chickens' necks are sliced and pigs are run through with a spear because of the difficulty of decapitating them. In a sacrificial context, any exceptions to the normal order of things are motivated by the demands of either the deity or the cult.
10. A series of stories about the origin of these spirits can be found in Maskarinec (2009).
11. This is perhaps more of a rule of thumb, with a particularly notable exception being the animal donated by the Dullu royal family in 2012, for example, which was roundly considered to be rather puny.
12. They were also offered to temples as *deuki*. The practice is officially forbidden today, but it has not completely disappeared in far western Nepal. *Deuki*s are girls of pure castes, offered on the occasion of a vow by their father to a temple, where they dedicate themselves to the service of the god. They may also be bought from poor families to be offered in this manner, I was told. A village of former *deuki*s adjoins the temple of Mehuli in Baitadi, and at the temple of Dehi Mandu, while it is difficult to investigate this taboo subject, forbidden by law, the women in charge of waving yak tails during the transfer of the Goddess's goods from her treasury to her temple are said to be *deukis*.
13. As for the women who are related to the groom, they are excluded from the wedding ceremony altogether. They organise among themselves a risqué

'counter-party', *ratauli*, which is forbidden to men, where they sing, dance and mime male sexual desires.

14. Schematically, the higher the caste in the hierarchy, the more *kanya dān* is followed.
15. While the government is seeking to put an end to this practice, which has been decried even by the international press, it has perhaps not accounted for the effects that the destruction of these menstrual shelters might have in this very poor region. Here the houses are of such modest size that it is not possible to separate the gods, the ancestors and the kitchen, as the middle class of Kathmandu do, in order to protect their domestic purity without forcing the women outside. It is therefore unsurprising to see women fighting with the police who come to destroy these refuges. We must also not forget that women simply sleep outside, under the veranda or in the cowshed, in rural areas where such shelters do not exist, and this has elicited almost no reaction from either the local or international press.
16. *Paśu* and *pankhi*, birds, refer to all animals in the compound *paśu-pankhi*. They are contrasted with humans by their lack not of soul or language but specifically of consciousness, *cetanā*, commonly defined as the ability to understand what is right and wrong, especially in matters of sexual relations. Their absence of consciousness, a young man told me, causes '*paśu* to have sex between brother and sister, mother and son, father and daughter'.
17. More generally, 'truth' is set in opposition to evil. Prasai (2008), for example, presents the rite with these words: 'Dashai is the festival symbolising victory of *truth* over evil.'
18. The Damāī are tailors and musicians; the Kāmī form a group subdivided into many subgroups of craftsmen in the region, including blacksmiths, coppersmiths, silversmiths, carpenters, potters, woodturners, bamboo weavers, and so on.
19. In Dullu, the Bādi are a caste of musicians and dancers, who also make clay pipes.

5

The buffalo sacrifice

An ethnographic approach comparing how the festival of Dasaĩ unfolds in various ancient kingdoms of western Nepal reveals the unique elements particular to each site. It also reveals the way in which violence, order and disorder are combined in singular arrangements, like the various elements of a sort of transformative group which we can observe changing as we move across the country. The festival of Dasaĩ (The Ten Days) otherwise known as the Durgā pūjā (Worship of the Warrior Goddess) is an annual celebration which takes place during the first ten days of the clear fortnight of the month of Asoj (September–October). It is a combination of family celebration, a gathering of the bloodline and/or village, and a royal ceremony, so that the practices associated with each collective intertwine at different levels. The ten days of the ritual are divided into a preliminary phase lasting seven days dedicated to the worship of the Goddess and the reading of her *Celebration*, followed by two days of sacrifices, first of goats, in private houses and clan temples, and then buffaloes, which take place in ancient palaces and the great temples dedicated to the Goddess. The tenth day closes the rite, and is an occasion for the renewal of positions of power and hierarchical relationships, as a prelude to the final warlike rejoicings.[1]

The reclusion of the first days

From its very beginning, the ritual suspends the ordinary passage of time. Throughout the country, all activities grind to a halt, with schools, universities, administrations, banks and most businesses closing for the duration of the festivities. Even the farmers interrupt their work in the fields, the only time they do so all year. The days before the ritual trigger a vast migration within the country, marked by the departure of three million people from the Kathmandu Valley alone.[2] All over Nepal people huddle together in crowded buses, hoping to get back to their villages in time. The rite is a symbol of prosperity and abundance, marked by the distribution of the *Dasaĩ kharca*, the equivalent of a thirteenth month of pay for civil servants and to a 'New Year's bonus' for private employees. It is the moment each year where everything is renewed and renovated, from paths, public buildings and private houses to one's own wardrobe, and it requires vast preparations of all the ingredients needed for the feast of food, and alcohol (for those whose caste authorises its consumption).

There is a feverish air hanging over the first day, devoted to 'the establishment of the [Goddess's] pot', *ghaṭasthāpanā*, as everyone busies themselves with the renovation of their houses in order to adequately accommodate her presence. Furniture is brought out into courtyards, from the trunks in the attic to the mats on the first floor. Young people who left at dawn, tasked with getting chalk powder and red clay to repaint the walls, come back with full baskets on their backs and a smile on their faces. Children run amok, calling out at regular intervals, as if not to forget, *Dasaĩ āyo, Dasaĩ āyo*, 'Dasaĩ has arrived, Dasaĩ has arrived', then race to join the group who are busy building a huge bamboo swing on the jutting pathway (see Figure 5.1). We hear the Damāī's sewing machine turning, stopping and starting again, working at a frenetic pace to finish five identical shirts for the neighbour's children as quickly as possible because all of his patrons have commissioned him at the same time.

At my friend Narmati's house in Darling, the inside walls and floors of the house have already been coated with a mixture of cow dung and clay. While they are busy putting things back in place, the eldest son is setting up the Goddess for the next nine days. The adolescent, who acts as master of the house in his father's absence, places Her in the form of a vase filled with pure water in the dark corner reserved for the lineage gods. His mother brings him two leaf-plates, filled with earth and sown with barley seeds, which he places at the foot of the vase. They will remain there to germinate in the heat and darkness. The teenager then sprinkles pure water and vermilion powder over the arrangement and plants a bunch of incense sticks from which swirls of smoke escape. His mother rejoins him to water the plate of seeds with a tiny copper receptacle. The rite is then over and will be repeated in the same way every morning until the eighth day.

Figure 5.1 A Dasaĩ swing in a hamlet of Rolpa district, 2011
Source: Author.

Everyone is now busy repainting the outside walls of the house, the bottom in red and the top in white, as a conch is sounded from the village temple in a call dedicated to the wish-fulfilling goddess, Mānakāmanā. There too there has been a major cleanup – the weeds have been pulled up and the walls re-plastered. A dozen onlookers stand around the Magar officiant who has just completed his own installation of the living presence of the Goddess, in the same form of a vase of water and plates of barley seeds. At the end of the nine days, these seeds will become the *jamarā*, the bright, almost fluorescent green shoots that will be distributed to the gathered devotees. The springtime origins of the rite are recalled by this act of planting of seeds, which seems a rather incongruous act for this harvest period, as the villagers explain. Barley, they add, is the cereal that brings the most energy; its cultivation is restricted to a few plots, and it is to be given exclusively to the oxen for ploughing.

Six or seven hours' walk away, in the ancient capital of the kingdom of Ismā to which the village of Darling once belonged, the rituals are more elaborate. The eponymous capital of the kingdom is now a village like any other, except for the presence of a building referred to as the 'fort' or 'palace', located at the top of a rocky outcrop. On the first day of the ritual, five officiants, three Brahmins and two Kshatriyas, settle there for nine nights, during which time they will fast. One of the Brahmins acts as chaplain, *rājguru*, and one of the Kshatriyas provides a royal presence, even though the royal dynasty ruling over Ismā was wiped out when it was annexed by the Gorkhālis in 1786. The Kshatriya in question takes on the role of a 'soldier of the king', and the villagers say that the ceremony cannot take place without him. On an already purified floor in the shrine, the officiants set up a vase of water coated with dung and sown with barley seeds, a lamp and a figure of Gaṇeś. Bhairam, a terrible form of Śiva who resides below the fort, is led there by his priest, a Kāṇphaṭa ascetic, and put near the other divine forms. The main deity of the kingdom, the Sword-god of the ancient kings of Ismā, Khaḍka devatā, will not join them until the seventh day.

In the same sanctum, a Brahmin reads a passage from the *Sāma veda*, accompanied with the prescribed hand gestures, *hātsar*. He then reads an episode of the *Caṇḍī pāṭh*, in Sanskrit, in a melodic tone, before rereading the same passage in Nepali, this time with no particular accentuation, producing an alternating effect which is reminiscent of the bard's delivery of the epic, switching between archaic chant and modern recital. The worship of the gods and the readings are repeated every day in the sanctum, which is renamed the 'House of Dasaĩ' for the duration of the ritual, as if the palace suddenly housed a new dwelling.

The rituals of the first six days are said to be 'hidden' or 'secret', *guptā*, just as the residence period of the five officiants in the palace is called a 'hidden stay', *guptābās*. This long seclusion evokes a gestation period and reminds us that there is an imperceptible germination of barley taking place alongside the readings. Time passes slowly and seems to be in a loop, but the passing of each day also acts as a kind of countdown, associated in turn with a specific form of the Goddess.

We can pick out certain features in the preliminary phase of Dasaī which accord with the list of preparations before sacrifice described in Hubert and Mauss's scheme, including separation, reclusion, fasting and deprivation. However, in Ismā these features are not limited to the sacrifier, but rather touch all officiants equally. Indeed, in this particular village the person of the sacrifier is poorly defined. Admittedly, there is the king's soldier, whose presence is mandatory for the execution of the rite, but what follows will show that he in fact takes on the role of sacrificator at the time of the execution itself, while all householders who make an offering of a buffalo at the fort become sacrifiers themselves, by their collective performing of the rite of commitment to sacrifice, *saṅkalpa*. Such a fragmentation of the function of sacrifier mirrors Hubert and Mauss's scheme: in their essay, the sacrifier is laid out as a unique person who may come to represent a group, whereas here we have an instance of a group who acts together to form a plurality of sacrifiers. In the neighbouring kingdom of Musikot, where the former royal family is still in place, the role of sacrifier is not limited to one person either, but is duplicated, by the presence of two kings who worship distinct gods and conduct different rituals within the same sanctum: one is a member of the Siṃha Ṭhakurī dynasty, representing the last ruling royal power; the other, a Sāru Magar, is a member of the Indigenous community whose ancestors ruled that land before being taken over by the former dynasty. As in Ismā, they are accompanied by two Brahmin officiants of different lineages, a doubling which is common in Nepal, designed to safeguard against the risk of the rite being cancelled in the event of the Brahmin's impurity should a death or a birth pollute his family.[3]

In Musikot, after the solemn entry of the officiants into the palace, the first ritual procedure, without which the Brahmins cannot install the vase of the Goddess, is 'tribal' in nature. The Magar king mixes rice and yeast in an earthen pot to initiate the fermentation of a beer that will be offered to Bhairam, a god attached to his clan and residing in the palace along with the five Sword-gods of the Ṭhakurī kings, albeit in a separate room. Only then can the Brahmins place the vase, the lamp and Gaṇeś, as well as Annapūrṇā, the goddess of abundance, in the form of a knife covered with a mound of rice. Afterwards, the Ṭhakurī 'king' beheads a goat in front of the five swords, while the Magar 'king' sows barley seeds and waters them, as he will do every morning thereafter. In the afternoon, the Brahmins give readings from the *Sāma veda* and the *Caṇḍī pāṭh*. In this case, despite the presence of two 'kings', the preliminary phase of the sacrifice is not designed so that the person of the sacrifier accumulates sacred merit either, which is in contrast to Hubert and Mauss's thesis. The two 'kings', who are both sacrifiers and sacrificators, claim to be 'at the service of the gods', as do the two Brahmin officiants.

These four men carry out the ritual actions according to their status and their specific relations to the different divine persons in presence: the Magar king is in charge of the worship of the ancient royal deity, which requires the making of beer, an act which is deemed impure by the Hindus, as well as conducting a similarly impure pig sacrifice, which the Ṭhakurī king or the Brahmin priests are again not able to perform without losing their status. The Ṭhakurī king displays his warrior nature by performing the very first decapitation in honour of the five Sword-gods of his ancestors, which he alone can pay homage to. Finally, the Brahmins 'install' the Goddess, as if they were the householders, and proceed to the readings that neither the Kshatriyas nor the Indigenous are authorised to do. We see here that all officiants of the ceremony share their complementary specialties.

In addition, while these preliminary days are indeed marked by the intensification of a 'formidable' energy, to paraphrase Hubert and Mauss, here it is the Goddess, not the sacrifier, whose *śakti* increases in a crescendo over time. Kanchā, a schoolboy from the village of Darling, summed up the process for me in these words:

> There are nine goddesses and the buffalo-demon, Mahiṣāsur. The Goddess wants to kill him, but Mahiṣāsur is very strong. So, as she repeatedly fails to defeat him, the Goddess gets angry, and from her anger another stronger goddess is born, and in the end, Durgā, who is the strongest, kills the buffalo-demon.

The journalist Sanjeeb Phuyal (2019) echoes Kanchā in his presentation of the ceremony, stating that its nine-day duration corresponds to the length of the fight led by the Goddess against the buffalo-demon, by taking on nine different forms. The intensification of the *śakti* in the ritual mirrors the various stages of the combat led by the Goddess as recounted in her *Celebration* (albeit approximately if we look closely at the text). This is felt in the real world, without, however, particularly affecting the sacrifier. Rather, in Musikot, the divine power manifests itself in the swords that are said to literally awaken during Dasaĩ, to the point that it becomes difficult to hold them when they are brought out on parade for the sacrifices, according to the royal officiants, who say that when they handle them, they begin to move of their own accord.

The divine presence is by then so strong that the music drives the assembly 'crazy', *pāgal*, and some people in the crowd go into a trance. By contrast, the two 'kings' of Musikot maintain a hieratic calm in the midst of the crowd, whereas in Hubert and Mauss's essay the sacrifier should be the main recipient of this excess of energy.

In the case of Dasaĩ, the sacrificial ceremony brings to life a process which is inscribed outside of it in the myth, namely the rise of divine anger, which intensifies as the narrative is recited, until being finally manifested in the bodies of the gathered crowd at the time of the sacrifices, at which point the written word becomes fully actualised in deed by the killing.

The breaking of the seventh day

On the eve of the seventh day, one of the officiants who has until now remained secluded in the fort of Ismā leaves the sanctum and heads towards the boundary of the kingdom, accompanied by a few men. The group makes its way to a place outside the main inhabited territory, on the banks of a river, and beds down for the night at the foot of a *bel* tree (*Aegle marmelos*). At daybreak, the officiant offers prayers to the tree and plucks three fruits from it, which he places in a cloth, while the other men go off in search of the plants they need to create the vegetable form of the Goddess, the *phulpāti*, 'flowers-leaves', which they wrap up in a bundle.[4] The *phulpāti* is then solemnly carried up to the capital in a wedding palanquin covered with a red cloth. Upon hearing of its approach, the palace officiants come out in procession, carrying a vase of pure water, and descend to the royal esplanade accompanied by musicians. The bearers of the *phulpāti* wind their way up the path, picking any ripe cucumber and fruit they see on their way, without having to ask permission, and placing them in the palanquin.

When they appear on the esplanade, they are showered with flowers, and they are greeted with cries of *jaya, jaya mātā*! 'Victory, victory to the Mother!' Making their way through the crowd, the carriers of the palanquin bring it up to the sacrificial post, making sure that the palanquin is touching the post, causing a new shower of petals to rain down upon them. Then begin 'cutlass' duels, which are in fact pantomimed with swords' leather sheaths, with the matches being arbitrated by the 'great men' of the assembly. Lastly, from a small temple adjoining the esplanade, the chaplain takes out the entirely wrapped royal sword, to much ado from the crowd. A new procession forms, snaking its way up to the palace, with the musicians at its head, followed by the officiants who carry the vase, the royal sword and the Goddess in her vegetable form (see Figure 5.2).

The vegetable Goddess only stays in the palace for three days, in the same way that brides do after their wedding ceremony, before they go back to their parents and decide, sometimes years later, to move in with their husband. For the period between the wedding celebration and the commencement of actual conjugal life, the groom finds himself in a situation over which he has little control. In the village of Darling, there was a Brahmin who regularly walked for hours in the hope of convincing his wife to leave her family home and return with him. The bride was resolutely unhurried, and with the opening of a new secondary school nearby, she had resumed her studies, which she intended to continue for as long as possible. The Dasaĩ ritual places the 'king' himself in this uncomfortable situation.[5] He plays host to the Goddess for only three days before she leaves, which is reminiscent of the many stories that teach that the relationship between the king and the Goddess must remain distant, even if she is technically his spouse.[6]

Figure 5.2 The vegetable form of the Goddess and the royal sword. *Phulpāti* in its palanquin, the 'king's soldier' holding a *khuḍā* sabre, the royal chaplain holding the hidden royal sword-god and a Brahmin officiant in the fort of Isma, on the seventh day of Dasaĩ. 1991.

Source: Author.

Further west, in the region of the Twenty-Two Kingdoms, the rituals shed a different light on what happens on the seventh day of Dasaī, which acts as a prelude to the blood sacrifices. Dullu, the former imperial capital of the Khas Malla rulers (twelfth to fourteenth centuries), which became one of the Twenty-Two Kingdoms at the fall of the empire, obtained the special status of a vassal kingdom within the Kingdom of Nepal after military unification by the king of Gorkhā, in the late eighteenth century. The kingdom of Dullu retained this status for two centuries, and the last king was granted the privilege of keeping his title until death. The rites thus continued to be practised there by an official royal power until the 1980s. The palace of the Dullu kings was destroyed in April 2002 by the Maoists, and the 'kingdom's' ability to conduct its sacred rites was deeply affected, but when I first visited the place in 2000, it was still inhabited by 'the king's little sister' who, like the other elderly villagers, had not forgotten the intricate formulas of the Dasaī ceremony.

At the threshold separating the palace from the royal esplanade stands a stone lion, which is said to represent the power of the Dullu kings, who looms victorious over an identical lion embodying the powerful neighbouring kingdom of Jumlā, who can be found a few yards from his vanquisher, condemned to lie forever on its side in defeat. On either side of the esplanade extends a small town dotted with ancient stone pillars. Near to the palace there is a temple dedicated to Kālīkā and to the Goddess of Victory, the protective deity of the dynasty, as well as a throne made of stone, from which the king used to dispense justice, and which remains a place of worship to this day.

This exceptional site is located at the top of a mountain surrounded by four rivers. On their banks, temples shelter 'eternal flames' of natural gas. All are considered to be the form of Jvālā Māī, the Flame Mother, while simultaneously also forming a constitutive part of her: her head, navel, feet, eyes, forehead and soul (see Figure 5.3). The kings of Dullu circumambulated these flames at the time of their coronation, and their cremation took place at the flame 'of the navel', which was used to light their funeral pyre.

The fire temples are maintained by ascetics of the Nāth sect who, until recently, chose one of their children to be their master, *pīr*, a term they translate as 'sufferer' because of the pain the child endures during initiation, wherein his earlobe is split in order to pass a large crystal ring through it. The *pīr* ruled from a throne located in a building adjacent to the fire temple, and only he was pure enough to conduct the rites. But since he was a child, he was supervised by a superior, *mahant*,[7] who was in charge of material affairs, for these temples

Figure 5.3 Ascetic Nāth priest in the temple of eternal fire, Dullu, 2003
Source: Author.

also formed a sort of capital, each of a vast domain from which the ascetics dispensed justice and even had weapons and prisons within their walls. The territory of each of the five main temples was exempt from taxes until recently, and those living within its jurisdiction had an obligation to render services and to offer a share of their harvest to its ruling priests. Still today the priest receives an additional tax from inhabitants of an even wider area, defined as those who use the sacred fire to light their cremation pyres. The ancient imperial capital is thus surrounded by five territories which are for all intents and purposes completely detached from the world, territories which are ritually fashioned into vast cremation grounds governed by ascetics.

During Dasaī, the royal palace of Dullu was transformed into one of these fire temples, and the king into an ascetic. This transfiguration of power took place on the seventh day. An emissary left the royal palace the night before, accompanied by a Brahmin, for Pādukā, the Flame of the Feet.[8] The emissary was a Kshatriya from the clan of the king's treasurers, but for the occasion he dressed as an ascetic and was referred to as the 'ascetic warrior', *jogī kṣetri*. He spent the night at the sanctuary and, at daybreak, received the eternal flame, which was transferred to him by the master of the temple, in the form of a large ignited wick. This warrior ascetic then brought the sacred fire up to the capital. Upon his arrival at the city limits, a place marked by the shrine of Māthurā Māī, he was joined by a delegation from the palace, carrying the 'sword of Kālīkā'. A goat was sacrificed at the point where they met, so as to 'open the path' to the flame, which was then solemnly led in procession to the palace, to be presented to the king.

Since the very first day of the ritual, the sovereign had secluded himself 'at ground level', that is, in a room on the ground floor of his palace where the Goddess and the seeds had been set up, and where the Brahmins gave daily readings of the *Caṇḍī pāṭh* and the *Rudri pāṭh*. In this room, the sacred Pādukā flame was used to light the king's *dhunī*, the fire of the renouncer, as opposed to the sacrificial fire, or *hom*.

Unlike what has been observed in the region of the Twenty-Four Kingdoms, the bringing up of the Goddess from the margins of the kingdom to its centre has no nuptial associations in Dullu. She is welcomed at the threshold of the capital by a sacred sword, as elsewhere, but the weapon here represents a form of the Goddess herself, rather than acting as a substitute for the king. Similarly, the quest for the flame goddess requires that the royal emissary, disguised as an ascetic, openly abandon his martial virility. This is also the case for the king, who is relegated to the status of an undressed, belittled recluse. The arrival of the goddess from the margins of the kingdom thus transforms the palace into a hermitage and the king into a renouncer. Here, the rite abolishes royalty itself, testing the limits of the void it creates in the world. It creates a kind of interregnum, no mean feat in a context where even the death of the king must not interrupt the continuation of the reign, with the new sovereign being enthroned by rule before the cremation of his predecessor. In contrast with the wild, vegetable goddess of Ismā, who comes to unite with the king and reinforce his power, the all-devouring flame of Dullu does not add to the existing order, but rather abrogates it and manifests Her own sovereignty, one which belongs to a higher order. For it is from Dullu, so say its inhabitants, that the Fire which destroys the universe at the end of each cycle of time comes, in its form of Kāl Agni, the fire of the apocalypse. This terrifying fire is housed in a small temple situated near the temple of the Flame of the Head, where it only lights up dimly from time to time and then goes out.

By transferring the powers from the limits of the kingdom into the palace, the seventh day of Dasaī has the double effect of abolishing the established boundaries of the kingdom and concentrating its forces within its centre. This torsion of space – which brings to mind the Klein Bottle, which has neither outer nor inner surface – marks the first outing of the royal weapon, the first public sacrifice and the first ritual fights. As in the episodes of the *Celebration of the Goddess*, the *śakti* of the Goddess intensifies with the arrival of this otherworldly form of herself, and in Kathmandu, the valley echoes with the salutary shots of the army, which welcome her arrival.[9]

The sacrifices

The *śakti* further intensifies on the morning of the eighth day, *aṣṭamī*, with the installation of Durgā in each household. At Narmati's house, in the village of Darling, the warrior goddess is represented by a pot filled with water, beside which is placed lights used to represent a multiple form of herself, the nine Durgā, as well as the tutelary deities of the lineage, in the form of ropes. Facing the altar, all the weapons and agricultural tools of the household are displayed. A goat is sanctified inside the house by the householder, who goes on to decapitate it. He then sprinkles the weapons and tools with the animal's blood and lays its head as an offering before Durgā's pot. The carcass is taken out and gutted in order to extract the liver. This auspicious organ is cut into pieces, grilled, then distributed in as many portions as there are people present, in leaf cups offered to all as *prasād*, or blessings of the Goddess. As soon as the liver is consumed, the master of the house removes the head of the goat from the altar, to cut it up along with the rest of the meat. While he is busy with this task, the teenager who has temporarily taken on the role as head of the family explains to me: 'What the gods want is the liver, *kalejo*. We immediately give them the blood and the head to "make them forget", *bhulāune*, as we give sweets to a child to make him forget what he wants. The head is like a pledge, a deposit, *bandhak*, before the liver is offered, which is why it can be taken back as soon as the liver has been offered in *prasād*.'

The sacrifice of the goat is followed by that of the plant version of the kid-goat, made of a flowering cucumber to which twig legs are inserted, and whose execution is obligatory, although no one can say why. Sometimes the sacrifice is that of a gourd, and in this instance it is said to represent a human death. This particular sacrifice is therefore performed in some places by throwing the weapon at it, so as not to be tainted with the sin of homicide, as is the case in Dullu, for example.

The village of Darling includes two Brahmin hamlets, where it was not possible for me to observe their worship, as I was not allowed inside their homes. The 'guru', a schoolteacher who was literate in Sanskrit, gave me a manual detailing the domestic procedures, which some people follow to the letter. This *Handbook of Autumn Worship to Durgā* (Rana 1975) was published by the Royal Academy of Nepal, giving it a quasi-official character. Unusually, it is not written by a Brahmin, but by a Kshatriya, and more precisely by a member of the Rana family, the prime ministers who usurped the royal power. The handbook describes the procedure of the sacrifice of a goat inside the house in detail, but makes no mention of any type of buffalo sacrifice during the 'autumn cult'. There is also another manual, written by a Brahmin (Subedi 1988: 18–19), but this one gives no description of any sacrificial procedure at all, merely mentioning the custom in order to advise the Brahmins against it: 'On this day [the eighth], without having eaten, it is customary to offer sacrifices in the temple. It is said that it is not right for Brahmins to offer a sacrifice, *bali*, and that they should offer a gourd or a *bel* fruit instead.'

If we had been left with these manuals alone, it would be difficult for us to imagine that the procedures described for an educated elite are in fact part of a much more remarkable 'customary' ceremony, including the royal buffalo sacrifice, since they are entirely omitted from these texts.

Through these handbooks, we enter a world where each gesture is to be accompanied by formulas, so numerous that it is impossible to learn them by heart, a problem which Rana's manual itself specifies, stating that they must be read out loud.

For those who follow its instructions, the legs of the goat must first be washed and then it is presented to the divinity. Libations are then made on its body using *kuś* grass, while saying: 'The gods made of Agni an animal and sacrificed him, and Agni won the world. This is why you are going to join the world of Agni. Drink this water.' Then the sacrifier touches different parts of the goat's body, saying: 'I purify your speech, I purify your head, I purify your horns, I purify your eyes, I purify your ears, I purify your mouth, I purify your throat, I purify your senses, I purify your whole body.' He sprinkles some consecrated rice on the animal and repeats: 'May your speech be satisfied, may your head be satisfied, may your eyes be satisfied,' and so on. He then expresses to the goat the wish that the parts of its body join the elements: 'May your buttocks reside in Water, may your eyes reside in the Light, may your ears reside in Heaven, may your snout reside in the Wind, may your bones reside in the Orients, may your mind reside in Brahma.' After speaking sacred syllables to the different parts of its body, the sacrifier again addresses the goat: 'I am going to cut you in sacrifice ..., you are the form of the sacrificial offering and I worship you like a god: join Indra's heaven by leaving this form for a divine form.' He has the goat hear the *gāyatrī* formula, which turns men into Twice-born, and proceeds to the rite of the commitment to sacrifice, *saṅkalpa*, asking that his faults be erased, his enemies annihilated and the goddess Durgā contented for a period of ten years. He then sprinkles the animal with water from tail to head, saying again: 'By your faults in a previous life, you were born an animal; in leaving this place, leave this world and join the divine world,' and then waits until it trembles. After having observed this, he sanctifies the sacrificial weapon, 'the sword', and awakens the Goddess in it through the repetition of numerous formulas. At the moment of death, the sacrifier addresses the goat one last time: 'Rise animal, you are the form of Śiva. Merge into Śiva by leaving this body, for the good of all.' Once the execution is completed, he offers the head of the victim to the Goddess, accompanying his gesture with the words: 'O Goddess, take this animal offered to you. Ensure that it attains paradise, and me too!'

The blood of the sacrifice must then be poured on nine mounds of dung glued to the wall of the house, each representing a goddess, or else be offered to nine people. Finally, the liver of the animal is cooked with ginger and offered to the Goddess.

The formulas of the 'literate' sacrificial ceremony, presented here in abbreviated form, are mostly addressed directly to the victim, who is purified and quieted, then informed of its fate, with the promise of a better future. The sacrifier successively dangles the promise in front of the animal of joining the world of Agni, the heaven of Indra or the divine world, of merging into Śiva, of attaining paradise, of dissolving into the immensity of all the elements of the world.

As soon as it has been purified, the sacrifier treats the victim as an interlocutor, alternately animal and divine, then makes it his disciple, anthropomorphising the animal into his 'spiritual son', by making him listen to the *gāyatrī* formula, before asking to obtain the same fate as his 'child'. This spiritual filial relationship established between the victim and his sacrifier completes the picture of the goat as a cherished member of the family that we have already mentioned, and which, in certain contexts, is explicitly formulated.[10]

The sacrifice of the goat is therefore a major transgression of the normal order of things, sending the 'spiritual son' to heaven so that his father or *guru* can join him there. This is an inversed model to that of the life cycle rituals, where it is the son who is indispensable for the funeral of the father, as he helps his soul to initiate his year-long journey towards the abode of the ancestors.

Once the domestic ceremonies are over, the chief of Darling heads to the temple dedicated to the goddess Mānakāmanā, where he proceeds to worship the sacrificial post, first placing the goddess of Heaven at its top and then the goddess of the Underworld at its foot. Then he decapitates a goat and dips the four cutlasses of the temple in its blood, in order to strengthen them for the buffalo sacrifices of the next day.

In the fort of Ismā, as in Musikot or in the palace of Dullu, Durgā is installed in the same manner as in all the domestic houses. In each of these places she receives a billy-goat, beheaded respectively by the soldier, the Ṭhakurī king and a 'minister of the king'.[11] Blood sacrifice thus becomes generalised with the arrival of Durgā on the eighth day, but in a dispersed way, being present in every residence, both ordinary and royal, and in every temple.[12] Its private, lineage-based character is expressed by the offering of the *alter ego*, the he-goat.

The night bridging the eighth and the ninth days brings forth an even more terrible form of the Goddess, Kālī, to whom a sacrifice is offered at midnight in many temples or ancient sites of power. On this night called *kāl rātri*, the 'dark night', 'night of death' or 'night of the end of time', darkness reigns supreme at midnight, while the moon has not yet risen. Sacrificing under such circumstances adds to the terror, for nighttime sacrifice is associated with human sacrifice. At the Gulmi Palace or the Ugra Tārā temple in Daḍeldhurā, it is said that young boys were once put to death on this occasion. The dark night is also associated with the sacrifice of Dakṣa and the immolation of his daughter. To mark this connection, in the region of Dullu, only goats brought by married girls are sacrificed.

When midnight strikes in Musikot, the two kings perform a five-animal sacrifice, *pañcabali*, in honour of Kālīkā, while men go into a trance to the sound of devotional *mālsrī* songs sung by Brahmins. Two Sāru Magars, of the Indigenous king's clan, are possessed by Bhairam, and two members of the royal Siṃha Ṭhakurī clan by the Sword-gods. In the village of Darling, a crowd of about fifty men grunt, gesticulate or howl, each possessed by his own tutelary deity. These sounds mix with the invocation of the names of all the gods of the territory, sung by a choir of men. With the appearance of the most dreadful form of the Goddess, the divine presence is thus manifested in its fullness, which activates all the gods, who, being 'thirsty for blood', seek to become incarnate.

On this night, a sacrificial slaughter takes place within the precincts of the royal palace in Kathmandu, where fifty-four buffaloes and fifty-four goats are executed at midnight. Meanwhile, special sacrifices are offered to the nine Durgā in the royal 'House of Dasaī', as well as in the chapel, where the goddess Tāleju (the former tutelary goddess of the Malla kings turned into the 'national goddess' after the capture of their kingdom by the Shāh of Gorkhā) is taken down from her temple at midnight.

On the ninth day, in the village of Darling, a crowd gathers on the esplanade of the Goddess's temple. The groups arrive in procession, the head of the family in the front, holding a bamboo pole adorned with a standard, followed by his son pulling a buffalo, then women and children carrying plates of fruit and cucumbers, and finally one or two drummers, if the family's means so permit. These processions converge towards the temple from the four cardinal directions, and are reminiscent of the formation of an army, as described in the epic, where each clan, under the aegis of its chief, joins the king for his expedition. Once they have reached the temple, the groups circumambulate it, make their offerings and then tie their buffalo to the post. Others arrive with goats or rams, pigeons or roosters. The first animal of each of the five species is officially offered by the administration of the municipality, which has made a collection from all the inhabitants for the purchase of a *pañcabali*, 'five sacrifices'. The offering of these so-called governmental, *sarkāri* victims inaugurates each series. The execution of the buffaloes opens the session with a solemn tone.

The chief of the village, wearing the sunglasses he reserves for special occasions, holds his hand on the animal's flank, surrounded by the important men of the village, to the swelling sounds of the Damāī band.

A Brahmin consecrates the animal by sprinkling pure water on its head using a bundle of sacred grass, while mentally pronouncing wishes of prosperity for the community: 'O Durgā devī, protect all those who live in our village, destroy diseases and misfortune, grant us a good climate, make prosperous our crops and harvests.' He then pours a libation on the animal's neck and steps back. Everyone watches for the animal's reaction. The sacrificator, a Magar soldier from the chief's clan, dressed in a Brahmanic loincloth, stands straight upright at his side, pointing a long cutlass to the sky. When the buffalo trembles, a movement which is greeted by a few 'jaya' in the crowd, a man grabs the rope attached to its collar and pulls it over the hole in the post to force the animal to lower its head and stretch its neck. The soldier grabs his cutlass with both hands, raises it high above his head, and brings it down with all of his strength, the momentum of which causes his feet to literally leave the ground, to decapitate the victim with a single blow (see Figure 5.4). He immediately wipes his blade on the animal's body, then dips

Figure 5.4 The execution of the first buffalo by a Magar soldier in Darling

Source: Author.

his fingers in its blood and makes a bloody mark on the tip of the blade and one on his own forehead. The head of the buffalo is taken to the temple, while its body is dragged around, then laid aside. In the meantime, a second buffalo has already been tied to the post.

I had come to the ceremony with Narmati's mother, and was wearing a velvet blouse and a printed *longi* skirt for the first time, at the behest of the headman who, a few days earlier, had asked me in a very serious tone to come dressed for the occasion in *longi* and *cholo.* We had joined a group of women squatting at an observation post on the temple embankment. They all had things to say about my new look, and then began to comment on the scene, lamenting that the sacrificator's loincloth had a stain on it, that some goats were too young, and that the buffaloes were looking at each other as they tried to free themselves from their bonds. The headman, who saw me, gestured for me to join him in the first row, which alarmed Narmati's mother. She put her hand on my shoulder, whispering *bho*, 'it is not necessary'. She disapproved of such proximity to the execution, although technically there was nothing to prevent women from standing closer. Nevertheless, I decided to step forward, and the crowd parted for me to make my way through, then closed up once more, forcing me to remain extremely close to the executions throughout the sacrificial session. In this inner circle, there were no remarks made about the clothes, the size of the animals or the conditions they were being held in. Instead, a spirit of collaboration prevailed, a collective wish for the good technical realisation of the executions, heard in outbursts from the spectators closest to the action: 'pull', 'harder', 'keep it straight', 'wait', 'strike now'. With each buffalo, there was the mark of blood, on the blade, on the forehead. The headman, who I ended up asking why the sacrificator was doing that, replied: 'It's because he's happy, because he managed to do it.'

The intensity of attention and the sense of collective participation decreased with the next series of sacrifices, of goats and kids, then of rams. The crowd began to disperse and the pigeons were either cut up or simply released at the temple gate, without an audience. The sacrifice of the chickens, which closes the 'massacre', *kāṭmār*, on the other hand, took place in a spirit of general jubilation. The men sprayed those waiting their turn with the blood which spurted from the chickens' necks, or else dropped their headless bodies at ground level, where they tried to escape, running and flapping through the crowd in vain, causing much jostling mixed with laughter and the cries of women who did not want to see their new best outfits stained.

Once the sacrifices were completed, the drummers positioned themselves in a line, two by two, and were promptly joined by the men of the assembly. Together, they formed a large circle and brandished both the actual weapons of sacrifice and other dummy weapons, to sketch out a few steps of a war dance, *saraĩ*, which they would resume in greater numbers the next day (see Figure 5.5).

Figure 5.5 War dance of Dasaĩ in a Magar village of Rolpa, 2011

Source: Author.

On the eighth day, in the ancient capital of Ismā, the householders sacrificed a gourd and a goat for Durgā at their domestic altar, where they had stored weapons and the tools used to sanctify them. Then, at the call of the town crier, they all went to the palace, carrying their offerings, because the astrologers had established that the ninth day would begin in the afternoon of the eighth. There was therefore no 'dark night' that year.

Those who brought a buffalo to the palace laid their standard at its gate, tied their victim to the post and lined up. Under the direction of the chaplain, they collectively performed a *saṅkalpa*, a rite which seals their commitment to sacrifice and makes them sacrifiers. The chaplain then sanctified the sacrificial post by tracing a star at its foot, offered the *prasād* of the palace gods and pure water to the elder buffalo who was tied to the post, before placing flowers around its neck, which was already covered with a white cloth, to make it even more pure. Finally, all the officiants of the palace circumambulated the animal three times.

Here the victim receives a peculiar form of consecration, in which each component is in direct opposition to the reality of sacrifice: the animal is purified but its meat remains impure; by being offered *prasād*, an act which is usually reserved for humans, it is in a way treated as one, only to be killed as a beast; finally, it is venerated as a divine being by the officiants who circumambulate it, before being put to death as a demon.

Much like the victim, Ismā's royal sword carries antinomian tensions. From being a particularly visible symbol of power, whose consecrated epithet is 'sparkling like lightning', the sword is here obscured to such an extent that no one has ever seen it. From its role as a mobile and transmissible regalia, it is turned into an object consigned to a little temple that is always closed, except for once a year, where only the chaplain is entitled to take it out, fully swaddled in cloth. Finally, it is during the sacrifice that the sword's antinomy is expressed in the most striking way, as it goes from being an instrument of death, the operator of the sacrifice par excellence, to its principal recipient, in a remarkable reversal of the place it occupies in the ritual scheme.

With the royal Sword-god being thus inaccessible in Isma, two other curved-bladed swords were taken out of the royal arsenal by the Kshatriya officiants to be used in the sacrifices. They soaked them in a mixture of rice and milk curds before entrusting them to the two elected representatives, one from each of the two municipalities, at the intersection of which the palace is located. The mayors held the weapons aloft in front of themselves, as if they were standing to attention in the front row of the sacrificial arena.

The 'elder buffalo' was led there and sprinkled with water. It flinched. One of the mayors then entrusted his sword to the 'king's soldier', who seized it and executed the animal with one fell swoop. The Untouchable Gāine and Damāī musicians, who had been playing with redoubled vigour since the sanctification of the buffaloes, now let out cries and rushed upon the blood of the animal to mark their instruments and their foreheads with what they called the '*ṭikā* of Durgā' (see Figure 5.6). It was then the turn of the 'younger buffalo'. The officiant, a Kshatriya in the prime of his life, was in turn given an ancient sword dating from the time when Ismā was an independent kingdom by his respective mayor, which had been freshly sharpened by the blacksmiths before the ritual. The crowd amassed, the musicians beat their drums with all the strength they could muster, all eyes fixed on the man who was brandishing his blade high in the sky, ready to strike. But the victim made a sudden movement, and the blow, struck with considerable force, hit the buffalo's shoulders. The slashed animal started to buck and wheel around, with the sword still stuck in its flesh, struggling in pain. The drummers stood up and started shouting vociferously, mad with rage, and hurled insults at the sacrificator.

To contain their anger, the mayor outstretched his arms, saying in a loud voice: *śāntī*, *śāntī*, 'peace, peace'. He was thrown off balance and some spectators then tried to flee, pushing those who did not want to miss the show.

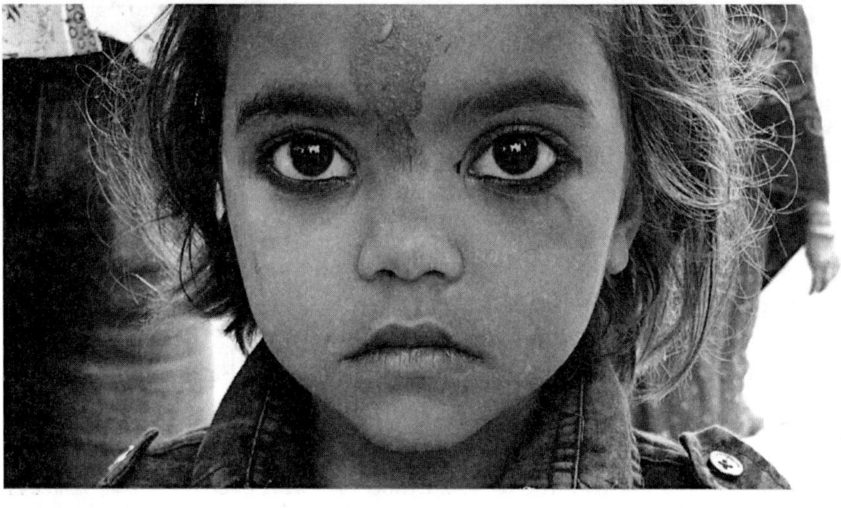

Figure 5.6 A girl wearing a *tikā* mark, Gaḍhī Māī, 2019

Source: Author.

I also turned around in the hope of escaping, but a hand grasped my arm to keep me in place, pointing at the Kshatriya who has just grabbed his weapon again and was about to complete the sacrifice. The death blow restored order and the musicians started playing again, while still grumbling among themselves. I had not understood their fury or why they were so involved in the proceedings, as they were usually so reserved in the presence of their patrons. My neighbour explained to me that the buffalo meat was theirs and that the 'fault' of the failed sacrifice had 'degraded' it.

The sacrifices continued and a total of thirty-two buffaloes were put to death. Goats and rams, pigeons and gourds then followed. At last, a pig sacrifice was offered to Bhairam as an aside, by a Magar officiant who killed it with a stone. The god's servant, a Nāth ascetic, was keen to point out to me that the victim was not actually offered to Bhairam, but to the demon he subdues under his feet, while he himself offers Bhairam a bread cooked with his own hands. The Magar did not agree, but did not tell me so until later.

At the fort of Musikot, the buffaloes are similarly led in martial processions, one by one, to the sacrificial post of the royal palace. They are bound to it, soon forming an assembly in the midst of the assembly of onlookers. The children approached them and men examined them. Soon the drumbeats focused everyone's attention, and people craned their necks to catch sight of the Sword-gods as they were brought out from the royal palace.

Only two of the five sword brothers are brought out each year. They are carried by the king and one of his relatives, dressed in a white loincloth, their foreheads marked with powders, their heads shaved except for one lock of hair, in the style of the Brahmin officiants. Thus transfigured, they carry the instruments of death and royalty, hidden with cloth, above the sea of people (see Figure 5.7).

They were preceded by the Indigenous king, who pushed through the crowd with a pot of earth in his hands, followed by the Brahmins. Behind them marched a line of men brandishing weapons from the fort's arsenal, fighting their way through the clamour and the shower of flowers thrown at them as they passed. Having reached the sacrificial site, they formed a circle around the central post, which the Brahmins sanctified by smearing the base and the top with cow dung, and by drawing diagrams with rice flour. Nearby, two Brahmins of the Ghimire clan recited prayers aloud to the Goddess in a trance state. They did not stop until the sacrifices were over.

The Magar king uncovered one of the two swords and used it to execute a set of five 'governmental' sacrifices, *sarkāri pañcabali*, including a gourd, a

Figure 5.7 Exit of the hooded Sword-gods for the sacrifices, Musikot, Gulmi, 1986

Source: Author.

ram, a billy-goat and the 'younger buffalo', which is the first to be killed here.[13] Then he made way for the Ṭhakurī king, who decapitated the 'elder buffalo' with the second royal sword. This is the only sacrifice he performs in public, emphasising its pre-eminence, even though the fact that the Indigenous rulers resided in these lands well before his ancestors is reflected in the privilege afforded them in offering the first animal. The Magar king then killed all the other buffaloes. Afterwards, the Sword-gods were taken back to the palace, where they would remain in obscurity till the sacrifices of the next year. A closing rite, *visarjana*, was performed in the courtyard opposite the sacrificial arena. It is addressed to the Sun, Sūrya, to whom the Ṭhakurī king, himself of the solar clan, offered one last billy-goat.

Of the buffaloes, nothing was left except bloody trails on the ground. The heads, placed for a short time in the sanctuary, in front of the Swords and the Goddess, were distributed to the blacksmiths and the drummers who provided 'service' for the rite, along with the meat of the two 'elder and younger' buffaloes; the other bodies were taken away by the castes working in the service of the patrons who offered them. They were cut up and shared among them separately.

Consecrations and warlike games

On the tenth day, a throne was established in the palace of Musikot, upon which the picture of the king of Nepal and his wife was installed.[14] A mark of consecration, *ṭikā*, made of a mixture of rice and milk curd, was smeared on it by a Brahmin officiant at the exact moment the radio announced that the king has been consecrated in Kathmandu. The officiant then went out to mark the sacrificial post, and finally threw a mixture of rice and curd from outside, through the window, in the direction of the palace gods. He then took some of the rice that was used to consecrate the throne and incorporated it into a dish of the same mixture, while the Magar king cut the barley shoots planted ten days before. The four officiants finally went out with these ingredients into the courtyard, in order to proceed to the consecrations in front of the assembly of the 'great men'.

The Magar king consecrated the Ṭhakurī king by placing a *ṭikā* on his forehead; the latter in return gave him a *ṭikā*; then the Magar consecrated the two Brahmin priests, before the Ṭhakurī did so in turn. The latter then gave a *ṭikā* to the mayor of the locality, while the Brahmins consecrated the members of the palace committee. Finally, the four officiants distributed marks to the men, then to the women, and lastly to the Untouchables, on whom they did not place the mark on the forehead, but rather in their hands, so that they had to apply it to themselves. Along with the *ṭikā* mark, everyone received a few barley shoots which they placed behind their ear. Finally, all those who came to the palace incorporated some of the royal mixture into their own, and went off to distribute the *ṭikā* marks among their families and employees. In this way, from the tenth day until the full moon, starting from the royal consecration, all the Nepalis go around in order to receive the *ṭikā* from each other.[15]

On the evening of the tenth day, a war dance was performed by the entire body of men, while the *phulpāti* was taken out of the palace and led to a spring to be immersed. Its journey outside the palace was protected by a rite conducted by the officiants, who went to a knoll outside the village, from where the Ṭhakurī king shot arrows with a miniature bow in the four cardinal directions while the Brahmins recited mantras.

The *saraī* or *sarāya* dance is performed everywhere as an extension of the rite, sometimes on the 'tenth day of victory', *vijayādaśamī*, sometimes on the following day or even later. This dance and music performance is described as a 'game', *khel*, which celebrates the victory of the Goddess and the strength of warriors.[16] The older generation say that in the past the dance opened the 'season of war' and marked the start of a military expedition to a neighbouring kingdom. The very name of the 'game', *saraī*, is locally related to the verb *sarnu*, which designates the action of displacement. The extension of the sacrificial rite that war represents is here manifested by the brief performance of the warlike dance in the immediate aftermath of the blood sacrifices, and its resumption on a larger scale the next day, as observed in the village of Darling or in Ismā. Through its warlike extensions, the sacrificial rite is not closed in on itself, but instead forms the 'entrance' to a sacrifice of a higher order, the 'great sacrifice', *mahāyagya,* of war.

In the village of Darling, the dance used to take place at night, in the headman's courtyard, but as he himself explained, it used to degenerate into violence, so he decided that it would take place in the afternoon, on the esplanade. As in Musikot, the dance is the occasion to dispose of the *phulpāti*. Its palanquin is now carried by two young virgin girls, led by the village headman and accompanied by a jester, up to a stream where its content is sunk under the water. The *saraī* dance thus represents both the departure of the Goddess and a departure to war, in a joining reminiscent of the chronicles which relate how the Goddess led the troops of Gorkhā in person during the unification campaign.

Interestingly, *saraī* is also an occasion to commemorate historical battles, as is the case in Ismā. In this ancient royal capital, on the morning of the eleventh day, the village crier calls for the people to gather on the esplanade, where the Damāī are already beating their drums. The crowd comes in great numbers, with everyone dressed in their finery, their foreheads adorned with a *ṭikā* of rice and their ears with barley shoots. Men wear their military decorations and brandish weapons, sticks or umbrellas in their right hands, and a handkerchief in the left, as a sort of shield. They form a circle around the sacrificial post, which is headed by the Nāth ascetic, who waves a small ball drum, *ḍamaru* and a bell. He is followed by the drummers beating their timpani, along with the dancers' movements. The circle turns slowly, 'in the direction of the movement of the sun', around the sacrificial post. For the people of the capital, the dances of the dependent villages, such as Darling, which turn counter-sunwise, are said to be 'backwards', a little as if the kingdom were coming to life like a vast war machine made of gears turning in different directions.

The men break off the progress of the circle at regular intervals to face each other two by two and mimic a fight, then resume their steps, singing in unison: *bhāi lo, khukuri, soli, bhāi lo*, 'yes, brothers, sword, shield, yes, brothers'. Suddenly, a group from the village of Chāp, located over the ridge, arrives in a flurry of dancing and brandished weapons. As soon as the newcomers are spotted, the men of Ismā gather behind an imaginary line, where they wait for the intruders, ready to compete with them in a race. The great men of the village stand at the meeting point, on either side of the path, in order to arbitrate. The Nāth loudly shakes his *ḍamaru* and bell, the Damāī sound out drum rolls. When the men of Chāp arrive at the allotted point where the Ismā men are standing, they all rush towards the sacrificial post, waving their weapons, and run around it, shoving their opponents' heads with their left hands to try to slow them down. The first man to get back to the starting line wins for his side.

This race, which mimics a raid, is said to commemorate the time that the people of Chāp once refused the tutelage of the king of Ismā and chose to attack him in his territory, where they ultimately lost. However, more than being a fight, the race is a competition, one which brings to mind a custom described in the chronicle of Gorkhā, which relates that in Liglig, on the day of *vijayādaśamī*, the 'tenth day of victory' that concludes the rite of Dasaī, the local peoples organised a race from the bottom of the valley to the top of the mountain, where their fort was located. All could participate, and the winner was given the title of king for the year. Drabya Shāh, the youngest prince of the neighbouring kingdom of Lamjung, tried his luck and was the first to reach the seat of power. This is how he obtained the throne of Liglig, from where, armed with a royal title, a fortress and a small army, he attacked the Magar king of Gorkhā and established his capital there in 1559 (Naraharinath 1964).

Sacrificial fights

In contrast to the region of the Twenty-Four Kingdoms, where Dasaī renews the ideal organisation of society in an orderly manner, in the Twenty-Two region the basic principle of the rite is disorder. In Dullu, the buffalo is not solemnly executed by a designated person in the midst of an assembly. Instead, on the ninth day, the victim, decorated with a wreath of flowers tied to its back, is taken to the stone lion guarding the entrance to the royal palace, which has been freshly painted for the occasion by a member of the royal family. In front of the lion is a small sacrificial post that the Brahmin sprinkles with water, before drawing diagrams with vermillion powder (see Figure 5.8). The buffalo is first consecrated there by the Brahmin, then by a member of the

Figure 5.8 The lion of Dullu
Source: Author.

royal family. All around them, the drummers beat their drums in a deafening way, while many men in the audience wolf-whistle (see Figure 5.9). When the animal has quivered, it is pulled through the crowd by a group of young men who beat it to keep it moving forward. Its passage provokes a concert of shouts that rises and falls in intensity, making it possible to identify where the animal is in the crowd.

Crossing the esplanade, the buffalo runs along the slope of the mountain, broken into a succession of terraces. Eventually it disappears from view, surrounded by those who try to cut it to death, in a great clamour. Young boys move like a flock of sparrows closing in on the action, forming a group that replicates in miniature the movement of the hunting group who charge in pursuit of the buffalo. In this year 2012, the animal was killed by a Kshatriya who stretched his arm up towards the sky to beckon the Brahmin priest, who rushed to the victim with a pot of pure water, and sprinkled it on the main wound of the victim on its neck (see Figure 5.10). The Kshatriya pointed to a secondary wound, on the animal's rump, which the Brahmin also immediately poured with water, to 'pacify and bless it', *śāntī svastī ko lāgī*.

Figure 5.9 Killing the pain. Helping the sacrificator decapitating a goat, a boy shouts and another whistles to 'kill the pain'. Eighth day of Dasaĩ, Dullu, 2012.
Source: Author.

The buffalo sacrifice riles the crowd up, many of whom are fairly tipsy by this point. A drunken old man came to talk about it as my recorder was on:

> When there were demons, *rākṣas*, they lived near here and went this way and that. And Kālīkā devī made the intoxication, *naśā*. And if you ask what the meaning of *naśā* is, it is said that Kālīkā devī made the beer and liquor, and Kālīkā devī, having made them, began to drink them and she began to slice all the demons that she met with her sword. With the *joś* of *naśā*, 'the enthusiasm of intoxication', one can do anything. With the enthusiasm of intoxication, Kālīkā devī killed the demons. After which the demon Mahisāsur began to drink blood. What sacrifice (*bhog*) does she eat, Sitā devī? What sacrifice does she eat, Lakṣmī devī? What sacrifice does she eat, Kālīkā devī? She eats incense, Sitā devī, she eats milk, Lakṣmī devī. She eats goat, Kālīkā devī.

As the old man suggested, men get drunk to give themselves the enthusiasm or courage to 'do anything', on the model of the Goddess in her

Figure 5.10 Sacrificed buffalo, its body decorated with a sheaf of flowers, Dullu, 2012

Source: Author.

Celebration. In this scattered, drunken mob, it is not always easy to understand what is going on. However, before the rite began, a Kshatriya did sum it up for me this way: 'When the buffalo is sacrificed, the *biṣṭa* [patrons] laugh and the *ḍom* [Untouchables] cry.[17] They cry because it's their defeat. They are from its party [the buffalo's].' In the crowd, such a division between pure and impure castes was not evident, and this was perhaps related to the fact that there was no longer a king in Dullu, that the sacred flame used for the rite had been washed away by a river flood in the 1980s, and that the palace itself had been destroyed in the early 2000s. I then interviewed one of the few members of the royal family still remaining in the village, who was in a state far removed from his status, because, as he told visitors by way of warning, it had been more than thirty years since he last washed, due to an allergy to water.

The man flatly refuted the existence of such a split between pure and impure castes, assuring me, 'We are united', and then added, 'But the *ḍom* argue among themselves after the sacrifice, at the time of meat sharing. One man wants more. Another says it has been stolen and there is a fight.' From being referred to as supporters of the buffalo-demon by one villager, the Untouchables were no better regarded by this prince, who spoke of them as scavengers.

The atmosphere of disorganisation that reigns over Dullu takes on a quite deliberate meaning when we consider the surrounding area. Indeed, the releasing of buffaloes into the crowd, unheard of in the Twenty-Four region, is the time-honoured way of offering the buffalo sacrifice throughout the region of the Twenty-Two Kingdoms. A similar ceremony is held in Lālu, in the district of Kālīkoṭ, a few miles north of Dullu. A member of the local royal family, Shāhi Ṭhakurī, described it to me. In Lālu, he told me, on the ninth day of Dasaĩ, the elder buffalo is taken to the temple of the goddess Kālīkā. There the animal receives a libation of pure water from the Brahmin, then from the king, and they wait for it to tremble. The king takes a sword and lightly slashes the animal's rump, then places a little salt in the wound. The buffalo immediately flees into the crowd, furious, and 'the king instructs his Kshatriya ministers to put it to death'. But, he added, 'the king lets all the men go, including the Untouchables', and they all rush out fully armed so as to join the fight. They chase the buffalo and strike it whenever they get close, each trying to kill it. Finally, when the buffalo is dead, 'the men start fighting among themselves, each saying: I am the one who killed it, I am the greatest. Then they come to the king, who makes peace between them and chooses the winner'.

The sacrificial combat in Lālu puts the Kshatriyas of ordinary rank, here designated as 'ministers', *kāji*, and the Untouchables in competition, in a conflict knowingly created by the king, who grants to those who are not warriors the opportunity to win over on the Kshatriyas. In this case, sacrifice forms a framework in which the king himself temporarily suspends caste rules, instigating a virile and warlike competition between his subjects in its place, where the best man may win, regardless of status. Far from creating a new cohesion within the crowd, uniting them against the same victim, the sacrifice instead further divides it, with each man seeking a chance at this most glorious of titles. This division also helps to strengthen the unique and separate position of the king, as arbiter, above all the chaos he himself has created. While competition is not totally absent from the rite in the Twenty-Four, it is only manifested in the events following the sacrifice, that is, during the warlike jousts, but not during the sacrificial execution itself.

In the Twenty-Two region, the rite subjects social organisation to distortions. It can render it clannish and thus more egalitarian, as at the temple of Tripura Sundarī, where thirty-two sacrificial posts belonging to the thirty-two clans related to the shrine, all identical, form the execution site for thirty-two buffaloes. In other places, such as Dehimaṇḍu, the ritual bestows honours on subordinates and excludes high-ranking persons.

The Dehimaṇḍu temple is dedicated to the goddess Nīgālā Sāinī, the Sister of Bamboo, and is located on the boundary between two rival ancient kingdoms, Upper Saḍaur and Lower Saḍaur, which arose from the split between brothers of the same royal clan, the Cand Ṭhakurī. To this day, the two rival branches meet there after marching down in two synchronised processions from their respective capitals. At the temple, they consult the augurs together with the oracle of the Goddess, a man of the Bohorā clan, who are Kshatriyas of lower status. The oracle passed away several years ago and the Goddess has still not chosen her new, official incarnation, but the temple's *rājbar*, the 'ruler of a religious domain', also recruited from the Bohorā clan, is still currently in charge at the temple of Dehimaṇḍu. This micro kingdom of the Goddess, ruled by a lower-ranking Kshatriya, acts as something of a buffer zone between the two rival Ṭhakurī kingdoms. Within the sacred mini kingdom, the devolution of power to lower status people is borne out by the prominent place accorded to a clan of Untouchables, the Lāvaḍ, who also count an oracle of the Goddess among them, who is in fact the only one currently in practice.[18] Anyone can come to consult him; however, this low-ranking oracle cannot sit on the great platform that serves as the throne of the Bohorā oracle. The Lāvaḍ, on the other hand, are the holders of a sacrificial post recognised as the 'main pillar', *mul khamba*, of the temple. While modest in appearance and difficult to spot among the forest of sacrificial posts which surrounds the temple, it is to this post that the first buffalo sacrificed at Dasaĩ for Nīgālā Sāinī is tied. The second buffalo is tied to the pillar of the Cand Ṭhakurī royal clan, which stands out from the others by its central location and its size. In this manner, sacrifice gives the Untouchables precedence over the *rājbar*, the lower-status Kshatriya king of the ritual domain, and grants them shared honours with the higher-ranking Ṭhakurī kings. The recurrence of this type of ritual inversion in the ancient kingdoms of the Twenty-Two region suggests a political will to make power 'untouchable', in both senses of the term, for those best placed to covet it, namely, the lower-ranking Kshatriya warriors, who are more numerous than the royal Ṭhakurīs.

Dehimaṇḍu and the two kingdoms of Saḍaur are located in the westernmost part of the Twenty-Two Kingdoms. It is a region where clan organisation is strong and caste rules, being stricter than elsewhere, have been used for strategic purposes. The sacrificial post or pillar, miniaturised in Dullu, makes a spectacular reappearance here. Inside the temple, the structure is supported by massive dark wooden pillars, called *kāl khamb*, 'black pillars', carved entirely with bas-reliefs. They form special insignia of power, and during the rite itself, each of the six temple officiants takes place at the foot of his designated pillar. Outside the temple, there are more than one hundred and fifty 'pillars' of varying appearance, as each person is free to place his or her own pillar of the shape, height and decoration of their choice, with their name and the names of their ancestors inscribed upon it. It would seem that the temple is more accessible than elsewhere. However, Ṭhakurī women are not allowed in the procession that leads their husbands and sons to the temple, echoing the rule that excludes them from wedding processions. In addition, the women of the Bohorā clan, that of the 'king of the temple', as well as those of the clan of Brahmin priests attached to the temple are all forbidden from approaching it.

The Bohorā men explain that their spouses, together with the Brahmin priests' spouses, struck the Goddess when they discovered her disguised in the form of a stone and have all been punished ever since. The Ṭhakurī 'kings' of the adjacent kingdoms, for their part, offer another reason for this prohibition, claiming that they are so beautiful when they arrive in procession on their horses that the wives of the temple officiants are kept away by their husbands so that they do not succumb to temptation. By way of proof, they add that the Goddess herself hides their beauty, causing a thick fog to fall when they approach her temple, even if, as a rule, the sun is shining when they set out. In any case, the result is that the women of the three most prominent groups connected with the temple are forbidden to approach it, even though the Untouchables may enter, provided that they remain on the lowest of the three levels of the temple hall. These women are also excluded from the sacrificial spectacle, even though it is held on the esplanade, outside the temple enclosure, much like the prohibition that excludes them from the sacrifices addressed to the tutelary deities of the clan, or to the gods of the territory, which generally include all men, including Untouchables, but exclude all women.

As with the reversal of positions of honour, the reorganisation of society along vertical lines which takes place during the time of sacrifice is undoubtedly not completely alien to the political organisation of the micro-states of this region, which were much less centralised than that of the Twenty-Four. The presence in these societies of peers pitted against each other in bitter rivalries, where the local sport consisted of ravishing the wives of the opponents, was clearly a source of conflict, and the alliances with the Untouchables, those men who, because of their status, could neither claim power nor enter into the game of assaulting spouses and fiancées, but could nevertheless help out, were very much indispensable.

On the ninth day of Dasaĩ, a huge crowd gathers in Dehimaṇḍu for the buffalo sacrifices. The devotees arrive in groups, with their beautiful buffaloes, their bodies completely anointed with oil, adorned with flowers and topped with a red band around their heads, making up a most spectacular procession. From the first steps of the sanctuary, they run alongside the animal in a race around the temple, stop to have it consecrated by the officiants, then make an offering of a performance by the drummers who serve their particular clan, who spin their tambours in all directions, while there are even some possessed individuals who dance to the beat. They then go to their respective pillars, which they have repainted before the rite, and decorate it with their standards. Depending on the whim of the sacrifier, the buffalo is either executed at the pillar or else thrown into the crowd, where a group of young Kshatriyas, recognisable by their yellow T-shirts, having been authorised by the temple committee to do so, chase the beast with swords to put it to death (see Figures 5.11 and 5.12). Here too, the sacrifices bring things to life: the oldest pillars among those surrounding the temple, which feature images of warriors dating back to mediaeval times, begin to shake when the blood of the buffaloes gushes out, according to the locals. The bodies of the victims are finally exposed at the foot of the temple, in a scene which resembles a battlefield (see Figure 5.13). There is a vaguely bacchanalian atmosphere to proceedings reminiscent of the scenes depicted in the *Celebration of the Goddess*, where the mix of blood and music turns the combat into a feast. Devotees dip their hands into the carcasses to adorn their foreheads with the mark of the Goddess, children play in the blood and young boys sit or stand on the bloody bodies to take selfies (see Figure 5.14).

Around the rite of sacrifice in Dehimaṇḍu, a balance of honours and opprobrium, of integration and exclusion, was set up. This balance worked to the detriment of women, even those of eminent status, and, conversely, to the benefit of the Untouchables linked to royal clans, whose power had always been insecure. Despite this, Dehimaṇḍu is one of the few shrines where the Untouchables have threatened to go on strike, refusing to consume

Figure 5.11 Cuddling the victim

Source: Author.

Figure 5.12 Mob sacrifice

Source: Author.

Figure 5.13 Mass sacrifices

Source: Author.

Figure 5.14 Collapsing with the victims

Source: Author.

the impure meat of the sacrificed buffaloes, a stance which caused an outcry and even beatings to be meted out in 2008. The sanctuary is located a short distance from the Indian border, and they were no doubt influenced by the Untouchables of Uttarakhand who led a similar emancipation movement with success. However, in Dehimaṇḍu, where the Untouchables do enjoy a special place of honour in the temple, especially during sacrifices, negotiations resulted in a resumption of traditions.[19]

Sacrificial order and disorder

As the distinct descriptions of the rite have emphasised, in each place, Dasaī̃ takes a variety of ceremonial forms, where, despite being organised within the same mythical and temporal frameworks, in the same caste society, and being ordered around the same royal power, the specificities of each area's history and their unique style of governance alter the assignment of roles and the way in which the animals are killed.

In Ismā or Musikot, the sacrificial ceremony is presented as a cult dedicated to the instrument of sacrifice, the Sword-god, the appearance of which provokes the exaltation of the crowd. From its status as regalia and as an emblematic weapon of the Goddess, this instrument of death has acquired an autonomy that recalls the deification and personalisation of the Sacrifice and its constituent elements which occurred during the Vedic period. It is humanised, it is a 'brother', *bhāi*. It is deified, 'he' is a deity, *devatā*. 'He' is treated as a living being, receives offerings, is anointed and washed, clothed and adorned, paraded. He is active – when he goes out, he shakes so strongly that he must be restrained, and his power extends to the heavens above, from where he chases the clouds away to allow the sun to shine. When he is finally unveiled for a brief moment, it is to accomplish the supreme act of killing the buffalo, a victim of formidable size and strength, from which he drinks the blood that makes him a living god.

With this sacralisation of the weapon of sacrifice, the means essentially become the end, in an act of translation similar to that of the Goddess who goes from being the perpetrator of the killing in the myth to being its recipient in the rite. In much the same way as the gods were devalued by the constituents of Sacrifice in the Vedic era, the instrument of sacrifice here somehow eclipses the Goddess, relegating her to the rank of spouse, as it eclipses the king also, who is placed at its service. It is only when he has been totally stripped of his finery and after having starved himself for a long time that the king is entitled to seize the weapon for himself, while this object of death, so full of strength and life, becomes the protagonist of a cult that he, the sword-god, addresses to himself, in a perfect loop which closes in on itself and devours its own tail. One might even be tempted to say that, just as the complexity of the rites was once able to absorb their meaning for the sacrifiers, or even the anguish of the sacrifier in the face of death, as Frits Staal and Charles Malamoud say, in Musikot or Ismā, the presence of the Sword-god is so strong that it captures all the attention of the participants and becomes the object of emotion of the entire sacrificial ceremony.

Further west, in the Twenty-Two Kingdoms, the preliminary phase of the sacrifice is marked by an activity of all the gods. In this region, where the lineage deities are not confined to the house, but have temples and rule over their territories, in all the sanctuaries, the priests, oracles and ascetics all observe a fast, including the king in his palace. When Durgā appears on the eighth day, the divine horde is satiated with goat sacrifices, then the royal cult takes over and puts an end to all the individual or lineage-based rituals. The killing of the royal animal, offered to the sovereign's tutelary goddess, provokes a unique gathering of all the groups that make up the local society. It does not take place in the royal palace itself, which lacks the requisite courtyard, steps and sacrificial post that we see in Musikot, for example, where a real sacrificial theatre is set up within the confines of the royal fortress. Continuing the movement initiated on the seventh day, when the powers of the otherworld are brought in the royal centre and abolish borders, and even the very reign of the king, the release of the sacrificial animal in Dullu and neighbouring kingdoms abolishes the limits of the sacrificial area and extends it outwards indefinitely, suggesting the idea of a power which knows no limits.

The way in which the execution is carried out in the sacrifice mimics the generalised violence of war, but here the idea of partaking in a collective killing that would annihilate all responsibility is out of the question. On the contrary, while it may seem collaborative at first glance, sacrificial killing here pits men against each other, for the glory of being the one to land the fatal blow, in a kind of indirect war of all against all. This turns the eventual sacrificator into a hero, but while in the orderly ceremonies of the Twenty-Four Kingdoms, he may smear himself with the blood of the victim as an uncontested hero, he finds himself having to defend his title from men of all ranks, including the lowest, in the sacrificial combats of far western Nepal.

The buffalo sacrifice offers a remarkable parallel with war, where similar breaches of the normal caste rules and purity prescriptions have been proclaimed by the kings throughout Nepalese history. Indeed, war is by definition situated outside the norms of Hindu law, as it inherently contains the notion of 'distress *dharma*', which allows for an infringement of the caste rules in life-threatening situations. Given this caveat, the ruler was able to periodically plunge his kingdom into a state of lawlessness. Among the most notable measures decided upon by the kings of Nepal, Pṛthvī Nārāyaṇ Shāh decreed that his soldiers would no longer have to abide by the rules of purity in order to eat, following an attack that caught them unawares and in a state of undress at a meal.[20] A few years later, another royal decree stipulated that yaks were essentially deer so that Nepali soldiers could freely consume their meat during the war against Tibet. The sacrificial ceremony also displays an abrogation of the usual social rules in some of the contexts we have examined, but in a framework which is more restricted in terms of both space and time.

Thus, when it is royal, sacrifice is linked to war in different ways, through the cult of weapons, the techniques of killing, in the form of 'games' and even more so in its unleashing of a controlled disorder. At the same time, from its very first day, the rite begins a process of 'fortification', one which applies to men, their weapons and their tools. It also applies to the collective, by the consecration of the occupation and the rank of each of its members and the reaffirmation of all that regulates them – the rule of the king, the power of great men, the dominance of the *pater familias*, that of the pure over the impure, of the Aryas over the Indigenous peoples, of men over women, as if these regulations were not so different from the implements which are also sprinkled with the life-giving blood of sacrifice. Such an exacerbation of oppositions and partitions makes the sacrifice a moment which fundamentally challenges the organisation of the group, by its unveiling of the violence at its core, a violence which is made as legitimate as the one which strikes the animal, by the demands of the divinity.

Notes

1. An initial comparison of the different forms of this ritual, a project which I initiated after having observed it in the first three sites discussed here in the late 1980s and early 1990s (the village of Darling and the former royal capitals of Isma and Musikot), was originally published in the form of a collective

work (Krauskopff and Lecomte-Tilouine 1996). The present study has been enriched by observations made in the 2000s and 2010s in the ancient Twenty-Two Kingdoms, which shed light on the overall schema of the celebrations. Remarkable recent publications on the buffalo sacrifice and on blood sacrifice in Nepal include Zotter (2021), Michaels (2016) and Torri (2016).

2. A number estimated for 2019 by Sanjeeb Phuyal (2019).
3. The impurity of death affects all members of the deceased's lineage. In the region of the Twenty-Two Kingdoms, it extends to all the 'pure' castes of the village, if the deceased is himself a member of that group. In contrast, the impurity that follows a birth affects only those living in the same household as the newborn.
4. The bundle is theoretically composed of nine plants, including the *bel*, banana and turmeric. The *phulpāti* is said to represent Bhadrakālī, the most terrifying form of the Goddess.
5. This custom did not spare the kings in Nepal. Pṛthvī Nārāyaṇ Shāh, the founder king of Nepal, was humiliated by having to wait several years after his wedding because his father-in-law, the king of Makvānpur, did not deign to entrust his daughter to him, leading the former to finally declare war against him (Naraharinath 1964).
6. The chronicle of the Gorkhā kings relates that the wife of Rām Shāh (seventeenth century) was worshipped as a goddess during her lifetime. The text tells that she exhorted men to fight against the powerful Lamjung army, that she marched at the head of their army and that, thanks to her presence, Gorkhāli soldiers were not injured by the weapons that struck them: 'Only their clothes were torn, or when the blow was very strong, only their skin was split' (Naraharinath 1964: 42). Offerings were presented to the queen after the victory, in recognition of her role. Other queens of Gorkhā were later honoured as incarnations, or 'parts', of her, thus tracing a strange line of divine wives without there being blood ties between them. The chronicle also underlines the impossibility of cohabitation with the Goddess. As soon as her true nature is revealed, she departs, often leaving with a stinging curse upon the king. Despite its limitations, the relationship that the king maintains with the Goddess in Nepal is considered matrimonial. The idea of their parentage, which is common in India, where the Goddess is often described as being a married daughter returning to visit her native residence, is not to be found in the Twenty-Four Kingdoms region of Nepal, to my knowledge.
7. Today, the *mahant* handles both ritual and economic affairs.

8. A river flood destroyed the Pādukā fire temple in 1981, and since then, the rite has not been practised.
9. In Kathmandu, the army, assembled on the March Field, fires a salvo while the Goddess (in vegetable form) is introduced into the capital. Before the abolition of the monarchy in 2008, the king, dressed in military costume, used to preside over the parade, while his chaplain and the chaplain's armed guard, accompanied by all high-ranking officials, went to greet the Goddess at the city gate and take her to the palace. The king joined her only at the moment of her arrival at the old royal palace.
10. Radhika Govindrajan (2018: 31–33) relates the case of a woman in Kumaon, who entrusted her husband's military career to the goddess Kālīkā and offered eight goats to her as a sacrifice when he retired with the rank of captain. She bought these goats from her sister and let no one but herself take care of them for two years, before offering them during the nine days dedicated to the Goddess. According to the author, it was important to confer the *gotra* (spiritual clan) of the family onto the victims before their execution, by the priest making an offering of water in their mouths. It is possible that this is a local peculiarity, but no one has been able to confirm this rite, either in Kumaon or in Nepal. This inclusion into the family would mean, says Govindrajan, that the victim commits itself to die for the family. The author expresses her own suffering at the sight of the sacrifice of one of these goats, while the woman who had raised them said that the goat was calling her, turning her head away and letting her tears flow. Yet she still ate the consecrated remains, while her nephew, who had arrived from the United States, refused them and accused the family of engaging in barbaric practices. The woman explained to her nephew how the kid-goat, raised as a son, had once been accepted by the Goddess in exchange for the son she was asking for as a sacrifice, adding that his suggestion to offer flowers or coconuts instead made no sense, as these items are not precious.
11. As in the village of Darling, in Musikot, the Brahmins and the Indigenous king anoint the royal swords with milk and raw rice to strengthen them for the next day's sacrifices.
12. In some regions, such as the ancient kingdom of Achham, the rites of the eighth and ninth days are switched: buffaloes are sacrificed on the eighth day, weapons and tools are sanctified on the ninth.
13. In addition, a pigeon was offered, which was later put to death at the palace gate, as is the custom for these animals, because of their great purity.

14. Observations of the rite were made in 1986 and 1990, while the monarchy was still in existence. Since its abolition in 2008, the deposed king continues to hand over the *ṭikā* marks from his personal residence, while the President of the Republic has officially taken over his role.
15. On the morning of the tenth day, at Ismā, the chaplain smears a *ṭikā* mark on the Sword-god and the other deities of the palace. He then goes out to distribute it, in no particular order, to all those who have come to receive the '*ṭikā* of the gods'. Here no hierarchy prevails. It is, on the other hand, strictly followed within the lineage, where the most eminent offer *ṭikā* marks to their inferiors, after the distribution at the palace. The rite ends with the chaplain bringing the sword back to its particular temple, cheered on by showers of petals, as on his arrival. The musicians then play a tune to which men perform a few steps of a war dance that they will 'play' all day the following day, the eleventh.
16. The term for dance, *nāc*, associated with seduction, has pejorative connotations.
17. As a reminder, the first term refers to pure castes, the second to impure castes.
18. The Lāvaḍ are specialists in the manufacture of objects woven in bamboo.
19. The sacrificial strike of the Untouchables is detailed in the following chapter.
20. We have encountered this historical episode, in comic form, in the vernacular epic, indicating that the latter is indeed a form of history, as the local people say.

6

Contestations of sacrifice

Boycott and litigation

The dissensions which go hand in hand with the unfolding of sacrifice begin to take on new forms which reach beyond the executions themselves, after the promulgation of the 1990 Constitution. This democratic turning point in the history of Nepal led to a weakening of the monarchy and to critics of the 'sacrificial' organisation of society. The questioning of consecrated forms of violence within a renewed political framework already occurred after the fall of the Rana and the opening of the country to foreigners in 1951. At that time, a first democratic regime which lasted from 1951 to 1959 led to the introduction in 1963 of a new code of law in which the notion of caste and its associated notions of social pollution and contamination were expunged. Following the 1990 Constitution, which re-established political parties that had been banned for thirty years, the Indigenous peoples organised themselves into associations to work towards their emancipation. From them emerged the very first organised protest against sacrifice, targeting Dasaĩ, the supreme moment of the reaffirmation of Hindu power. The Untouchable castes, now federated under the name Dalit, also created associations for the defence and promotion of their group, which advocated boycotting the consumption of sacrificial remains. And animal sacrifice finally became the object of growing opposition in urban and educated circles, who began to contest its violence. In this arguably more diffuse type of activism, the opposition to sacrifice is the most radical, in the sense that it does not target the place or role of a group in the sacrificial system, but its actual core, the ritual killing of animals itself. From this point on, conflicts over sacrifice became more than disputes over local issues of power and governance, with each of the protesting groups supported by an ever-growing network, the most extensive of which being the 'anti' animal killing, who combine followers of a purified Hinduism, as practised in India, and international animal rights organisations, both of whom advocate vegetarianism.

In this second context of democratisation the Nepalese Maoist party developed during the second half of the 1990s, growing so large that they ended up eclipsing the entire political landscape. The Maoists sought to restructure all of Nepalese society and thus banned animal sacrifice, but they did not eschew violence, instead transferring the legitimacy of royal sacrifice to their new ideal of martyrdom. Because of their own particular logic behind the use of violence and blood sacrifice for its own ends, we will consecrate the last chapter of this book to this movement. In the current chapter, we present the various contestations of sacrifice which have appeared in Nepal in successive waves, although it must be noted that none of them entirely ceased when the next one appeared, but rather each movement created a precedent for the other. The following pages may give the impression that sacrificial practices are on the decline in Nepal. This is certainly the case in urban or semi-urbanised areas, even if we lack quantifiable data in this regard. In parallel, a sort of 'sacrificial modernity' is also increasingly perceptible in the levels of mass tourism to Goddess shrines located in places far from cities and sometimes difficult to access. Such is the case of Manakāmanā in Gorkhā, access to which has been facilitated by the construction of a cable car specially equipped with a receptacle for sacrificial victims, where 2 to 3 million devotees visit each year, or, more recently, Pāthībharā in Taplejung, which is now visited by 350,000 pilgrims annually, despite the steep path leading to the shrine, located at an altitude of 3,800 metres (Bhattarai 2019).

Social networks, so often a bastion of politically correct, right-on opinions, unanimously condemn blood sacrifice and, during Dasaĩ, only the 'anti' post images of sacrifice. The bloody photos that freezeframe moments of abject horror are often not commented upon and form a 'bia-graphy'[1] on their own, that is a visual depiction of violence which speaks for itself. This does not mean that there is no debate, and the main arguments can be drawn from online discussion forums, where everyone can express themselves freely under cover of anonymity. Let's look at the answers to the question, 'Are you in favour of the custom of sacrifice?', posted on the sajha.com forum in August 2005. The forum is aimed exclusively at educated Nepalis who are just as comfortable in English as in Nepali, as shown by the multilingual wording of the question, written half in the first language and half in the second: 'Do you support Bali Pratha?', *bali prathā*, the custom of blood sacrifice. There are thirteen posts which respond to the question, written in an English that is also peppered with Nepali or Sanskrit terms.

The first, by 'Bullish', suggests offering coconuts instead of animals, 'as in India', and to stop killing innocent animals in the name of god. Bullish, however, does not condemn slaughter and advises those who want meat to go and buy it from the butcher. 'Shree5', who is apparently angry with the king whose title he has usurped for his pseudonym,[2] agrees '100%' with Bullish, and launches into an intellectual tirade to support his idea that the Goddess is the mother of all creatures and cannot be satisfied by the murder of one by another. We will see later that this argument is taken up by the judge of the Supreme Court when examining the practice of sacrifice. Bullish finally introduces himself as 'a proud vegetarian' and adds a second post to clarify that he is, on the other hand, fully in favour of cannabis consumption as a mark of devotion to Shiva.

'Anti-Monarqi' joins the chorus of 'antis', when 'Hushpuppy' bursts into the discussion to 'troll' it.

> Oh *sacrifice*... well I'm so used to it... being a girl, I'm not supposed to watch the whole ordeal... but every now and then, specially dashain back home... just to watch *the he-goat being put to death*, and the blood gushing out their neck and onto my feet, gives me so much high... just like hunting, it gives you an adrenaline rush... To make it short, I don't like halaal but *sacrifice* as in Hindu style is not bad. Then again if you visit all the slaughter houses where they hack animals and poultry you never wanna eat meat again.. but again all people in this thread are non veg...so this discussion is so void.[3]

Hushpuppy clearly sets out to provoke with this post, and it is unlikely that she is a girl, as she claims, because hunting is usually a male affair in Nepal. Beyond the excitement she expresses, she responds to those who think that animal killing is legitimate for butchery but not for sacrifice, saying that they are wrong, and that this hidden violence is abhorrent. When she realises her mistake in thinking she was only talking to 'meat eaters', as the majority of Nepalis call themselves, she adds a second post.

> oh i just realised shree5 is a veggie which is good..I could never be.. [...] well you were talking about Laxmi and Saraswati not being responsible for sacrifices...Laxmi pujas have always been clean..but even for

> Saraswati puja, we sacrifice ducks, and some people eggs. [...] Whenever the brahmins looked at my *horoscope* and saw if the year will have any mishaps, not only they asked for more *donations* but there were years that I was responsible for over half a dozen sacrifices.. the naughtier I got the worse it'd get.. [...] there were other occasions, if you had a new car, if you were travelling somewhere, ..its only been few years away from home and i am already missing the craze.. [...] Also if you know that some Devis actually want sacrifices, specially the kumaris over each corner of Kathmandu have had many accidental sacrifices.. Nepal as a whole is bleeding right now.. not properly though.. I think to end all the trouble there otto be a great DEVI puja cause she seems pretty mad.. Damn I didn't realize that i was sssssssssssoooo into these stuff.

Hushpuppy, having confessed her taste for meat and her excitement at the sight of sacrifice, now endeavours to show that the practice is perpetrated not only by those who condemn it and do not perform it themselves, the Brahmins, but also by the deities themselves, who make sure they receive their due share. She says that in the end the whole country (which was then, in 2005, living through its bloodiest episodes of the People's War) is plunged into the destructive madness of the Goddess. She proposes to put an end to this by appeasing her through worship, without saying if this worship should include sacrifice or not.

Deftly side-stepping all of this, Shree5 repeats his theology, supported by quotations in Sanskrit, to defend the idea that Hinduism rests on a single principle: the existence of an energy shared between all living beings, managed by *dharma* and its opposite force. *Dharma* consists in making beings happy, harming one of them is the definition of sin. Everything else, such as the caste system or the custom of sacrifice, are later inventions and political stratagems which are unrelated to religion: 'Perhaps the ancient kings wanted to show off their power, sort of traumatize or glamorize or whatever and retain their "*throne*" and thus began the *custom of sacrifice*,' he concludes.

'Dalli Resham', whose icon is a little Buddha, explains that he eats castrated goat but is opposed to blood sacrifice, then 'ZalimSingh' calls Shree5 out on his interpretation of tantra, and 'KLPD' declares that they are for the practice of sacrifice, because it helps contribute animal protein to people's diets. Shree5 answers them all: *tantra*, he says, comes from the observation that the 'supernatural' is not always good, yet he does not condemn meat consumption, nor perhaps even domestic sacrifices, ending his speech with this qualifying statement, 'regarding *sacrifice* in the temples, well, it kind of offends me. *That's it.*' For 'Neupane', sacrifice offered to deities is bad, but there are 'many evidences' that it works. 'The work', he says, is not done by the deity, but by 'the souls who guard the temple or environment', who take possession of the sacrificed souls and in return achieve the purpose of the sacrifice. This would not be known to ordinary people, who simply think: the deity has done this for me because I have offered them many goats. Bullish, finally, returns to the chat to propose a new substitute for sacrifice, which would entail buying a goat intended for the butcher's block, and giving it back its freedom, with a bell around the neck, at the temple of Pashupati. 'At least it will give blessings for saving its life.'

This discussion highlights the ideal of non-violence shared by the members of the forum, including the most transgressive of them, Hushpuppy. All announce whether they put their views into practice through their own diet or not, but it is notable that no one, apart from Hushpuppy, specifies whether they have ever offered a sacrifice themselves, particularly to the tutelary deities of their lineage. These cults, generally 'bloody', are obligatory, sometimes on pain of exclusion from the lineage group. Among these educated young people, killing for meat is acceptable, in contrast to sacrifice, which tarnishes the image of the gods. Their views are thus diametrically opposed to the ancient Hindu precepts which prohibited the consumption of non-sacrificial meat. The effectiveness of sacrifice is nevertheless recognised, and reveals a belief in a sort of occult forces which are associated with subordinate spirits and political power, even in the purified Hinduism of Shree5. The silence that follows Hushpuppy's comments is indicative of the discomfort she creates by failing to proffer a higher justification for sacrifice, nor any substitutes for the victim that might be considered more acceptable, such as offering a coconut, or by purchasing an animal destined for death in order to save its life.[4] Alongside these individual criticisms of sacrifice, of an informal nature, a political current focusing on sacrifice have developed.

The 'boycott' of Dasai

The first formal contestation of the royal sacrifice arose from the emancipation movement of the Indigenous peoples, which emerged after the instauration of the 1990 Constitution. This enshrined the freedom of association and expression in law, allowing these peoples to organise themselves to defend their rights and identities. The following year, in 1991, the results of the first census taking 'castes and ethnic groups' into consideration provided them with a measuring tool to fight against their domination, with figures to back it up. The over-representation of Brahmins in all the state bodies and political parties in Nepal became the main object of their struggle, and they therefore directed their attacks against what they called 'Brahmanocracy'.

Beyond the criticisms that this group crystallised by clinging onto its dominant position, it is remarkable that when they were published, the socio-economic indicators of the castes and ethnic groups very accurately reflected the hierarchy of caste society in Nepal. Take the most telling indicator, life expectancy. In 1996, it was 60.8 years for the Brahmins, 56.3 years for the Kshatriyas, 53 years for the Indigenous people and 50.3 years for the Dalits. The average number of years of school education followed the same hierarchy, ranging from 4.65 for the Brahmins, 2.8 for the Kshatriyas, 2 for the Indigenous peoples to 1.2 for the Dalits. Finally, income amounted to 1,533 rupees for the Brahmins and 764 rupees for the Dalits, with the intermediate values of 1,197 rupees for the Kshatriyas and 1,021 rupees for the Indigenous people.[5]

The census simultaneously revealed to the Indigenous peoples that they actually wielded considerable political weight by their number and that they were the most acculturated of the ethnic groups, as it revealed that they made up a third of the country's population, scattered throughout the national territory, with the exception of the former region of the Twenty-Two kingdoms. The Magar alone accounted for 1.5 million people in 1991, nearly a quarter of the number of Indigenous peoples and more than 7 per cent of the country's total population. And this group had been particularly underestimated in the previous censuses, which had only counted speakers of the different languages of Nepal, showing that an important number of Magars had lost the use of their ancestral Tibeto-Burman language. Thanks to the new census, the Magars therefore discovered the scope of their linguistic assimilation and interpreted it as the result of a 'cultural genocide' which was consciously orchestrated by the Hindu rulers since the establishment of their kingdoms on their territories during the fourteenth–sixteenth centuries. Throughout the description of the Dasaĩ rituals, we have encountered Magars in roles that emphasise their ancient ties to power, such as village headman, king or sacrificator. However, the specificities of each group's history were not taken into consideration by the Indigenous movement in Nepal, and this is for a variety of reasons. On the one hand, the associations representing them were federated under an umbrella association, which gave it a somewhat monolithic character. This federal association has been especially influenced by the Indigenous peoples from eastern Nepal, the Rai and the Limbu, whose history is rather different to that of other groups within the country. Indeed, they remained free of the yoke of Hindu rule all the way until the unification of Nepal in the eighteenth century, and they then retained a form of autonomy over their territories even after this, as granted by King Pṛthvī Nārāyaṇ Shāh in exchange for their peaceful rallying to his domain. The Indigenous peoples of the eastern region also benefitted from access to education at an earlier date than others, due to their proximity to Darjeeling, and Indigenous intellectuals from their ranks started to promote their distinct identity as early as the 1920s.Their hold over the federation of Indigenous peoples has thus meant that important issues, such as the impact of Hindu power on the Indigenous groups of central and western Nepal, such as the Magars, have not been addressed.

On the other hand, even within the Magar group itself, the historical narrative recounted by their 'organic intellectuals' who emerged in the 1990s generally omits the period corresponding to their subjugation, and even more so the episodes of collaboration with the Hindu authorities, to focus on their origins and their Indigenous customs. This situation places the spokespersons of the group at odds with its own members, many of whom were rather reluctant to put their instructions into practice.

An opposition to Dasaĩ appears early in the Indigenous publications, making it one of the foundational pillars of the movement. The idea is said to have emerged as early as 1988–1989 among the Rai and Limbu of eastern Nepal, according to a 1992 article in the inaugural issue of *Lāphā*, the first Magar newspaper to be published nationwide.[6] The article states that in 1991, the Indigenous association known as the Kirant Cultural Forum denounced the government policy 'that establishes Dasaĩ as a national holiday and thereby perpetuates its compulsory nature', considering that it amounts to 'destroying another's house to build one's own fence'. The Magars also announced in this paper their decision to boycott Dasaĩ, in order to ensure that their indigenous culture be protected, and presented the imposition of Hindu culture, rituals and language as a 'burden' that the Hindus put on 'their indigenous donkeys'. However, this same journal, one year later, places the beginning of the movement among the Rai–Limbu a little later, to around 1990–1991, and specifies that the directive was followed by the Magars along with some other groups, in 1992 only, and formally implemented in 1993.[7] The boycott of Dasaĩ thus spread from east to west in the space of two or three years after the promulgation of the November 1990 Constitution. The movement ostensibly gave all Indigenous peoples, or rather, their representative bodies, a means to fight against their oppression and assimilation. However, the boycott was not widely followed, prompting a closer examination of its message.

First, the Indigenous claims do not denounce the violence inflicted upon animals but only that which they undergo during their actual execution. As the Magars see it, the Dasaĩ ritual explicitly re-stages the conquest of their ancestral territories by Hindu populations, whom they call 'Aryas', with the buffalo sacrifice re-enacting the killing of their ancestors by the latter. The Magars see their forced participation in this ritual as a particularly perverse device of the Hindus, one which forces them to celebrate their own defeat; specifically, as they put it, 'to laugh at the death of their father and mother' and even to wear their blood on their foreheads, in the form of the *ṭikā*.[8] The violence of sacrifice takes on an extreme dimension when read in this light. It transforms the ritual from being a bringing-to-bear of the violence necessary to defeat the forces of evil, to a particularly monstrous celebration of the murder of parents in front of their own children, a celebration which is imposed upon them by the murderers themselves – a monstrosity reminiscent of the myth of origin examined in Chapter 3, in which the tribal ancestor is forced by his Hindu brothers to kill his own mother and consume her flesh. The Indigenous interpretation recasts the buffalo sacrifice as the very worst of sacrileges for these people who value their ancestors so highly. These deep roots form indeed the foundation of their identity and of their relationships with the world they inhabit. Their territory, they say, is 'soaked with the blood and sweat of their ancestors': this is what makes it fertile and *theirs*, in their understanding. The relationships they maintain with the invisibles are entirely modelled on those they maintain with both their parents and ancestors: it is one based on respect and gratitude for the life they have bestowed upon them.

The Indigenous reading of the buffalo sacrifice intensifies the violence which is inflicted on their group by their participation in the ceremony, while simultaneously ignoring the violence inflicted on the animal, which is not even mentioned. This observation leads us to ask whether sacrifice may merely produce a symbolic violence, or should we consider that by its combination of a principle of substitution and real violence, which is keenly felt in the bodies of those who participate in it, even as spectators, sacrifice can never produce anything purely symbolic? We will leave the question open for the moment, and see if we can begin to flesh it out as we continue our ethnographic exploration.

At the same time as it diverts the violence of sacrifice inflicted on the animal, the Indigenous arguments behind their call to boycott Dasaĩ also detach it from its religious basis. Therein may lie the reasons for its failure. Indeed, the call to boycott Dasaĩ was barely heeded in the mountainous provinces of western Nepal. Even in more urbanised areas, such as the Dang Valley in the Terai, it was so poorly adhered to that in 2006, the Nepal Magar Sangh made it known that any Magar wearing a *ṭikā* would have to pay a fine of 5,000 rupees to the association. This was reported to me by a young Magar resident of the city of Tulsipur, who felt it was unfair to deprive her of the festival, and who did not even seem to be aware of the rationale behind the movement. Beyond the generalised reluctance to give up the main festival of the year, the Magars' political history and their proximity to ancient Hindu power without doubt also played a role in the boycott's failure, because this contradicted the idea that the buffalo sacrifice celebrated their defeat. In the village of Darling, for instance, political power has been held by Magar headmen since the village's foundation in the nineteenth century and the rite is organised entirely by them. Elsewhere, as in Isma, for example, the Magars act as sacrificators for a deity who is directly connected to royal power. Further, at Musikot, the cooperation between the Magar and Ṭhakurī kings is so tight that such a reading could not be imposed. As for the Twenty-Two region, the question of Indigenous subjugation simply does not arise there, since it is exclusively inhabited by caste groups who consider themselves to be both Indigenous and Aryas.

In fact, the Magars formed a significant part of the Gorkhāli army before unification. As early as the nineteenth century, they were referred to as a 'military tribe' by British army recruiters, who integrated them into their own troops in important numbers. In the barracks of the Gurkhas, blood flows freely during Dasaĩ, as it is essentially a martial festival where the stiff courage needed for combat is celebrated and the values of the 'warrior tribes' are glorified. The paradox at the heart of the call for a boycott of Dasaĩ by the same Indigenous peoples who celebrate it as warriors to much fanfare has been noted by C.K. Lal.[9] To resolve such a paradox, it is not necessary to deny the religious character of the sacrifices offered by the military, as Lal (2009) proposes, but it is important to analyse the basis of the Indigenous boycott, which entirely omits religion from its arguments. There is no mention at all of the Goddess, nor of her fight against the buffalo-demon. Let us examine, for example, what a student branch of the Nepal Magar Sangh (Anonymous 1993, *Lāphā* 7: 6, my translation) says about the festival:

> Dear Magar brothers and sisters, the closer the Hindu festival of Dasaĩ approaches, the more an atmosphere of injustice sets in among us.... According to Hindu treatises, the great Dasaĩ joyously commemorates the victory of the Hindu prince Rāma over the non-Arya Rāvaṇa, from the land of Lankā, whom he beheaded by trickery. So we are foolish to rejoice over this injustice committed by the Arya community on the Non-Aryas. When we place red *ṭikā* on our foreheads on the day of *vijayādaśamī*, we rejoice in displaying the blood of the Non-Aryas. Is there any other people in the world who celebrate their own defeat?

Here, in place of father and mother, the sacrifice is said to celebrate the annihilation of Rāvaṇa, whose alleged kinship with the Indigenous peoples of Nepal is based on structural similarities, as he too is a 'non-Arya' who is defeated by Aryas. In the same journal, Pradip Thapa Magar (1993: 12) strengthens this link by presenting Rāvaṇa as the 'lord of the Kirants', a term that the Indigenous peoples of Nepal use to refer to themselves collectively. The Aryas killed him and then rebranded him a demon, he writes. From this emerges the equivalence of the opposition between Aryas and Kirants on the one hand, and Aryas and demons on the other, without there being any mention of the gods. In the next article, M. M. Thapa Magar (1993: 13) provides the reason for this: Rāma is not a god, but a prince, and his cult only began in the sixteenth century, he explains. In other words, the story is a political one for the Magar activists, the sacralisation of which dates from the period when Hindu populations imposed their power upon the Indigenous peoples of the Himalayas.

The argument for the boycott focuses entirely on Dasaĩ's 'secondary' narrative of the *Rāmāyaṇa* and the war between Rāma and Rāvaṇa.[10] In choosing to associate Dasaĩ with the epic and thus with 'historical' time, the Magar intellectuals do not even touch upon the main myth, contained in the *Celebration of the Goddess*, that the ritual incorporates and actualises. In so doing, to use a typically Magar metaphor, they seem to have deliberately 'shot wide of the mark' so as to avoid discussing the legitimacy of the ritual as a device which actualises the Goddess's fight against the forces of chaos. This deliberate omission is perhaps not surprising, given the fact that Indigenous peoples, as warriors, maintain a special devotion for the Goddess, as she is the patroness of armies. Many tell tales of her interventions at the most perilous moments. It is to her that they entrust their lives in desperate situations and it is she who they thank back in the village, by offering her the five sacrifices. Was aiming at the Goddess simply a step too far?

By choosing a peripheral target, the Dasaĩ boycott slogan did not achieve the desired effect, but it did, however, cast a veil of suspicion over the ritual and led many Indigenous people to question its meaning, so that it could no longer be taken for granted as pertaining to the natural order of things. Nor were the arguments raised by Indigenous people after 1990 forgotten after the upheavals of the revolutionary decade, from 1996 to 2006. Even recently, the scholar and activist K. B. Bhattachan (2016) affirmed that refusing to participate in Dasaĩ was 'punishable by exile and even the death penalty' until the end of the Rana era in 1950, and that it is still a compulsory celebration in the sense that it gives rise to national holidays and is the subject of lessons in school textbooks, whereas the ritual occasions of Indigenous peoples are not acknowledged at all by the government.

While it changed Dasaĩ only slightly, the Indigenous movement nevertheless led to a major reform of the state's conception of the society it governed, one which forced it to recognise the distinct nature of Indigenous peoples, after several centuries of forced assimilation into caste society. The Indigenous movement was so powerful that it caused the dominant castes, Brahmins and Kshatriyas, to claim the status of autochthonous people in turn, thereby short-circuiting the advancements that such a status originally promised.

The perverse dimension of the buffalo sacrifice denounced by the Indigenous peoples applies even more directly to the Untouchable castes. Much like the Dalits, buffaloes are considered impure beings, whose milk and dung cannot be used in rituals (unlike those of the cow). Their meat cannot be eaten by castes located above the limit which divides the 'pure' from the 'impure' castes – apart from the notable exception of the Newars of the Kathmandu Valley. In the Twenty-Two region, even accidentally consuming buffalo meat may have led to degradation, as the Damāī attached to the temple of Nīgālā Sāinī, testify about their ancestor, Dhanik, a pure-caste patron who became Untouchable. They tell how one day, upon his return from a hunting trip, Dhanik brought a young buffalo carcass back to the village, thinking that he had killed a tahr (*Hemitragus jemlahicus*). He ate a piece of it and offered some to the villagers, as is customary. Quickly realising his mistake, the villagers refused the meat with horror and summarily rejected Dhanik.

He was then asked to leave or play the drum at the temple of the Goddess, a proposition he quickly accepted, thus making him and his descendants members of the Damāī caste.

In the Twenty-Four region, by contrast, the prohibition on eating buffalo meat is less strict, and some Magars consume it without falling into Untouchability. This is the case for children, especially girls, who are at least permitted to eat buffalo until they marry, but they must cook and eat it outside of the house, so as not to pollute it or its inhabitants. Such a loosening of caste rules before marriage is observed in all strata of society. Even in the families of vegetarian Brahmins, children are given pure meat, such as lamb, and even those animal products which are known to pollute the initiated, such as eggs or chicken. However, buffalo is a notable exclusion from this list. Among the Magar, where the consumption of chicken is customary, this type of tolerance is transferred to buffalo meat, with the difference being here that there are entire Magar clans who choose to consume it, not just specific members of the clan. Until the 1990s, this very much stigmatised them, to the point that these clans were known as the 'Magars who eat buffalo', and intermarriage with them was prohibited by those Magars who refrained from eating buffalo meat. Today, food prohibitions are less strictly respected, especially in urban areas, where restaurants offer such prohibited products, as long as they are consumed discreetly.

Much like the impure castes, male buffaloes have been designated victims. They are bred with the sole destiny of being beheaded during Dasaī. In the mountainous regions where they are poorly domesticated, these animals serve no other purpose, apart from a few being selected for breeding. The females, on the other hand, are the main providers of milk in this region where the 'cows' (they are actually zebus) do not generally give more than 1 litre per day at best. The female buffalo therefore represents a sound economic investment, whereas the male is considered a financial burden.

Those who offer buffalo in sacrifice force the impure groups to eat its flesh and thus contribute to reinforcing their similarity. In many tales, opponents are even tricked into eating this forbidden meat or else are forced to do so, and lose their status. These old stories open cracks in the idealised conception of caste society, which presents social status as something inherited, which can only be disturbed by wilfully transgressing its rules, an act which is punishable by degradation. These stories say in their own way what Dalit intellectuals today are trying to communicate – that caste rules are violent and used as weapons. Dalits have never accepted the principles of caste, but have been led to accept them by force, writes the Dalit author Amar Bahadur B. K. (2008: 6).

The injunction to consume impurity is usually hidden during the buffalo sacrifice, so much so that the Dalits may even be presented as the main beneficiaries of the ritual. However, it is when we observe the reactions in the event of their refusal to accept this impure meat that we understand that this is no ordinary gift.

At the Nīgālā Sāinī temple in Baitadi, Dalits decided to organise a 'boycott' of the sacrifice in 2007, just after the end of the People's War. The movement was initiated by politicised Dalits of Maoist affiliation, at a time when the leader of the revolution was in charge of the country and had a large majority in parliament. The boycott was not designed to refuse attendance at the ceremony itself, or to wear the *ṭikā*, as proposed by the Indigenous leaders, but centred around a refusal to play the role of recipients of buffalo meat. The boycott was called the 'Carrion Boycott', *sino bahiṣkār*, which may be perceived as a rather strange name, given that the Dalits are allowed to butcher and consume the buffaloes offered as sacrifices shortly after their execution. But in Nīgālā Sāinī, between 250 to 300 buffaloes, each weighing 500 to 1,000 kilograms, are sacrificed, and it is impossible to butcher them all quickly enough, as the owner of the teahouse facing the temple recounts:

> It takes time because the Dalits argue a lot among themselves: some are four brothers, others are six brothers, and they have to divide the shares equally among themselves. The villages of some of them are far away and they have to come and go with their load on foot. In addition, the meat has to be cut into small pieces so that it can be preserved for a while, because they cannot eat it all at once. They make skewers of it, and eat it for a very long time, more than a month, then it starts to smell and it is called *sino* (carrion/gamey meat). The temple people tell them: 'hurry up and take it away', but they, on the other hand, are slow to do so. Otherwise, they can start taking it away ten to twelve hours after the sacrifices are over.

A man from the Lāvaḍ caste, the main Untouchable caste attached to the temple, explained that in addition to the meat, the Dalits are responsible for clearing everything away, including the skin and bones, implying that the gift does not come without strings attached, but he did not elaborate on the issue, nor on the conflict at the heart of the boycott, and immediately added that the movement did not last. To understand the reluctance of those Dalits who live in the village to publicly air their grievances, one must remember that they are largely dependent on their patrons for their subsistence. Their own meagre plots of land usually only yield enough food for one or two months of self-sufficiency per year, and the rest comes from crop shares allocated to them by their patrons in exchange for services, or by paid labour. In Nīgālā Sāinī, the Lāvaḍ distanced themselves from the boycott because they feared that they would no longer have access to the bamboo growing on their patrons' land, which is essential for their caste occupation of basketry. The importance of these economic ties underscores, albeit indirectly, the 'aboveground' nature of Dalit activism. Like the Indigenous movement, it comes from the restricted circles of educated Dalits who live in urban areas, where anonymity and the absence of client relationships allow some Dalits to improve their conditions.[11] This schism is reflected in their overall lack of unity. The Dalits are divided in their struggle, starting with those who have defined themselves by this name since 1990, and those who refuse it because they consider that it merely perpetuates their status, with its alleged derivation from the verb 'to fall'. I once heard an argument for the latter stance formulated in a striking way by a young Untouchable boy, challenging a Dalit activist: 'Sir, we are not Dalit, we are human beings, *mānche*.'

It is therefore not surprising that the Dalits' boycott of sacrifice does not have the systemic character of the Indigenous boycott, but rather wells up in a more haphazard manner. On the other hand, like the Indigenous boycott, the narrative used to justify the Dalits' cause also focuses on a secondary object – the refusal to eat the 'carrion' of sacrifice, without explicitly denouncing sacrifice as a device that reaffirms the shared traits or even identities between Untouchable castes and the impure and demonic animal.

A report by the Human Rights Council (OHCHR 2011) on the conditions of Dalit people in Nepal, especially focusing on the Baitadi region, discusses the boycott organised at the temple of Nīgālā Sāinī. The investigation and drafting of the report were entrusted to several Dalit defence groups to enable them to express their views. In October 2007, the report says, twelve members of the Dalit community were beaten and robbed of their belongings by eight men for refusing to clear away the carcasses of buffaloes after their sacrifice at a local temple (OHCHR 2011: 54). An explanatory note states that Dalits are expected to eat the meat of the sacrificed animals, which is considered 'holy', even if several days have passed since the sacrifice, meaning that the meat is often 'rotten'. The police refused to register the Dalit complaint, the report adds, and only complied after pressure from local human rights defenders, supported by the OHCHR. In a rare development, three of the men were eventually tried and given prison time. However, only the man with the shortest sentence actually carried it out, while the police never went after the main defendant, who even managed to get a job in a ministry only a few months after his conviction.

The account of the boycott given by the teahouse owner, who is not Dalit himself, put it this way:

> The Maoists issued the main order (*nārā*) of the carrion boycott (*sino bahiṣkār*), telling all Dalits not to eat the meat of dead buffaloes, saying: 'You eat buffalo meat and that's why you have become Dalit.' After that, there were quarrels, conflicts, and it was a fight. Then the members of the temple committee announced: 'If you don't eat the meat of the dead buffaloes, we will send it to Kathmandu and other places.' Then all the Dalits answered with one voice: 'Don't send the buffaloes from here, we will eat them.' In this connection, there was also a fight in Tallo Soḍar, where there were injuries. The Dalit leader, Guje Lāvaḍ, died eight to ten months later, and the Dalits were very resentful. But here at the temple, Dasaĩ has resumed as it was before, without any difference.

The villager's account successively evokes 'carrion', 'dead buffalo meat', and finally 'buffalo meat', the ingestion of which turns the person into a Dalit, thereby bringing the activists' overarching framework of health and hygiene back to its local reality. It also underlines the utter dependence of the Dalits and their inability to negotiate the improvement of their conditions with those who can simply dispossess them if they dare to protest.

In contrast, the United Nations report describes the Dalit's sacrificial boycott as a refusal to eat gamy meat.[12] This line of argument, which sidesteps questions of religious and social impurity, is not specific to the Baitadi context. It can be found in other Dalit-led sacrificial boycott movements, such as the one that took place in October 2014 at Gaḍhī Māī, a sanctuary where a gigantic sacrificial session is held every five years.

One journalist who followed the incident (Acharya 2014) states that an assembly of 'Dalit leaders' decided to boycott the consumption of the sacrificial animals, which they consider 'degrading' due to the fact that the buffaloes are only directly butchered the day after they are slaughtered, 'which is not hygienic'. The journalist adds that a Dalit leader said the boycott was also aimed at putting an end to another type of discrimination against the Chamar, a caste of Untouchables from the Terai region who are traditionally the recipients of the sacrificed meat, and are 'perceived as people who can only afford buffalo once every five years', that is, when the ritual takes place.

The concerns around hygiene shown by Dalit leaders in both Baitadi and Gaḍhī Māī is in clear response to a new form of discrimination affecting these castes, one where status impurity is reformulated in terms of 'dirtiness', coupled here with concerns about not appearing to be economically disadvantaged, the second modern stigma of the Untouchables.

The justification for the Dalit boycott of this sacrifice nevertheless avoids the crux of the matter – the asymmetry of the buffalo sacrifice, which reaffirms the division between pure and impure groups, the very building blocks of the caste system itself. It is true that, apart from the impurity of the meat in question, the buffalo sacrifice may appear to benefit the Dalits, as a Brahmin from Dullu argued, claiming that they should be grateful for the largesse of their patrons during Dasaī̃. He concluded with the formula: 'The Brahmins get the sacrifice done, the Kshatriyas do it, and the Dalits reap the benefit (*samāune*).' In this formulation, the Dalits are analogous to the gods, and while this can be read as a classic Brahmanical denial of reality through the inversion of things, one nevertheless even finds traces of this view in the OHCHR report, written by Dalits themselves, who write that the sacrificed buffalo meat is simultaneously 'holy' and 'rotten'. Strange as it may seem, it is probably not inaccurate, for while it is possible to see laughing youths irreverently desecrating the bodies of sacrificed buffaloes at the temple of Nīgālā Sāinī, it is inconceivable that their meat would be thrown away, and the idea of refusing its consumption is so disturbing that it has led men to beat Dalits who refused to do so to death.

More fundamentally, the Dalit's hygiene-based argument to boycott sacrifice, much like the Indigenous peoples' political boycott, does not touch on the religious basis of the buffalo sacrifice, and avoids mentioning the figure of the Goddess altogether. Attacking her is probably equally unthinkable for both of these groups. Many Dalits have a special devotion for the Goddess, especially the castes of musicians. Some are willing to do anything for her sake, as Lālu Rām Damāī, a bard currently attached to the temple of the goddess Tripurā Sundarī in Baitadi, told us when describing the circumstances of his taking office. Lālu was a soldier in the Nepalese army when, one day, he received 'a call from the Goddess', he explained. She asked him to abandon everything to come and play music at her temple, with these simple words, 'a person is needed here to play the *huḍko* drum'. 'The Goddess requisitioned me, I had no choice...,' he said, before adding, pensively, 'today I would have 15 or 16,000 rupees in pension.' As if to compensate for this shortfall, Lālu went on to describe his triumphant bus ride home, during which he, a Dalit, seated as always in the back row, was invited to come and stand at the front by the passengers when they learned that he had left his post in the army and was going home, with his turban on his head, to put himself at the service of the Goddess.[13]

The 'anti' movement against the cult of Gaḍhī Māī and the judge's response

Unlike the boycotts led by Indigenous peoples or Dalits, which have never targeted sacrifice as such, a current advocating the end of all blood sacrifice, supported by animal rights groups and vegetarian Hindus, has taken off in Nepal over the past twenty years. Locally, the followers of this movement are called the 'antis' and we will explore this movement by looking at its most notable action, the public interest litigation (PIL)[14] it brought to the Supreme Court to ban sacrifices at the shrine of Gaḍhī Māī, which is said to be the place where the largest number of animals are killed for the gods on the planet. The Supreme Court's verdict was delivered in 2016, in a text which is of great interest not only for what it says about the cult itself but also for its more general discussion on animal sacrifice.

The shrine at the heart of the dispute is dedicated to the 'Mother of the Fort', Gaḍhī Māī. It is located 5 kilometres from Bariyārpur, in the district of Bārā, not far from the Indian border. A festival, *melā*, is held there every five years in November–December. It sees five million pilgrims come in attendance, three-quarters of whom are from India, according to the author of the introductory booklet to the shrine, which was sold on site at the *melā* in November 2019.[15] Five hundred thousand animals were reportedly sacrificed there in 2009, at the peak of the celebration, according to figures put forward by Human Society International. This society, with the help of activists such as Manoj Gautam, president of the Animal Welfare Network Nepal, worked to limit the number of sacrifices. In 2009, 100 volunteers were trained and deployed to encourage people who had brought an animal to kill as an offering to instead let it live (Smith 2015: 34). The Indian authorities were also involved to ensure control over the passage of the buffaloes across the border, and as a result, the number of sacrifices was reportedly reduced to 30,000 by 2014 (Gupta 2019). Manoj Gautam stated at that time that the next *melā* would be 'bloodless', so confident was he in his strategy of getting the temple management committee to ban sacrifices in exchange for financial assistance to promote the site, as well as a museum and school, which were to be built with the support of the Indian Embassy and American fundraisers (Smith 2015: 35). Indeed, there were many voices echoing Gautam's words, announcing that there would be no more sacrifices in 2019, or even that the practice had already been banned by 2015 (Jones 2015: 474) – or by 2014, as the French-language Wikipedia page devoted to Gaḍhī Māī states.

A visit to the temple during the *melā* of November–December 2019, three days before the sacrifices began, showed that there were already some 500 buffaloes herded into the sacrificial enclosure. According to the priest Mangal Chaudhari, interviewed after the *melā* by telephone, eventually 8,000 were sacrificed, a figure to which must be added the goats, roosters and other animals whose numbers are impossible to quantify, since, unlike the buffaloes, they are not registered and are put to death by their owners in the vicinity of the shrine. It is possible that their numbers may have actually increased as a result of the obstructions put in place to limit bringing buffaloes from neighbouring India. The decline in numbers of sacrificed animals during the cult of Gaḍhī Māī is thus real, but still relative. The great numbers seen at the *melā* itself is in fact a relatively recent occurrence. Sixty-two-year old Mangal Chaudhari has seen the change with his own eyes.

> In the past, there were only 400 or 500 buffaloes, and it was since 2024 [that is, 1967], as I remember, that it started growing. The population has also increased, so people are offering more buffaloes. When I was young, there were only 50,000 people coming, now it's five million, and the *melā* had to be lengthened too. Before, it was only a week long, and then we made it ten days, and since 2009, it's a month long – it's getting bigger.

The development of the cult, he says, is due to the power of the goddess, who grants wishes in exchange for sacrifices.

> Those who have been married for a year and still have no children come to the temple, eat consecrated rice and get a child. They are happy and come back to offer an animal as they had promised. Otherwise, there are

> those who have an illness, those who do not have a job, those who want to go abroad, to America, to Australia, and who do not have a visa. They say to the Mother: if I have the visa, I will offer a sacrifice. That's why there are so many people here. They come to make a wish for a sacrifice, and their wish is granted. You can come whenever you want to the temple, but for the vows, you have to come during the *melā*, and they come in great numbers.

The introductory temple booklet, for its part, states that this fervour for the Mother developed because she originally protected children and young people (Chaudhari n.d.: 5).

The various steps of the ritual show that the cult of Gaḍhī Māī has essentially been grafted onto a village ritual which was addressed to their local territory gods by the Tharus of the neighbouring village. With the increasing popularity of the goddess, the jungle which had previously been dotted with small indigenous shrines has now become a vast religious domain, although the officiants are still Tharus from Bariyārpur.

Gaḍhī Māī is presented as a form of Kālī, who is said to originate from the royal fort of Makvānpur, one of the Twenty-Four Kingdoms. She is said to have been brought back to the village ten generations ago by Bhagwan Chaudhari, the ancestor of its present-day priests. As the story is told by Mangal Chaudhari, his ancestor Bhagwan was accused of murder when a fight broke out in Bariyārpur following the intrusion of a thief into his house. He was then taken to the prison in the fort of Makvānpur, where he was locked away in chains. In desperation he prayed to Kālī, the tutelary deity of his lineage, for whom he had a great devotion.

> The Mother of the Fort spoke to my ancestor as a mother speaks to her child, for one day, two days, and on the third day she appeared to him and told him that she was a form of Kālī. She promised to deliver him if he offered her five human sacrifices in return. Bhagwan made the promise, the jailers fell into a deep sleep, his shackles came off, the padlocks opened, and he fled, taking with him the stone, *silā*, of the Mother of the Fort. He placed it in the courtyard of his house and honoured it with a trident carved from a *khimti* stone, which is still there to this day. He took the remaining pieces of the stone and carried them into the forest to the site of her present-day temple. Normally, a human sacrifice is required for this goddess. Even today we do it, our medium, *dhāmī*, does

it. He lives in Rautahat and only comes for the *melā*. For him too, his grandfathers did it before him. But here, for human sacrifice, there is no need to behead a man, only to offer his blood.

The priest here refers to the custom of offering five drops of human blood to the goddess, along with five animal sacrifices, 'instead of the five human sacrifices' she had originally requested, and which Bhagwan Chaudhari was ultimately unable to offer (Chaudhari n.d.: 5).

The main temple of Gaḍhī Māī is raised on a small mound planted with century-old trees, in the middle of what was once a forest. It is flanked to its west by a pond where devotees perform their ablutions. To the west of the pond are the sanctuaries of the four 'soldiers' of the goddess, answering to the names of Janginaṭ, Chaṭhunaṭ, Gangārām and Motirām,[16] and to the south is the temple of Kaleśvarnāth.[17] About 200 metres eastward from the temple stretches a vast enclosure surrounded by high brick walls, known as 'the esplanade', *maidān*. This is the arena of sacrifice. The buffaloes are herded inside to wait for the Seventh Day, where they are executed, away from the crowd, by members of a committee, each of whom holds a 'permit'. No one else is allowed in. Walking north along the wall of the esplanade, one comes across the funeral home, *samādhi*, of the cult's founder, Bhagwan Chaudhari.

Finally, at the end of the enclosure stands a mound surrounded by a low wall with a large ficus tree planted in the middle. Called *brahmasthān* or *daivikstbān*, 'divine place', it is inhabited by Baram Bābā, 'he who is invisible, but who sees everything, and who protects the earth, *pṛthvī*, and its inhabitants', as Mangal Chaudhari describes him.

Mangal's son, Shiva, adds that Baram Bābā and Gaḍhī Māī are 'like father and daughter', but his father denies it, assuring that they have no family ties. Baram Bābā lives there in the company of a cohort of local deities, and Gaḍhī Māī herself is taken there on the Seventh Day for sacrifices.

When the *melā* begins, all the sisters of Gaḍhī Māī are invited to attend by the performance of special rites beneath two *pipal* trees at the gate of Bariyārpur, where the village ends, at the edge of the forest of the goddess. Gaḍhī Māī is the eldest of a group of seven Mothers, including Saṃsārī, Joralāhi, Sabhe, Ramanākamanā, Gaḍbāḍā and Rājdevī Banaśakti, the 'royal-goddess-power-of-the-forest'. A ritual boundary, *lakṣmaṇ rekhā*, is drawn there by the medium of the shrine, which the women of the Chaudhari priests' family must not cross. Like the wives of the priests of the Sister of the Bamboos in Baitadi, these women were also punished at the time the goddess was first established.[18]

In the village, Gaḍhī Māī has a small consecrated 'place', *sthān*, in the courtyard of her priests. When the Seventh Day begins on the stroke of midnight, the goddess's stone is carried from her temple to the sanctuary of Baram Bābā. Sweets and rice pudding are offered to her there and a 'sacrifice of the embryo', *garbhe bali*, is performed. A hole is dug, wherein an egg and a new trident are placed for the goddess. They are immediately buried. The medium, *dhāmī*, goes to tour the temple, and when he returns to the sanctuary of Baram Bābā, he has become possessed.

> The Mother comes into my body. When *śakti* comes, only my eyes see, I no longer feel my body and it is *śakti* who speaks. My body does not tremble. I sit for five minutes in meditation, I pronounce a formula and the flame of the Goddess's butter lamp lights up by itself. Then the sacrifices can begin, first here [at Baram *sthān*], then the buffaloes [in the enclosure]. They must stop when the flame goes out. This year, there are fewer buffaloes, India has stopped them at the border, but the important thing is the human sacrifice and the five sacrifices that are made here [at Baram *sthān*]. Likewise, others worship the statue, *mūrti*, of the Goddess, because they do not know that it is the stone, *pātthar*, which is very powerful, *śaktiśālī*. In the evening, I offer five drops of my blood, from my forehead, from my tongue, from my chest, from my arm and from my thigh. Here, it's like that, you need human blood every day.... But I can't tell you the names of the gods who live here in Brahmasthān, it's forbidden, they are our gods.

The *dhāmī*, who is evidently in a hurry, entrusts us to a devotee who lives at the sanctuary all year round. Pacing back and forth on the divine mound, he decides to give us a guided tour, perhaps not having fully understood the parting words of the medium. To the north of the mound, he explains, Rājdevī Banaśakti Māī, the royal forest goddess, is worshipped; to the south, the spirits of the wild spaces known as Jākha-Jhākhim;[19] to the west Kaṅkālī, the goddess of game; and near the steps, King Harapati.[20] On the Seventh Day, a strange collection is offered to them as a *pañcabali*, opened by the sacrifice of a wild rat, *jaṅgali musā*, followed by a billy-goat, a pig (for Kaṅkālī), a rooster and a pigeon. The rat must be brought by the *dhāmī*. 'The rat is wild,' says Mangal Chaudhari, 'but the *dhāmī* does not need to go to the forest to capture it; it comes of its own accord to present itself to his village.' He puts it this way as if to say that the animal offers himself voluntarily as a sacrifice.

The *pañcabali* is followed by the sacrifice of buffaloes at the sacrificial post facing the shrine of Baram Bābā. Each branch of the Chaudhari clan offers its own, bringing the total number to seven today. Like the trident of the goddess, the sacrificial post must be changed at each *melā*, and only the priests' buffaloes may be sacrificed there (see Figure 6.1). The post is extremely eye-catching because it is massive, cut into a ball in its upper part, and slightly curved. 'It is carved from mango wood and must have the size and shape of a man,' says Mangal Chaudhari. His son Shiva adds that it is in fact a representation of Mahikhāsur, which is merely the local pronunciation of Mahiṣāsur, the buffalo-demon. Shiva Chaudhari explains that buffaloes are offered to the demon because this animal is his 'vehicle' and that he himself has taken on 'this disguise' in order to make trouble for the gods. 'That's why he's tied to the post, *maulo* and killed,' he adds. 'Also, in our local language, we call the post Mahikhāsur. That means we cut off Mahikhāsur on the seventh

Figure 6.1 The sacrificial post of Gaḍhī Māī

Source: Author.

day.' Asked about the shape of the post, Shiva Chaudhari explains that it must be curved, *bango*, because Mahikhāsur is a demon. 'Mahikhāsur himself is curved: he is a demon. His teeth are curved, his mouth is curved. Everything is curved in Mahikhāsur. He is the guardian of Gaḍhī Māī and that is why the family has to give him a buffalo.' His father, Mangal, attempts to reconcile his explanation with his son's, saying: 'The post should be made in the form of a man (*mancheko akharmā banaera*) and have a head, but its head should be a little bent, for it should look like a demon.'

The various identities that are projected onto the sacrificial post interlace to bring together human, demon and buffalo in a blurring of appearances that merge to create a single artefact. Grafted on it we see the intertwining of traditions relating to the human sacrifice requested by the goddess, the killing of the demon who has become the guardian of the goddess, as well as the execution of the buffalo, which is attached to the demonic entity that has borrowed its form. This clustering allows for divergent readings of the ritual, which are not mutually exclusive, leaving interpretations open. In contrast to the prevailing view, which makes the 'human sacrifice', the 'five sacrifices' and the buffalo sacrifices offerings to Gaḍhī Māī, the devotee we spoke to, for example, maintained that the Goddess does not drink a drop of blood, but instead honours her 'guests', *pahunā*, with these offerings. According to him, the buffaloes are all offered to the demon Mahikhāsur, who thus takes a prominent place as a guest of honour, gorging himself with the blood of thousands of his own animal form.

The end of the rites conducted by the Tharu officiants at the Baram Bābā shrine marks the beginning of the sacrifice of thousands of buffaloes in the vast enclosure. The butchery takes place there behind high walls and closed doors, with signs all around indicating that it is forbidden to take pictures. It is not easy to see what is going on inside either, except by climbing the wall or by standing on the small shrine of Baram Bābā, which offers an overhanging view of the esplanade, but to which access is restricted. The sacrifices of the goats take place the next day, dotted throughout the area, performed by those who have brought them.

The preceding description makes it easier to address the points raised in the PIL brought before the Supreme Court, which formally requested an end to all sacrifice at the sanctuary.[21] Presented in no particular order by seven plaintiffs, these points may be grouped into two categories: criticisms of sacrifice and its effects, which are more pertinent to this work, as well as sanitary questions.

The plaintiffs' presentations argue that the cult is only 'two to three hundred years old', or even more precisely, '260 years old', and go on to recount the story of the origins of the shrine, presented here as factual evidence, even though they admit that the story is based on 'popular beliefs' (*janabiśvās*). They explain that a landowner (*bhumipati*), imprisoned by the king of Makvānpur, had a dream in which he learned that if he went to the temple of Gaḍhī Māī and offered blood there, his wish would come true. He was released from jail by the goddess, headed directly to her temple and pierced his body in five places to offer her his blood. Over time, 'thousands of animals were offered as sacrifices' in place of the gift of his blood, through a 'degeneration of tradition' that the plaintiffs attribute to 'superstition'.

The delegitimisation of the cult is based here on its lack of antiquity, knowing that Nepalese law specifically protects religious 'traditions' and not innovations. The argument is taken up again with regard to animal sacrifice, which is presented as a 'degeneration' of this 'recent' tradition. The story presented ignores the five human sacrifices initially demanded by the goddess, which the offering of the five drops of blood replaces. Likewise, the cult's description fails to mention that this human blood offering continues to be performed today as a prelude to the animal sacrifices and that the latter therefore do not replace the former. The self-sacrificial mutilation, by being deprived of other historical antecedent by the plaintiffs, is cast by them as a model in itself and, furthermore, a morally acceptable one, akin to a Brahmanic vision of (self) sacrifice. They sweep aside the Cornelian choice of sacrifice, replacing it with a violent form of asceticism that elevates the soul by detaching it from the body. Nevertheless, the goddess's request remains clear, because five human sacrifices designate a plurality, and demands more lives than can be given by one individual alone. For the plaintiffs, who ignore this rather important detail, animal sacrifice has come to replace self-harm or self-sacrifice, due to the effect of 'blind belief', *andhabiśvās*, a term rendered in the official English translation as 'superstition'.

In their view, this 'degenerate' and 'superstitious' tradition developed within a given cult is made even more suspect by the identity of its founder, who is presented as a *bhumipati*, or 'landlord', the archetypal figure of the exploiter in the modern imagery of the Indian subcontinent. At no point is it made clear that this is a Tharu or indigenous cult, and, as we shall see, the rite will only be assessed by the plaintiffs, as by the judge in his response, in relation with the most orthodox Hindu textual tradition of ancient India. From the point of view of 'traditional Hindu Vedic' philosophy, the plaintiffs say, 'the offering of animal sacrifice is a *mahāpāp*', a concept rendered as 'great sin' in the official English translation, but which more accurately corresponds to 'major moral fault'. Animal sacrifice, according to the plaintiffs, is indeed defined as the 'murder, *hatyā*, of innocent living beings, *nirdoṣ jīva*'. Their criminalisation of animal slaughter leads them to the idea that its 'evil influence' gives rise to 'criminal thoughts and character' (*āparādhik cintan caritra*) in everyone, including women and children, in a sort of reciprocal feedback loop. Sacrifices offered to Gaḍhī Māī must finally cease because they turn this site which is so 'pure', *pavitra*, where the goddess stands into 'a slaughterhouse', and, beyond that, they spread a negative image of Nepal and the Hindu religion to the rest of the world. Here again, no mention is made of the fact that the site where the execution of the buffaloes takes place is not actually public, but rather hidden in an enclosure surrounded by walls so high that the images that are broadcast have required great acrobatic skill and a good amount of determination in order to take them.

The plaintiffs go on to argue that the sacrifices are done 'in an extremely barbaric manner' (*barvarātāpurvak*), that is, they point out, without water or food being offered to the animals before their execution. Yet when the gates of the enclosure open, fodder and troughs full of water are clearly visible in front of the rows of buffaloes, at least today. Likewise, the technique of slaughter by decapitation is regularly practised outside of a religious context, meaning that sacrifice is no more barbaric in this respect than ordinary butchery. Shiva Chaudhari also pleaded with us in defence of sacrifice with this argument: 'How many buffaloes are killed in the Kathmandu Valley each week? Surely more than in Gaḍhī Māī once every five years.'

The second line of argument presented by the plaintiffs concerns the environmental pollution and risk of spreading diseases attributed to the sacrifices, the fact that the health of the animals is not checked, that an examination to verify that they are not 'pregnant' is not done, as well as there being no quarantine imposed upon the buffaloes which have been imported from India nor any post-mortem evaluation of the quality of the meat. All of these accusations are levelled exclusively at the treatment of the buffaloes, while the slaughter of billy-goats or other animals does not seem to raise any health concerns. The request to verify that the buffaloes are not 'pregnant' is very surprising, and may even suggest that the text of the case was not written by Nepalis, since there is no question, to my knowledge, of offering female buffaloes as a sacrifice anywhere in Nepal. In Gaḍhī Māī, the prescriptions are especially precise in this matter: only uncastrated male buffaloes with both testicles intact may be offered, as the priest Mangal Chaudhari told us.

All the institutions concerned, including the office of the prime minister and then various government ministries, responded to these complaints in turn, asserting the right of religious freedom and the existing health provisions. A right of reply is then given to the administrative committee of the temple of Gaḍhī Māī, which, for its part, declares that the ritual addressed to Gaḍhī Māī has involved the offering of five sacrifices 'since Vedic times', and that worship of the Goddess, 'a form of *śakti*', is usually done 'by means of sacrifice' (*baliyukta*), so that prohibiting the practice would be an infringement of the law that protects 'religious traditions'. Finally, the committee refutes the pollution attributed to the sacrifices, the absence of prior examination of the animals and the lack of care before their execution.

The judge's statement, in attempting to answer the question of whether a ban on sacrifices at the temple of Gaḍhī Māī should be pronounced or not, goes far beyond the case in question. From the outset, he displays his disapproval of blood sacrifice. In his eyes it is a practice for which a certain section of Hindus 'retain a passionate attachment'. However, he continues, these are modern times of 'science and conscience' (*vigyān ra cetanā*), where one cannot continue to respect 'conservative superstitions' (*ruḍhivādī andhabisvās*) that run counter to the 'modernisation of society'. One must, he says, abandon the 'wrong' (*galat*) things to adopt the 'right things' (*asal kurā*).

After this praise of progress, the judge turns to tradition to examine the place of animal sacrifice within it. He reiterates his position that the 'view of non-violence' is prevalent in the 'great texts of the Hindu religion', which do not depict any person of quality (*sajjan mānis*), such as a sage or god, offering an animal in sacrifice. Indeed, it is demons who sacrifice not only animals but also men. The judge uses these 'facts', which seem so trivial for a Supreme Court judgment that they come across as vaguely ridiculous, to give a sentence which nevertheless has serious consequences: considering that 'actions such as murder and violence' (*hatyā, himsā kārya jastā*) indicate a demonic nature, 'it does not seem logical to associate the practice of sacrifice with religion (*dharma*)'. Now, if sacrifice does not fall within the realm of religion, the law that previously protected it as such can no longer be applied to it. Likewise, according to the judge, the suffering that animal sacrifice causes to many people 'who have internalised the precepts of non-violence and vegetarianism' is related not only to the religious domain but to 'social understanding and tolerance'.

The judge then sets out to deconstruct any religious justification for sacrifice, after identifying three distinct motivations for it – some people consider that offering sacrifice makes the Goddess happy, others believe it is necessary to obtain power (*śakti*), and finally some think it must be performed for the liberation of animals, he says.

To those who think that animals should be liberated by offering them as a sacrifice, he does not answer, but to the first point he proclaims that the Goddess is widely considered 'the Mother of the World and of all creatures', and that a mother experiences maternal feelings and compassion for all her children. 'How could a Mother be made happy and satisfied by the sacrifice of her own children in her own name?' he asks.

He argues against the second point by explaining that many people hold power without offering sacrifice, and that others, 'who delight in sacrifice', are 'in a state of weakness that is painful to see'. 'Obtaining power is a matter of personal ability, hard work, perseverance, self-sacrifice,' he declares, thereby deftly severing the link between power and blood sacrifice, *bali dān*, and reattaching it to the notion of renunciation, *tyāg*, a term that is ironically rendered as 'sacrifice' in the official English translation and thus confuses its reading.

'Social progress will not be possible as long as the retrograde idea prevails that the source of power lies in an invisible and imaginary realm to which the name of religion is given,' concludes the judge, who declares in his final statement that sacrifice is 'incompatible with a modern civilised state'. He sees in effect another danger in animal sacrifice, that is, its possible drifting towards its 'most extreme form of degeneration', that is, human sacrifice. For this reason, he says, 'it is necessary to maintain control over the practice of animal sacrifice, by preventing or prohibiting it' and to substitute an acceptable type of 'sacrifice' which this time he refers to by the two expressions *bali dinu* and *tyāg garnu* joined together: the 'sacrifice/renunciation of our demonic tendencies', a list of which he details: 'profit (*kāma*), anger (*krodhha*), envy (*lobha*), delusion (*moha*) and jealousy (*irṣyā*)'.

Having seemingly reached this point of no return in his argument, the judge suddenly switches gears. 'Is it appropriate to immediately prohibit the practice of sacrifice at the temple of Gaḍhī Māī?' he asks again, in a formulation somewhat different from the first, this time highlighting the immediate effect that his decision might have. Sacrifices are offered everywhere in Nepal, he notes. Certainly, in Gaḍhī Māī, 25,000–30,000 buffaloes are sacrificed in one day, he continues, but this also means that the faith of thousands of people is involved in the court's decision. Neither the 'social context' nor 'reality' should be overlooked, and so for the time being it is therefore more appropriate to take steps to limit the sacrifice and 'make the public aware', even if it will eventually be necessary to prohibit it entirely.

The judge thus advocates working for the recognition of animal rights in Nepalese law (which currently only protects the cow and the bull, as well as a list of wild animals), and in the course of his description actually attributes them with the qualities of language, sentience and even a 'soul', in the English translation, which perhaps deliberately modifies the meaning of the term *prāṇ*, breath of life, which the judge actually used. He further considers that sacrifice has the same 'terrorising' effect on animal victims as it does on humans: 'It has become commonplace to make everyone terrorized [by sacrifice], whether the people watching or the animals,' he writes.

Despite his harsh criticism, the Supreme Court judge's decision ultimately only ensures that animal sacrifice be conducted in hygienic and non-cruel conditions. He also puts an end to any direct or indirect government support, in order to 'discourage [it] or not encourage it'.

In this landmark judgment, it may be surprising that, in a country that purportedly adopted religious neutrality in 2008, the only authoritative references cited are the Dharmaśāstras and the Vedas, and this to deal with a cult whose officiants are all Indigenous peoples. It is true that the judge only evokes this textual body of Hindu orthodoxy in an incantatory form, in support of a progressive and somewhat Manichaean morality. Not much attention is paid to the content of the texts themselves, but the judge nevertheless draws his arguments from them to define animal sacrifice as a demonic practice, one which is antithetic to *dharma*, in a judgment where morality, law and religion come together. In response to the invocation of *śakti* by the temple committee of Gaḍhī Māī in defence of animal sacrifice, the judge is especially severe. He vilifies this particular stream of Hinduism that promotes sacrifice in order to gain divine force, despite it being the majority view in Nepal. He declares that true power is born of work and renunciation and has nothing to do with some imaginary force, reducing the Supreme Śakti to the state of a good-natured Mother.

The judge nevertheless recognises some virtue in sacrificial violence, when it is applied to the self, thereby allowing an individual to kill their own demons, in a passage where the law gives way entirely to morality. His praise of self-sacrifice as opposed to animal sacrifice echoes the position of the plaintiffs, who denounced the transformation of the early ritual human mutilation into animal sacrifice.

As in the Indigenous or Dalit boycotts, the judgement also makes no mention of the Goddess's mythology, of her battle with demons, of her worship in her most terrifying form of Kālī, as practised in Gaḍhī Māī, and when it comes to citing examples of demons, only Rāvaṇa and Kaṃsa are mentioned by the judge,[22] leaving the buffalo-demon entirely in the shadows, in spite of his centrality in this ritual. In their own ways, like the Indigenous peoples and the Dalits, the 'antis', that is, the plaintiffs and the litigating judge, avoid speaking of the heart of the matter altogether. As much as the former groups chose to read sacrifice in a wholly political light, this lawsuit was intended to appear depoliticised, and it is therefore not by chance that the Court's main decision consists of the prohibition of any further government aid to the *melā*.

The 'antis'' approach offers a fairly typical example of what Indigenous people denounce as 'Brahmanocracy', by imposing a wholly Brahmanical vision of sacrifice onto an Indigenous village community which has long asserted its identity and nurtured its hopes for the future through its blood ties with the invisible powers that inhabit its territory. Their sacrificial traditions attract crowds in ever-growing numbers, who all come to reap their own benefits from it. It is noteworthy that, whereas the 'superstitions' of the Indigenous groups are severely dealt with, the faith of the attendees, according to the judge, should not be violated by the law. His final judgment in their favour will allow Indigenous traditions to be maintained in spite of their 'demonic' violence, at least for a while longer, and within a more standardised framework.

After the boycotts, failed attempts at shaking up the system, where one category of participants refused to play their prescribed roles, this Supreme Court judgment is reminiscent of the whispering of women during the execution of sacrifice, who deplore the fact that humans behave like demons towards animals. Here it is a strong voice and the word of authority which rejects and severely condemns the immorality of the sacrificial practice, but nevertheless respects the faith. Just like the women's hushed voices, it rises up only to fade away immediately, after having said what there was to say, but not daring to impose itself.

Notes

1. From the ancient Greek term *bia*, violence, force.
2. This title *Śrī 5*, which systematically precedes the king's name, means 'five times honourable'.
3. Passages noted in italics are in Nepali in the original text.
4. It is common to set cows free in holy places, such as in Swargadwari, the 'Gateway to Heaven', in Pyuthan, where more than two hundred such cows graze in the sanctuary's forest. This is a gift which also eliminates the evil of coercion against the sacred animal, whose 'killing' is still punishable by prison in Nepal, in spite of the abolition of state Hinduism, by virtue of its status as a national animal. Every Nepali must release their cows from their bonds when they show signs of weakness. Until the 1960s, the code provided that the householder whose cow died while being tethered should himself be tied up in his stable and fed with grass for a while, explained the old chief of the village of Darling.
5. ILO (2005: 95).
6. Anonymous (1992: 5).
7. Anonymous (1993: 6).
8. It is in these terms that Dasaĩ is presented in the description of the ritual practices of the Magar country published in *Lāphā* (7: 4–5) and Anonymous (1993). On ethnic politics in Nepal, see Hangen (2010).
9. C. K. Lal writes in the *Nepali Times* (471, 25 September–1 October 2009): 'Ironically, those who gave Dasain pan-Nepal acceptability – the Janjatis of the mid-mountains from the east and west – have begun to call for its boycott.... As long as these indefatigable fighters continue to serve abroad, Dasain celebrations there will retain their secular character.' N.B.: 'Janjati' is now translated as 'indigenous people', after having been initially translated by the term used in China, 'nationality', when the neologism was coined at the turn of the 1980s–1990s.
10. In India, sectarian development has given rise to antagonisms that are expressed in the same way. Thus, the Jains have a version of the *Rāmāyaṇa* which glorifies Rāvaṇa, the demon of the Hindus (Thapar 1995).
11. On the importance of anonymity in urban areas for the improvement of Dalit conditions, see Pariyar and Lovett (2016).
12. The report emphasises this detail, noting later that the Office of the United Nations High Commissioner for Human Rights (OHCHR) supported a Dalit organisation in the two years following the 2007 and 2008 incidents

in order to monitor discriminatory practices such as 'forcing Dalits to eat rotten buffalo' during Dasaĩ (OHCHR 2011: 89).

13. The expression of caste status by which row of seats they are permitted to sit at is still common in the area where Lalu lives, as noted in the OHCHR report (2011: 14), which deplores that Dalit children are relegated to the back rows of classrooms in Baitadi.
14. Since the 1990s, civil society in Nepal has been at the forefront of this new type of legal action, called public interest litigation (PIL).
15. The booklet, written in Hindi by Manoj Kumar Chaudhari, 'a member of the family of Gaḍhī Māī priests', is undated (Chaudhari n.d.: 7).
16. These soldiers receive the rather unusual offerings of dried fish and, for two of them, alcohol.
17. Names are spelled as they appear in the booklet written by Manoj Chaudhari (n.d.).
18. The story goes that the founder of the temple, Bhagwan Chaudhari, was so holy that when he left his home, the food that was placed on the ground at home in his name flew straight into his mouth. One day, after he had left his home, his young daughter-in-law, 'who knew nothing of the things of the house', boiled milk and placed it scalding hot in the courtyard in his name. The milk instantly burned Bhagwan Chaudhari's mouth, and in anger he cursed all the wives of his clan to be banned from the shrine of Gaḍhīmāī.
19. A name which is derived from Yakṣa, that is, a class of gods linked to wild spaces who were venerated in ancient India, and who guard treasures.
20. The (classificatory) father of the first king of the Kharore dynasty, who reigned over Mithila from the sixteenth century onwards, bears this name (Jha 1997: 159).
21. The text of the litigation is available online in its English translation (Supreme Court of Nepal, 2016, Gadhimai Verdict. English Translation. The Jane Goodall Institute Nepal. Judgement of August 4, 2016, Certified translation on August 8, 2019). I would like to thank Chiara Letizia here for providing me with the original Nepali text. She recently published an article on this subject: Letizia and Ripert (2023).
22. Kaṃsa is the maternal uncle of Kṛṣṇa, who tried to kill the latter.

7

Self-sacrifice versus sacrifice in the revolutionary struggle

The relationship between sacrifice and violence took a spectacular turn with the advent of the People's War, which lasted from 1996 to 2006. The struggle was led by the Maoist party of Nepal, at the heart of which developed a true mystique around the concept of violence. Blood sacrifice, *bali dān*, became the iconic symbol of the revolution. From the very start, it expressed both individual commitment and the movement as a whole. It differs in this respect from sacralisation of violence after the fact which can be found in other contexts, such as the use of the term 'holocaust' to designate the Nazis' Final Solution, or the titles of martyr conferred after the end of hostilities in communist China.[1] With the outbreak of the People's War in Nepal, violence was considered sacred from the very beginning, and commitment became the expression of its most venerable form, that of sacrifice. This attribution of holy meaning to violence happened as the war was being fought and then, just as quickly as it appeared, faded away with the ending of the war. The People's War was declared on 13 February 1996 by the Communist Party of Nepal (Maoist), at that time still only a small group, and ended a decade later, on 21 November 2006 with the signing of a peace agreement, in the manner of the great wars of yesteryear. By starting and ending so decisively, the People's War parenthetically takes on the form of sacrifice as defined by Hubert and Mauss, with its formalised 'entrance' and 'exit'. Much like sacrifice, this war was detached from ordinary time and its inherent violence modified the experience of its duration. The staccato rhythm of attacks removed any comforting structure from daily life. This kind of suspense and uncertainty, which imbue the animal sacrifice with its proper meaning at the moment of the consecration, become generalised in the People's War. In one fell swoop, terror spread across the entire territory, in a sort of sacrificial invasion, from the more targeted dread of blood sacrifice.

The idea that war is a vast sacrifice is nothing new in the Hindu world, but it is not merely a rhetorical equivalence. In contemporary Nepal it is still understood that the death of a warrior in battle does not besmirch the purity of the members of his lineage, in much the same way that the death of the renouncer who sacrifices himself by leaving the mundane world does not creates impurity for his kin. According to Article 45 of the treatise on impurity written by the Nepali pandit N. Sharma Dhakal (1963) entitled 'On Death in War', no period of impurity is induced by death on the battlefield directly. If one dies as a result of a war wound, the number of days of impurity to be observed by the members of the deceased's lineage varies with the number of days between the injury incurred in battle and his subsequent death. If this is greater than seven nights, then the warrior's death triggers the standard ten days of impurity marked for any death. This strange arithmetic shows how war forms a context in which violence is sanctified, one which abrogates the usual norms governing Hindu purity.

The equivalence between war and sacrifice was expressed even more explicitly well before the revolutionary period, by the Nepalese novelist H. C. S. Pradhan (1970). War, he says, is the greatest form of sacrifice.[2] This is true only of defensive war, he adds, while wars of aggression are not sacrifice, but 'massacre', and the soldiers 'butchers'. Pradhan, however, sees an exception in the war of aggression against oppression and exploitation, which he calls 'excellent' and whose nature, in truth, is defensive. We thus find in war the same relativity that looms large over the framing of violence, in its infinite feedback loop, and the same idea of a 'violence that is not violence' when it is considered just, while it is an abomination when it is not.

The evaluation of war within Nepal's Maoist movement also places considerable emphasis on the polarities of violence. Rajan, a fighter in the armed wing of the CPN(M), summarised the military instruction he received within the party in a booklet, where he presents the origin of life as a sort of survival of the fittest characterised by struggle.[3] He then describes the different 'stages' of organised forms of violence and their development up to the present day, where peacetime has in fact proven to be the worst form of violence, one marked by terror, theft and exploitation of the people (Rajan 2006). The party was purposefully created to put an end to this concealed violence in the most explicit way possible, which is why its founder made the army its main organising structure and war its main form of struggle.[4] In the eyes of the revolutionaries, the use of armed violence reveals class violence, which is maintained by the state. It works to dismantle its democratic and humanitarian facade, revealing the exploitation and oppression of the people hidden beneath. The war machine clarifies positions, exposing reactionaries and revisionists, whom it drives out to regions under state control, while simultaneously attracting new recruits.[5] It is, as Comrade Ananta (2004) puts it, a 'total war', because globalisation has turned the revolution loose on the global stage, further expanding the overwhelming sense of sacrificial invasion.

In the Maoist view, the struggle must also be prolonged infinitely, in order to reach a state of 'permanent revolution', which is to be ensured by an 'ocean of armed people', who are the only ones who can prevent counter-revolution and the return of class violence. Each struggle encountered at each moment of their life, which is the first level of the lifelong fight, represents therefore the ideal outcome for a person, with the difference being that one passes from a personal struggle on the path towards death where the strong overcome the weak, to a battle which is fought on equal terms. Revealingly, Prachanda very concretely proposed distributing a weapon to every Nepali citizen in order to achieve this type of equality. This declaration took place during a political meeting which I attended on the symbolic date, as chosen by the leader, of 11 September (2009).

The revolutionary struggle took place within a society where both the acquisition and manifestation of power traditionally took place during the royal sacrifice, during which time the ruler demonstrated his power of death, was anointed, and then led his people into battle. The self-sacrifice of the revolutionary martyr was introduced as a kind of counter-sacrifice, in many ways similar to the vengeful suicide of those who are cut off from sacrifice and the ultimate power of death itself (see Figure 7.1). Led by Brahmins, and including women for the first time in history, as well as a considerable number of Indigenous peoples and Untouchables, the People's War brought together not only those who were excluded from the royal sacrifice but also those who considered themselves its victims and boycotted it. In this way, it brought about a reversal of perspective and assigned all of that negativity formerly attributed to demonic forces to the ruling monarch, while the revolutionary leader placed himself at the head of an ascetic organisation of self-sacrificers. He was pointedly not involved in the violence that the others who joined his movement readily accepted. As we shall see, he remained invisible throughout the hostilities.

We then witness the birth of a true mysticism around violence and death in the writings of the revolutionary recruits. By placing heavy emphasis on bloody imagery, this new type of religiosity blurs the lines between the real

Figure 7.1 A Magar fighter of the People's Liberation Army, Gulmi, 2005

Source: Author.

and the ideal. The mysticism is bedded in the space between ordinary life, on the one hand that of the dominated or the 'living dead' who are chained to their material form, and on the other the all-spiritual life of the revolutionary until the 'fall' of their 'material form'.

Between these opposite forms of existence – between life and death, a detestable materiality and a sublime spirituality – Maoist mysticism opens up a new plane of reality which, by dint of its interstitial position, evokes the ritual domain. One can access this realm through self-sacrifice, which liberates people from oppression and transforms them into 'new humans'. Thus 'reborn', they also describe themselves as 'living dead', *jiundo lās*, using the same expression used to speak of the dominated, but inverting its polarity: entirely detached from the material, including their bodies, they depict themselves as living people who have 'embraced death', much like the renouncer who ingests his own sacrificial fires, the fires of his own cremation, and whose real death, essentially nullified, is now nothing more than a prolonged meditation.

Such a framing of the revolutionary condition brings an unexpectedly spiritual component to Marxist–Leninist–Maoist ideology, which is famously based on atheistic principles. This particular version developed in the nebula of small armed collectives and 'families' of cultural warriors that constituted the military and cultural branches of the party in Nepal. It was expressed in the diaries, poetry, songs and performances of its members, and spread through the 'campaigns' of the party and its clandestine press. It makes use of a number of images and idioms that are specifically targeted at the domestication of violence within the very socio-political organisation that it aims to destroy. This includes the hijacking and recasting of its most highly authorised form, sacrifice. This contemporary reworking of sacrifice is important, because it shows how sacrifice can renew itself and rebuild its relationship with legitimate violence. Sacrifice itself becomes a set of inter-relational practices, thus highlighting that its reach can go far beyond the religious realm. To understand such a movement, it is necessary to situate it in the context of events that accompanied its rise.

Milestones in the political history of Nepal

The history of Nepal is atypical and often out of sync with the rest of the planet. The revolutionary movement took root in a kingdom that had never been colonised, remained closed to foreigners until 1951, and where the abundant polytheism of Hinduism was the official state religion until 2008. The revolution developed in the 1990s, fed by a purely ideological fervour, long after this type of movement had ceased in other parts of the world, and its turning point was marked by an unprecedented historical event, the bloody massacre of the royal family by the crown prince on 1 June 2001.

Born from the military unification of about fifty warlike kingdoms and indigenous territories by the Shah dynasty of Gorkha at the end of the eighteenth century, the kingdom of Nepal continued to wage wars of expansion until the armed intervention of British India in 1814–1816, which fixed its borders once and for all.[6] The creation of the post of prime minister then poisoned domestic politics and culminated, in 1849, in the seizure of power by a hereditary line of prime ministers, who operated in parallel to the royal dynasty. For a century, these Rana ministers confined the king to a ritual role, but continued to rule in his name. Their regime ended in 1951, following a popular uprising organised by Nepalese political parties which had been clandestinely created in India, supported by Prime Minister Jawaharlal Nehru. The king regained his power and was expected to establish a democracy. Political parties were legalised, but King Mahendra soon accused them of creating instability. He promptly banned them and instituted a non-party system called the Panchayat in 1960, which lasted for three decades, until a popular uprising led by students convinced his son, King Birendra, to promulgate a constitution that restored political parties in November 1990.

There was much excitement before the first general election in 1991, which, for the majority of the population, was their very first. People were eager to learn about the programmes and turnout was very high in political meetings. The Nepali Congress and the Marxist–Leninist party dominated proceedings, while the revolutionary Communists were a small group by comparison. Nevertheless, from the very beginning, they stood out for their artistic performances and their use of violence. In November 1990, a friend suggested that I go to a rally in Baglung which would bring the various parties together, but warned me: 'There will be the Maoists (Masal, as they were called then): they are the ones who sing the best, but there will be a fight because they bring their *khukuri* cutlasses!' With this combination of art and violence, the Maoists captivated the crowd and laid the foundations of their organisation, built on a blend of terror and seduction.

The Communist Party of Nepal was itself founded in India as late as 1949, and a pro-Chinese faction only broke away in 1974, more than a decade after the Sino-Soviet split. This faction was not recognised by the electoral commission in 1994 and went underground. In March 1995, a new faction broke away from the main group and took the name of the Communist Party of Nepal (Maoist), or CPN(M), its English acronym. The new party was created in order to lead an armed struggle, under the leadership of its two key figures: Prachanda, who gave his name to the party's strategy, the Prachanda Path, and Baburam Bhattarai, its ideologue and spokesperson.[7] In November 1995, a first large-scale police operation against the Maoists, widely known as 'Operation Romeo', helped fan the flames of general hatred towards the government in what would become the revolutionaries' base region, the districts of Rolpa and Rukum, inhabited predominantly by the Magar group. Barely a few months after its creation, the CPN(M) presented forty demands to the government in an ultimatum and, even before the end of the deadline, officially declared war on 13 February 1996.[8]

The party's first actions were aimed at destroying police stations in the base region and at hunting down opponents, the 'big men' of the villages, often former headmen who had joined the conservative Nepali Congress party. A year after the war began, in 1997, the party announced the creation of an armed wing, the 'Special Task Force', which was still only comprised of sixty fighters. Over the following years, the attacks on government forces grew in scale, culminating in the attack on fortified military camps by a veritable army of thousands of soldiers equipped with automatic weapons. In January 2006, 6,000 soldiers led the charge on the district capital of Tansen.

The call for the King's sacrifice

The massacre of the royal family on 1 June 2001 and the coronation of Prince Gyanendra, the king's younger brother, represented the turning point of the People's War. While his elder brother, King Birendra, had remained unmoved during the first five years of the conflict, under Gyanendra the government declared a state of emergency and deployed the royal army on its own territory in response to the first Maoist attack on an army camp in November 2001. The king was the supreme commander of the army and any attack on the latter was an attack on the former. A face-off took place, and the Maoists confiscated several long-held privileges of the king, such as his role as head of justice and recipient of land taxes. They created parallel governments at the village and district levels in the western part of the country, and introduced collectivisation in certain 'model villages'. This gave the rebel leader the opportunity to gradually establish himself as an alternative, legitimate sovereign compared to a king who had been relegated to nothing but a miserable butcher, and was thus transformed into an ignoble version of the warrior king. This process was in fact initiated from the very beginning, upon the declaration of war by the Maoist party. Indeed, the very act of waging war gave the Maoist leader a form of sovereignty. Royal sacrifice had been an opportunity to re-establish order within the social structure. War, on the other hand, its extension, created a certain flexibility for the caste system, because it transcended its bounds, having offered exceptional destinies to otherwise modest peasants for many years. From the nineteenth century onwards, many of these people were able to earn untold riches as salaried soldiers in the British army, to cross the seven seas and be decorated with the highest distinctions, notably during the two world wars. These essential roles that the army and war played in social regulation – and even more so in stoking the dream of social improvement – had puttered out in Nepal, only to be skilfully revived during the People's War. Indeed, for several years prior to the outbreak of the People's War, the Nepalese army no longer recruited below the SLC and, given that its pass rate was particularly low in rural areas, many soldiers' sons were summarily excluded from the future they so keenly aspired to.[9] The Maoist party, on the other hand, offered a career to all, whatever their caste, social status, gender or education. In Dailekh district, they even revived the old tradition of hiring one person per household. Following in the footsteps of the great conquering and reforming rulers of yore, the leaders of the People's War in turn repealed fundamental laws. Women, who traditionally did not even hold the right to kill a chicken, and whose recruitment in the Nepalese army was entirely forbidden,[10] were now enrolled en masse. Children, previously excluded from the fighting, were also integrated. Finally, the revolutionary movement, led by two Brahmins, did not show mercy on the 'cows and Brahmins' protected by the Hindu king and law – Brahmin teachers who refused to acquiesce were cruelly executed, and according to the villagers, the Maoists used to feast on cow meat and often forced the population to consume it in order to destroy 'superstitions'.[11]

In addition to the social advancement offered by military engagement, arms confer sovereignty, as Michel Foucault (1994: 1471) puts it. The warrior maintains a direct and unique relationship with the divine, since his or her commitment constitutes a sacrificial gift in and of itself, because they give their own person to the cause. This being said, war itself is triggered by the sovereign, who thus acts as a sacrifier for all ensuing hostilities. In the past, the king used to take part in the battle himself, taking on the dual functions of sacrifier and sacrificator, as he does in the buffalo sacrifice. Unlike any other form of sacrifice, however, war is not orientated in any one direction, simply offering the most extreme of choices, either to make an offering for sacrifice or else be offered as a sacrifice. Not even the king was excluded from these starkest of options.

It is important to understand how the supreme sacrifier and sacrificator could suddenly appear as a butcher who executes his own people, and how some of them eventually came to call for his murder. The pendulous swinging of the roles of the king, alternating between the ideal and the monstrous, echoes his paradoxical nature. Entirely devoted to the well-being of his people and his kingdom, the king is simultaneously the very model of both the one 'who enjoys' and the keeper of the power of death, in a tightly intertwined knot, so much so that the terms for 'reign', 'enjoyment' and 'sacrificial offering' are all expressed by the same Nepali term, *bhog*.[12] Similarly, the king is the guarantor of the law but neither he nor his family are subject to its rule. Thus outlawed, transgression is required of him by the rituals he must perform, without which, according to the founding myths, he cannot establish his reign, and cannot accede to the throne with each passing generation.

In the origin myths of the Shah of Gorkha or the Malla of Kathmandu, in order to establish his rule, the king must desecrate and degrade a prince, his brother or even his son, by forcing him to offer an impure sacrifice that transforms him into an Untouchable or tribal servant in charge of royal worship. In the ritual practices, for each generation, the advent of the new king requires the desacralisation of a Brahmin, who must ingest part of the body of the deceased king and thus become an Untouchable who is swiftly expelled. The process of the transference of impurity, which continued until the very last royal coronation, in 2001, allowed the new king to not be touched by the impurity of his father's death, but at the cost of not fulfilling his filial duty to him (Lecomte-Tilouine 2009b).

The king, finally, is surrounded by fearsome relatives, in the person of his wife and his brothers. Since the middle of the nineteenth century, the queens of Nepal came from the Rana family, the usurpers of power, who had established this rule of alliance in order to consolidate their position. Birendra's wife, Aishwarya, was no exception. From the beginning of her reign, she was seen as having a dangerous influence on the king. In the 1980s, as she was driven around in her black sedan with blacked-out windows, protected by her sunglasses, the townspeople whispered among themselves that she was going to the airport to retrieve all the gold seized by customs officers for herself. The villagers said that she was organising hunting parties in the royal reserves, in which she herself participated, an activity strictly forbidden to women. The rumours about her grew as the situation in the kingdom deteriorated. During the 1990 riots, it was rumoured that she had tried to poison her husband so that he would not re-establish a multi-party system.[13] Naturally, the population first blamed her after the massacre of the royal family, [14] but the queen herself had also died and so could no longer be accused of such crimes. The people then turned their attention towards the younger brother of the sovereign, Gyanendra, and suspicions about his role as instigator of the bloodbath grew stronger over time.

Structurally, everything seems to predispose the king's brother to crime – as a member of the royal family, he is placed above the law, but unlike the sovereign, he has no responsibilities to fulfil and no model role to play. He thus merely soaks up all the negativity directed towards royalty, with many crimes being imputed to him. Gyanendra was no exception – he was known as a drug dealer, but also as a trafficker in works of art, a doubly sacrilegious crime, because it also implied these objects' prior theft from a temple. The transfer of the crown to the king's brother is in itself an event which can only come about as a result of misfortune, either by the premature death of the king or the absence of a male heir. People say that the younger brother was not born to be king and that he was not educated for it. In the case of Gyanendra, his succession had simply never been imagined by anyone, since Birendra had two sons. On the other hand, portentous omens soon announced the inevitability of the end of his reign, having long been announced by the gods.[15]

Gyanendra therefore ascended the throne in a particularly bad set of circumstances, combining an ongoing revolution with the mass murder of the entire elder branch of the dynasty. In addition, the long chain that once linked the sovereign to his subjects, to use Tocqueville's formula, had been broken in 1961 by the Panchayat regime, which had replaced the former village headmen delegated by the king by representatives chosen by open elections. This inversion of the top-down direction of political power detached it from its sacred aspects and from the person of the king, who was no longer its source, nor its model. Although he remained at the top of the pyramid, the king appeared from then on as merely the ruler of a clique of courtiers who were all hoping to curry favour with him so that he would appoint them to those positions that were still his to give. However, the Panchayat reform took several years to come to fruition, with the former village headmen retaining important roles until the late 1980s.[16] All the while, the parties continued their activities underground, especially in the universities.[17]

When Gyanendra was crowned, three days after the palace massacre, a bloody image became immediately and indelibly attached to him.[18] Far from trying to shake it off, the king seemed to embrace this terrible image of murder and blood, and use it to revive old patterns for both obtaining and deploying royal power.

As the father of a prince who was accused of several homicides, at the first Dasaĩ after his coronation, the king went on a tour of his kingdom to offer sacrifices to all the gods who were historically connected with his dynasty. He visited Lasargha, where his ancestors would have made their first stop when entering the Himalayan territory, then Gorkha, the kingdom built by the founder of his dynasty, and Nuwakot, a stronghold inhabited by a goddess who granted her favours to his ancestor Pṛthvī Nārāyaṇ Shāh and enabled him to conquer the Kathmandu Valley. Similarly, on his first official visit abroad, Gyanendra had a set of five animal sacrifices offered to Kamakhya, the famous goddess of northeast India. He made headlines in India, in papers such as the *Indian Express*, which published articles with titles such as: 'Nepal's king leaves bloody trail behind him'. Unmoved by these reactions, he had a second sacrifice offered the very next day at the Kali temple in Calcutta.[19] He then dismissed his prime minister and appointed a new government, making use of a vague clause in the Constitution. While most of the family had already been exterminated, he nevertheless increased the annual budget allocated to the royals by the state, and when he decided to occupy the royal palace which had been the scene of such a macabre event, he had it surrounded by armed soldiers, thus cutting it off from the world in the very heart of the capital.

The king thus adopted an attitude which was widely perceived as offensive, but this display of the most terrible face of royalty was not supported by a military display of its strength, because the royal army was already struggling to fight against the rebels. He therefore sank into darkness, helped by the Maoists and their army of cultural warriors, who composed increasingly biting verses about him.

> He killed him by immersing him in a pool of blood,
> And by the taste of blood, he enjoys a heavenly pleasure.
> Turned into the puppet of the White House,
> The butcher brought up in Narayanhiti's palace
> Has turned the beautiful country into a land of butchery,
> He has made himself the Great King of butchery.
> It is time to burn the emperor at the stake,
> It is time to throw the emperor into the grave, ...
> Let us exterminate the emperor by torture,
> Let us make his throne his bed of torture.[20]

Sucked into a regressive spiral, Gyanendra dug his heels against the sweeping tide of history, preferring to continue sacrificing to the most ancient gods of his lineage, to unleash the war, which was buried deep in the ritual vestiges of the past, and to appeal to those who had supported the monarchs in the past, such as Surya Bahadur Thapa. A vast protest movement against this 'royal regression' began to stir up the urban population of the Kathmandu Valley, leading in May 2004 to the resignation of the prime minister, followed by that of all elected officials who still held municipal roles. Apart from the army, who remained loyal, the king no longer had any support. Towards the end of 2004, five major political parties asked him to carry out constitutional reforms, joining the Maoists in calling for the independence of the army.

By this point it was no longer possible to hold elections and after a few failed attempts, Gyanendra fully embraced the role of tyrant which had been simmering away since his accession. He took over all powers on 1 February 2005 and accompanied his move with a show of force designed to instil terror, ordering the arrest of all politicians, the cutting off of all mean of telecommunications in the country and the suppression of press freedoms. He thus became the ultimate despotic incarnation from a bygone age, even cutting himself off from any remaining royal supporters, and a consensus was quickly formed among the political parties to abolish the monarchy altogether. These parties formed an alliance with the Maoist party in December 2005 and organised huge demonstrations in April, which finally convinced the king to relinquish his power on 24 April 2006. A peace agreement with the Maoists was signed a few months later, on 21 November 2006, and elections for the Constituent Assembly were held in April 2008. Against all odds, the CPN(M) won.[21] Nepal was duly declared a federal republic 'without religious parties' at the first session of the Constituent Assembly.

The Maoist ideology, which contributed to all these transformations in great part, maintains a complex relationship with violence. It made no real imprint upon the Nepalese political scene until it took up arms. Violent action was considered vocational and those who joined the party dreamed of taking part in it, to the point that the leading members recounted how difficult it was to convince some to take on positions within the political branch of the party. The People's Liberation Army (PLA) was in fact becoming larger and better equipped than the Naxalites in India or the Shining Path in Peru, yet its members insisted that their most formidable weapon was only ideological.

The Prachanda Path

Maoist thought was initially brought to Nepal by a handful of educated young people who had access to Marxist literature in Hindi and Nepali translations, which modified some of the key concepts of Marxism. One of the most important of these, the 'proletariat', was translated as *sārvāhara*, 'those who have lost everything', which does not adequately capture class poverty, and which also allows anyone who gives up their possessions to instantly become proletarian, regardless of their class. In Nepal, those who got rid of the greatest number of worldly goods acquired the most notoriety, such as Mohan Bikram Singh,[22] the father of Maoism in Nepal. He went about re-distributing the land which had been acquired by his own father in less-than-ideal circumstances back to the people, in a gesture strongly reminiscent of Brahminical renunciation, *tyāg*, thus reassociating himself with the surplus merit that such an act confers. Caste status received the same treatment, allowing two Brahmins to mobilise the population to fight against caste discrimination.

With the advent of the conflict, it was no longer possible to live one's political ideas from the comfort of one's armchair, because now it was required that adherents leave everything and 'walk in the party', that is, to engage in an itinerant life outside the country's inhabited areas. These travelling Maoist groups of ten or fifteen people could rely on a network of supporters, whose homes they took for overnight shelters, and even more on forced hospitality in remote hamlets. Despite their small size, these groups were structured, with members including a leader, a co-leader, and a member of another of the three branches of the party: a political commissar or activist from among the fighters, or a fighter from among the artists, and so on.

In leaving the world of 'the old government' behind, the revolutionary community's mission was to fight against its organisation, starting with caste and patriarchy, but it also had to get rid of all individualism in order to bring forth 'political consciousness', *rājnītik cetanā*. The translation of consciousness as *cetanā*, which conveys the idea of intelligence and knowledge, has inflected its meaning. Kamal, a cultural warrior, described his involvement as being the result of a long history of oppression in his village, which, he said, had made his father rebellious, *bidrohī*, but without 'political consciousness', because he had no access to education. The importance of the latter in the movement was expressed in the strong involvement of primary and secondary school teachers, as well as in the place given to literacy and education within the party.

The development of 'political consciousness' was part of a process of self-improvement expected of party members, in order for them to transform into 'new men'. This was ensured by the implementation of continuous instruction and training sessions, the practice of discipline, as well as by seances of purification, *śuddhikaraṇ*, where each person exposed his or her weaknesses and made self-criticism, before going on to criticise the party and its cadres. It was thus only through the group that individual evils were absorbed, ensuring perfection for the organisation as a whole.

The party members have always claimed that weapons were secondary to the ideology that drove them, namely the invincible thought of their supreme commander and party secretary, encapsulated as the Prachanda Path. This path presents itself as a synthesis of Marxism, and its main contribution is the concept of 'fusion', which proposes to combine the strategy of the Soviet armed insurrection with that of the protracted Chinese People's War. It is also a synthesis of the history of Chinese Maoism, aimed at simultaneously carrying out its two successive phases, armed revolution and cultural revolution.

Indeed, from the beginning of the People's War, entire formations of 'cultural warriors' led campaigns to transform society, fighting against 'indecent feudal culture', and introducing communist values through song, poetry, choreography and drama. Through their art, the Maoists demonstrated their ability to generate strength, vitality and modernity. In the remotest places, they captivated audiences with their use of locally unknown musical instruments such as the guitar and harmonium, amplifiers and ultra-modern weapons that no one had ever seen, which were entrusted to them to be exhibited as trophies during martial dances, where the revolutionary artists dressed in military costumes.

Conversely, in the PLA, many fighters wielded 'the gun in one hand and the pen in the other', as they put it, and contributed to an unexpected enrichment of the key concept of the Prachanda Path by this 'fusion between the pen and the gun'. They composed texts before leaving for the battlefield, recounted the battle in narrative or poem form and addressed their fallen comrades in verses or tributes, which allowed everyone to participate in the war in the most intimate way possible. In this literature, war is cast as an apocalypse orchestrated by warriors who rejoice in their own suffering, who grow by defeat and strengthen themselves by their losses, forming an anti-world in which the supreme figure of the martyr, *śahīd*, leads the way towards the realisation of the ideal of a classless society.

Revolutionary martyrdom

'[*Ś*]*ahīd* is the "big word" of the Maobadis,' my friend Mohan explained to me without giving another definition, as he read me an account of a Maoist attack. He had paused after reading it, thinking that I had not understood its full meaning. The term was indeed not yet familiar in rural Nepal, but with the revolution, the language had become loaded with 'passwords', in Madame de Staël's phrase, those words which signal political affiliation, such as the Maoist *spaṣṭa cha*, 'it is clear'. The martyr, *śahīd*, had already had a brief existence in Nepal before the People's War began. The term, of Arabic origin, means 'witness to the faith', much like the Greek *martur*, which gave martyr. It was secularised in 1930s India, where *śahīd* was used to refer to victims of the independence movement. In Nepal, its use did not appear until a decade later in the 1940s, during the anti-Rana struggle, which had been organised from India, and it had then reappeared sporadically during anti-Panchayat actions, especially during the 1990 movement which finally put an end to that regime.

The figure of the martyr thus developed in Nepal exclusively during struggles against the incumbent government, with no religious dimension, as in Islam, nor nationalist one, as in India. While the term is borrowed from Arabic, the *śahīd* of the People's War also draws on a second source of inspiration, revolutionary China. One can see this in the repeated use of the image of the martyr's death as being heavier than a mountain by the Nepalis, with Mount Tei from Mao's formula being replaced by Mount Everest. There are also references to Islamist movements and to suicidal political actions that are contemporary with the People's War. Finally, the Maoists of Nepal also found figures who embodied their notion of martyrdom in the Hindu world, notably Abhimanyu, as evidenced by this couplet addressed to him by a Nepali revolutionary soldier:

> By the supremacy of self-sacrifice,
> They were defeated and you were victorious.
> By the drops of your spilled blood,
> By your convictions, your ideals,
> By the lacerations of your wounds.[23]

Abhimanyu is a tragic hero of the *Mahābhārata* who decided to break through the circle of the enemy, knowing that he could not come out alive. This episode is fundamental, in that it is said to mark the end of adherence to the rules of war and the beginning of the Dark Age we now live in. Indeed, the enemies all fell on the young man instead of challenging him to a series of face-to-face duels, as was the rule. On the other hand, since the narrative is from the point of view of the *dharma* camp, that of Abhimanyu, the anomaly of his suicidal enterprise, which also breaks the ordinary rules of war, is hidden. The couplet describes three traits – the strength of self-sacrifice, of the ideal and of violence inflicted to the body – that define the revolutionary martyr, even if they are not always all present. Only the death by the enemy of the Maoist soldier or activist combines all three traits, but people killed by government forces or any party members succumbing to accidental death were also seen as martyrs, with the former receiving a kind of bloody baptism by their brutal death which expresses the revolutionary cause, while the latter meets death while themselves being fully committed to it.

Like Abhimanyu, the Maoist martyr pushes heroism to its limit, so that the latter notion is no longer used except in adjectival form, as a qualifier for the '*heroic* martyr'. The martyr thus subsumes the hero of yesteryear, giving new meaning to the combat in the process. Heroes, both in the great pan-Hindu epics and in those of western Nepal, are supermen, endowed with qualities beyond those of ordinary men – they are stronger, taller, more skilful or more cunning. The 'heroic martyr' of the People's War, on the other hand, has no special talent. He is weak. He describes himself as poor and poorly armed. It can even be a woman. But he or she fights for a cause that carries an extraordinary strength with it, one which allows the fighter to transform weaknesses into an advantage, defeat into victory and death into new life. Similarly, in the Maoist accounts of battle, conditions are often described as unfavourable, whether it is raining or snowing, or the night is either too dark or too bright, and the revolutionaries have the task of 'transforming the obstacle into an asset', according to their established formula. Their weapon is immaterial and eternal, so nothing can affect it. Like a kind of *ātman*, the ultimate reality that forms the self for Hindus, the revolutionary cause is both integrated within each warrior and yet remains external to them:

> Soldiers may have their eyes gouged out, their legs broken, [but] the eyes and legs of the revolution remain intact. [24]

Through holding onto ideals that ultimately surpass him, the martyr escapes the rules that constrain ordinary men, and 'embraces death'. This means that the forces of coercion can be diverted, and he can definitively withdraw from the power of death, previously the sole prerogative of the sovereign. The absolute counter-power of the martyr turns absolute power into a counter-productive force, which not only cannot touch the person who has already offered his or her life, but also reinforces that very thing it is fighting against, as the verses of this young female fighter testify:

> O enemies, do not try to burn my head,
> for I am already ablaze with the fire of the revolution.
> Don't laugh at me, placing thousands of corpses before me,
> for I am a traveller who crosses the ocean of blood,
> using their bodies as a bridge.
> Do not try to bind me with iron chains,
> for I am already bound by the philosophy of equality,

of justice and freedom.
Do not try to make me beg for my life in alms,
for I have already embraced death. [25]

The revolutionary commitment is thus a deliberate severing from the ordinary world, in order that the utopia of the future can be forged through violence and sacrifice. Like a self-sacrificial renouncer, the revolutionary warrior detaches himself (*tyāg garnu*) from his family, his ego and even his 'material form', which does seem to suggest the existence of one's *immaterial* form, in the purportedly atheistic ideology of Marxism. Again, like the renouncer who ingests his sacrificial fires, the Maoist warrior holds the fire of fury, *ākroś*, within them, which consumes from within and purifies. Their commitment is a blood sacrifice (*bali*) or an offering to the sacrificial fire (*hom*), which inverts traditional values and transforms death into the greatest achievement, in the beautiful, desirable form of the martyr's glorious death which brings eternity.

The blood of the martyr is life-giving: it forms blood-seeds (*raktabīj*) which spring to life as soon as they fall to the ground, giving birth to new warriors. It irrigates the soil of the motherland so that the revolution can flourish, strengthens it and forms the blood foundations (*ragatko jug*) of revolutionary constructions, often named after fallen comrades. It traces a path for the willing to follow. It is clear, then, that through this abundance of images, the idea that death represents an annihilation of the being is entirely refuted in the revolutionary war, as is also the case in animal sacrifice.

Sacrifice
They are eager to go to the front,
because they know
that death in war is not death
but the bloody seed
from which Communism will grow, shining.
Now I see a life without price in my death...
because I have understood, in truth,
that it will be a priceless sacrifice for Communism. [26]

The Maoists also address their loved ones in anticipation of the moment of 'the fall of their material form', enjoining them not to commemorate them with tears, but by their continued action towards the realisation of 'their dreams'.

Those who take over from the fallen address them in return, as if to pacify them, like this example from Simana Sharma, written to her martyred sister:

> Comrade Shyam,
> Your great unfulfilled ambitions,
> I will fulfil them without fail;
> I will carry the gun of your shoulder.
> The red flag that you waved in your hand,
> I will raise it.
> On the bloody path that you have traced,
> I will walk. [27]

When the revolutionary takes the 'sacrifice' of commitment upon him- or herself, they smear their forehead with the blood of the martyrs, or with vermilion powder in lieu of blood, and then tie a scarf of a particular type around their head, known as the *kaphan* or *kātro*, which is worn by mourners at the time of a relative's death. This becomes a sign of *self-mourning* worn by the newly committed warrior. The combatant once again dons the *kaphan* for armed action.[28] Their actual death is minimised – it is simply the 'fall of one's material form', while the immaterial part ascends to the sky and settles there in the form of a star. The revolutionary headband itself is often decorated with a star, so that both planes are reflected – on earth they are the star bearers, and in the sky, their accomplished, celestial forms. Only these 'stars' are celebrated by the party, in homage ceremonies to which their families are invited, while no decoration or celebration rewards the acts of bravery of those still alive. The mother of the martyr is the guest of honour, heaped with praise for her sacrifice which makes her the mother of 'thousands of sons and daughters of the party'. It is the spilled blood of the martyr which this mother uses to weld a family together, one united by blood-ties unrelated to kinship. This life-giving blood creates alters, as the saying goes, 'kill one, a hundred will be born'.

The definition of life and death is here reversed, for life under autocratic rule is death, while death in the People's War gives access to eternal life. However, we should not assume that the Maoists have simply fallen under the influence of manipulators, or that they were victims of a more diffuse force such as mimicry, or of the strange disease called 'martyropathy'.[29] They were part of a sacrificial machinery that gives life through death and blurs the meaning of both in a collective construction. It is again poetry that expresses this idea most powerfully and, as we will see, this is not by chance:

> When the waves carry away our sobs,
> When the walls are painted with human blood,
> Then it seems to Man
> That only destruction is good
> And death desirable,
> And that only the gun makes a poem pretty.[30]

Fusion of the pen and the gun

War, in all its technicality, becomes the main source of inspiration for the combatant-poets:

> Yes I am here
> To dig tunnels under your camp,
> To make powerful anti-personnel mines,
> So that they explode under your tanks.
> I'll unwind the detonator wires
> And dig you a fresh grave.
> I am present
> In the INSAS and SLR assault rifles
> In the flash of explosions.[31]

For the Maoist literary critic Pandav Thapa (2004), revolutionary poetry forges with the people and shares its vitality with them: 'its [touching] eyes become their eyes', its tongue 'let the people's cries and outpourings of blood be heard', it 'fills their parched insides with sap', 'lives in the hearts of the people as a pulse' and acts as 'a balm upon their wounds'. This power of poetry stems from its 'vigorous' (*ojapurṇa*) form of expression, which contains magical energy (*jādumayi śakti*), as Tarakant Pandeya (2006), another Maoist literary critic, puts it. Its energy, he adds, comes from the processes that govern melody, such as metre, repetition and alliteration, which create 'regularity', while its beauty lies in its 'original' terms, in its 'allusive and surprising' style, its 'deviant' language and 'processes of inversion' (*biparyās*), as in these verses which he cites as an example:

> Van beats sighs, mallet crushes suffering,
> Cutlass cuts misery, sadness sits on the stool.

Pandeya does not comment on the verses he has chosen, where two registers both evocative of the peasant life are mixed – tools and feelings – but here the former are used to fight against the latter, in a detour of their usual functions.

Maoist poetry thus builds a universe which is not simply a vehicle of revolutionary ideas and feelings, but a form of expression which is itself revolutionary. Powerful and effective, it breaks with the conventions of language and opens onto 'a reflected life, [one which is] more important and sublime than reality', as Pandeya puts it.

It spreads to all, forming a pact for life and for death between comrades, in their collective quest for immortality.

Saral 'Sahayatri', writer and commander

Saral, a brigade commander in the 3rd Division of the PLA, is the second of nine children. He 'entered politics' at the age of ten and joined the PLA at eighteen in 1999. He took part in numerous operations, always carrying a notebook in which he wrote poems, tributes and stories whenever he could. When he was sent 'to the front', he sometimes entrusted his precious notebook to his comrades so that they could keep it in a safe place, making sure his works were safeguarded if he himself were ever to disappear. These facts are given in the preface to his *Stories of the Revolution* ('Sahayatri' 2008), before Saral himself addresses the reader:

> I thought it would be instructive to explain how I wrote these stories. One day, Comrade Kavita [Poetry], our section commander, asked me, 'Sushil (at that time my name was Sushil), if I become a martyr, what will you write about me?' I hesitated for a moment and replied, 'And you, if I become a martyr, what will you write?' She laughed lightly and her answer remains engraved in my memory to this day: 'My name is Poetry, so I will write a beautiful poem about you.' Then I replied, 'I too will write a beautiful story in your memory'. I was unable to provide Kavita

> with the inspiration to write a beautiful poem about me, but she became a martyr on the Rumjatar front and I immediately composed a text in her memory. I had only been wounded, and I wrote part of this text while my comrades carried me on a stretcher through the mountains. Before that, I had already written a few lines, but no stories.

The scene reveals the concern that both fighters share, to be immortalised through textual tribute. If death in combat transforms revolutionary warriors into martyrs, then only their comrades can compose the text that ensures the posthumous life to which they all aspire. This important task makes each of them not only warriors but also potential writers, likely to have to one day fulfil the duty of memorialising those who offer their material form by 'inscribing their name in history'. In this way they aspire to be like the old heroes of the epics, whose names still ring through the Four Ages thanks to the living word of the bard. Here both the request for and the promise of assistance in the quest for immortality are reciprocal and openly formulated, a phenomenon which is specific to Nepal's People's War, where it was not a question of one or two martyrs whose posterity would be assured by the media, but of thousands of people engaging in action with this objective explicitly in mind. Only the witnesses, called upon to write, could thus ensure this collective quest for immortality.

Saral explains that he wrote many texts during the war, most of which were lost, reduced to ashes by the enemy or left to rot in some place he could not return to. This loss is painful for Saral and makes him think of the number of other texts that must have disappeared in this way. However, he sees it as a necessary sacrifice, much like the giving of a life: '[I]t seems to me that, just as it takes the sacrifice of hundreds and thousands of soldiers for the revolution to advance one step, it takes the sacrifice of hundreds of creations, *sirjanā*, for the creation of a single soldier to survive.' His collection is one such surviving creation, whose value lies in all those creations to which it bears witness.

The gun and the pen are the only two ways to fight a battle effectively, Saral explains. The revolutionary embraces both, bringing about a fusion that is itself revolutionary, in that it breaks with the conventional division of the great social functions, expressed in the Hindu world by the opposition of *brahmaṇ* and *kṣatra*, spiritual and temporal power. The fighter-writer describes what has been done, but he is also the one who did that same action. In perfect fusion, he composes while fighting and writes immediately after the battle, sometimes even while being carried away from the battlefield on a stretcher, thereby closing the sacrificial loop linking speech and action entirely in on itself.

Revolution on the move

Diaries, field reports and tributes to martyrs present the revolution as a progression in which revolutionaries join as 'travellers'. These 'new men', as they call themselves, see the world with new eyes. On the way, the different aspects of the landscape they pass through form metaphorical images of the revolution: the anti-proletarian fog dissipates into the revolutionary sky, rivers allow them to hear the sobs of the people, climbing the steep slopes of the mountains reminds them that the People's War is progressing step by step towards the summit of victory. In this worldly poetics which is capable of absorbing everything, the poets describe themselves as itinerant ascetics, always on the move, on steep paths, through mountains and forests, detached from the material and from their ego. However, in the perception of the villagers, they are more akin to wandering spirits of the wild. They thus occupy spaces both beyond and below the ordinary world.

By its mobility and inverted values, the Maoist movement evokes the Deleuzian 'nomadic war machines', which develop in the interstices of the state and manifest themselves in uncontrollable forms, such as indiscipline, riot, guerrilla or revolution. Escaping the state apparatus that exerts its power by fixing people and things in space and controlling their circulation, these machines promote deterritorialised conditions of existence and associated values, such as speed and secrecy (Deleuze and Guattari 1980: 499–500). In the Maoist movement, these traits are essential not only to the functioning of the machine but even more to its expansion. It exercises its power in a manner in strict opposition to that of the state, by uprooting the population and pushing them towards an uncertain destination, which is couched in the terms of destiny. This is what the Maoists called capture, *kabjā*, which consisted in acts of destruction and subtraction more than occupation or fixing, and took on a wide range of forms, from the destruction of signs of the state's presence (police stations, town halls, prefectures and tax collection centres) to the kidnapping of people. These might be members of the legal or justice systems or class enemies, as one may expect in the context of war, but also teenagers by the hundreds, in order to subject them to 'training'. These might also be entire villages, corralled into party construction work or, more rarely, to force them to serve as 'volunteers' in armed actions. Lastly, it may even be the inhabitants of an entire region, who are required to attend large-scale party meetings.

These abductions transport the individual into a parallel plane of existence, where the adventure takes on its full meaning of 'what can advent'. They are lived as an experience of imminent death and derealisation, where this loss of bearings, in the context of a utopian society without ties and without ego, give way to intense and contradictory emotions of terror and excitement.

Joining the party brings a similar experience to the revolutionaries, who enter an invisible, mobile and secret organisation, which rears its head at moments of violent action or artistic epiphany. At the head of this universe is Prachanda the Terrible, whose quotations pepper the writings and speeches of all party members, but who himself remains invisible.

The invisible leader and his manifestations

Prachanda went underground early in his political career, in around 1980 or 1981, that is, fifteen years before taking over the leadership of the CPN(M) to wage the People's War. Few people were even aware of his actions throughout the duration of the movement. Kulman, a Magar cultural warrior from the base region who joined the party in 1996, toured the province with his troop to conduct campaigns. He participated in all major party rallies as the head of the 'Jaljala cultural family', which was responsible for performing at such occasions. During a Chinese revolutionary choreography training session in the Punjab region, he even managed to forge a ritual friendship with Prachanda's son. Even so, he did not see Prachanda in the flesh until the Chunbang meeting in October 2005, almost ten years after hostilities were declared. Despite this, Kulman never doubted his existence, and always carried his portrait with him on his missions, drawn in pencil on the flyleaf of his personal notebook, facing his own photo, which was hidden by a small paper flap stuck with tape, as if to erase himself in front of the leader's image.

The faith in the existence of the invisible leader conferred a special power on his word, making it into a purely dematerialised force. His 'underground' nature, *bhūmigat*, brought him closer to the most powerful deities and shamans, those who were born 'by breaking ground', an expression meaning that they were born of themselves and more precisely, in the case of shamans, that they did not receive instruction from a human master. Like them,

Prachanda never mentioned intermediaries between himself and the Sacred Fathers of Marxism–Leninism–Maoism.

Outside Maoist circles where faith remained utterly untainted, the reality of Prachanda's existence was the object of doubts and many people were suspected of being the 'real' Prachanda, even the king, who could well have taken this disguise to better fight his enemies, the mainstream political parties.[32]

In the physical absence of Prachanda, his words were publicly delivered by the party's number two, Baburam Bhattarai, which, far from leading to the idea that Bhattarai was 'the true face of the Maoist insurgency' as has been said, gave Prachanda an air of omnipresence. Though invisible, there were two photos of the leader which were circulated with such reverence that they evoke rare, precious and immaterial powers. These pictures, reproduced in all formats, from the intimate medallion placed in a locket to the giant parade poster for all to see, took on an iconic value. His image was also inserted into all sorts of photomontages, allowing the leader to appear, with his fist raised, sometimes at the head of the combatants, sometimes with the people or with a given group, such as women or Indigenous peoples. Prachanda was thus able to gain a real omnipotence from all this.

The strange leadership duo of the Maoist party generated a veritable liturgy at its very highest echelons. The leader was pure speech and his will was absolute – his formulas were 'quotations', his projects 'decisions' and their public revelation 'proclamations'. This disembodied voice which triggered the great sacrifice of war is thus reminiscent of Vedic Speech, coupled with Sacrifice. It is remarkable that this power only materialised in the flesh when he announced the end of the war sacrifice, before his assembled party at the Chunbang meeting in October 2005, where Prachanda declared his 'decision' to pursue the revolution in non-warlike ways from then on, and that he was now willing to play the parliamentary game. It was during this assembly that Prachanda was photographed anew and even filmed weeping at an opera that depicted the martyrdom of a combatant.[33] Kulman, who took part with his troupe of cultural warriors, told me that the play was a 'true' story, with the martyr's own partner and child playing themselves. The end of war-sacrifice is thus displayed as a sudden crash into reality, where Speech becomes embodied and the violence of the martyr's sacrifice exposed, bringing tears to the eyes of the very people who orchestrated it.

Prachanda's first appearance before the public in Kathmandu would take place later, on 16 June 2006, five days before the peace treaty, and would mark the beginning of his desacralisation, notably by becoming the butt of much of the derision that the 'bourgeois' media had saved up for him.

The capturing machine

Initially just as invisible as its leader, the Maoist party itself only appeared fleetingly in the base region, in violent, sudden and rapid actions which usually took place at night, often catching people off-guard. Party members strategically targeted the police stations and 'big men' of this remote region, so as to clear it of what they considered to be hostile presences. Despite the Maoists being hidden deep in the surrounding forests, they were nonetheless perfectly aware of what was going on in each locality within this region which they claimed as their own, as if they were seeing the world through a sort of panopticon. For their part, the local forces of order responded to the party's targeted violence with their own kind of blinded violence. Posted there by administrative ill fortune, the police were forced to adapt to the challenges of the region, but without 'discerning' *cinnu* anything, as a woman in Darling told me. They brutalised respectable individuals and innocent young people whom they confused with Maoists, and soon aroused general hostility in the area.[34] The Maoists, on the contrary, were actually the ones who came to intervene in households where a disturbance was reported. For instance, if a man in the region had two wives, the Maoists would come in under cover of night and divide his property up, giving half to the first wife. If another man drove his sister who was pregnant by a man of a lower caste away from the village, they would surround his house and force him to apologise to her. Their methods were harsher with usurers, seducers and especially with informers, who were often mutilated or even executed.

Working in parallel to these factions, the cultural branch of the party was in charge of campaigns of 'construction'. Kulman, who led a family of cultural warriors, was still in school as war began to brew in the northern region of Rolpa. It was here that he was introduced to revolutionary culture and, shortly thereafter, his village was the scene of unbridled police violence and was renamed the Village of Martyrs.[35]

Musician, singer, actor, dancer, choreographer and composer, Kulman is also a photographer. With a small plastic camera bought for 500 rupees (around 4 dollars), he took hundreds of pictures of the revolution, convinced, he says, that even his children could not believe what they had done. Kulman can recall all his campaigns in great detail – in 1996, he ran one calling 'for the centralisation of forces', then one 'for the capture of weapons'; the following year, he contributed to two campaigns which attempted to explain the objectives of the People's War, and so on. He was also in charge of composing operas, poems, songs and speeches on the theme of each campaign, and of organising meetings in his sector.

In a wandering troupe consisting of a dozen artists, accompanied by a few fighters for their security, they travelled through the mountains and arrived unannounced in a random village. Banners were quickly unrolled, fabrics stretched out to form a stage, school benches were brought out for the ceremony to take place. The performance followed a strict protocol: it opened with a welcome song, followed by a salute to the great martyrs and a minute of silence with fist raised. Then the show would begin, which alternated between speeches and entertainment, including songs, dances and operas. Finally, the ceremony closed with a farewell song, the promise to 'meet again on the battlefield' and the handing over of some object as a souvenir.

In the moments before the ceremony began, Kulman was able to compose a song or an opera for the occasion, featuring a story which had happened in the village of the day. He was careful to make the villagers feel acknowledged and included by giving them places of honour and gifts, such as embroidered handkerchiefs or miniature bows.

To understand the significance of these campaigns, we must look at the scene from the villagers' point of view. These unwitting hosts to the revolutionaries had to put up with them organising a visible and noisy demonstration in their homes on their behalf, an activity which placed them all in danger of death. Indeed, the police often took advantage of such moments to fire into the crowd, sometimes from a helicopter, in the belief that all those attending a Maoist meeting must be Maoists. In such circumstances, it is thus understandable that the revolutionary spectacle was a particularly disturbing experience for the local people. Who to fear? Those who expose you to death, but who themselves incur this risk to tell you about a better world, or those who have been ordered to destroy this movement with brute violence?

Over time, the Maoist meetings became true apogees of the party's power and the number of participants expected to attend grew exponentially – thousands of villagers were brought by force, sometimes having been marched there over several days. At the end of a long pilgrimage towards the unknown, the emergence of the 'ocean of the party' from the mists in the middle of nowhere formed a striking and unreal spectacle. Many people compared it to a dream.

Flags, banners, armed fighters and huge crowds were a source of wonder to all, even the party members themselves, who were used to living in small groups. Thus immersed in the deadly camp, the population lived these moments very intensely, and many of them signed up to join the travellers on the Prachanda Path, by simply following a group who were leaving at the end of the ceremony. Usha left this way, when she was only eleven years old. As she explained to me, she knew nothing about politics, but she liked the revolutionary songs and wanted to follow artists. She then chose to join the base region from her village in eastern Nepal, where she received military training, becoming a child soldier.

The show could touch even the most seasoned combatants. The commander of the 5th Division of the PLA, Comrade Abinash, who himself confesses to being 'hard-nosed and unemotional', recounts in his memoirs how he organised an ambush that went wrong, with one of his comrades being killed in the action. On his way back, he came across a village where a cultural family was giving a theatrical performance that 'made him relive what he had just experienced', which overwhelmed him (Abinash 2003: 47). The performance exposes death in all its reality and also exposes the audience to death in one gesture. It creates a sort of augmented reality for all concerned, sublimating both the action and its actors, who have already been sublimated by the war. As Abinash (2003: 55) writes: 'Now to read the history and the life of "great men," *mahāpuruṣ*, one need not go far, for events produce them. The stories of revolutionaries are being written from our homes.'

The repeated abductions of the population periodically uprooted it from the certainties of its foundations – social position, property, family and caste ties – while the party strove to blur the limits of its own organisation and used a number of methods to get as many people involved as possible. This is how Patiram, a Dalit from the blacksmith caste, joined the party: 'Men gave me things to keep and I couldn't refuse, but if the army had come to search my house, they would have killed me. I was afraid of that, so I set out, taking nothing with me. I carried papers [for the party], I did this kind of work and I travelled very long distances.' These 'long distances' are no mere figure of speech, and to get some idea of the kilometres traversed, we can cite the memoirs of a Maoist teacher (Kandel 2009), who recounts his journey in December 2004 from Chitwan to Rolpa-Rukum where, with a group of seventy people escorted by some PLA fighters, they were to join a meeting of revolutionary teachers. They walked for twenty-two days, he says, while other groups arrived after fifty-five days of walking. If we count the return journey too, we begin to understand why young Man Kumari was worried about agricultural production and a possible famine. This villager from Gulmi told me in 2009: 'I was wondering if we weren't all going to starve, and I told them: You don't even give us time to work. Every day you take us to a meeting and soon how will you be able to beg your food from us?'

Like Usha, who had been swept away by the art of the Maobadis (or Maoists), hundreds of teenagers were abducted from their villages to be trained in Marxism–Leninism–Maoism, to learn a few songs, and sometimes even to be initiated in the handling of weapons. It is difficult to know how many of them ultimately stayed, but of the seven schoolchildren abducted by armed men from a village in Gulmi when I was there in September 2005, only five returned after a two-month absence; one of the other two joined the PLA and the other the cultural branch of the party.

The population was also taken away to serve as 'volunteers' during major armed operations, to carry both equipment and the wounded, supervised by members of the political and cultural branch of the party, who themselves served as 'volunteer' cadres.[36] It was in these circumstances that the change to these people was the most extreme. Bhim, a 'volunteer' villager who fled with the revolutionaries when they were pursued for several days by the army, recounts how he had to rely on his new revolutionary comrades for his survival, the necessity creating a firm solidarity with those he had previously feared.

The party members themselves lived in perpetual motion, without knowing the purpose of their movements. The method, no doubt adopted for security reasons, turned the party into a mystical order, in the sense of an organisation requiring total commitment, complete trust in its agents, and blind obedience to directives from an invisible voice.

The memoirs of Comrade Dhruwa, also known as Himmat Baral Magar, published in 2010 as *Samar yātrā* (Journey of War), offer a glimpse inside this mystical journey.

Journey into unknowing

Dhruwa was born on 10 December 1980 in a village of Gulmi District, western Nepal. He became a member of the party in October 1998, shortly before his eighteenth birthday. At the time, he was not particularly politicised, but was seeking an 'ideal', *ādarṣa*.

Dhruwa recounts the circumstances under which he 'set out on his journey'. One day, some young men came to his house with a message from his brother that only said: 'Follow the bearers of this message, they will lead you to me and we will talk.' He set out without asking any further questions, following these strangers who became his guides, thus showing his 'confidence', *biśvās,* which is synonymous with religious faith in Nepal. Dhruwa gives the date of 'that day when he left home', the title of his first chapter, as the date of his commitment to the party. His journey leads him from one surprise to another along the way, until he eventually reunites with his brother, who, having been involved for a year, tells him that he must join the Young Communist League. This prospect hardly appeals to Dhruwa, who is afraid of speaking in public, but he again complies.

During his early tribulations, Dhruwa undergoes a personality change. He is no longer the man he used to be, because he is now perceived as a supernatural being:

> People would approach us to see if we were human or not. They would approach us, anxious and terrified, asking, 'Do the Maoists behave like humans? Do they walk the same way we do?' Indeed, they had heard that if you see a Maoist in one place, he is in another at the same time, that Maoists could jump from the highest rooftops, that they are very strong, very smart and very fast.

This popular perception gives Dhruwa a power which he is fully aware of but from which he derives no personal benefit, because, as he says, he is constantly forced to lie about his identity.

Dhruwa is then subjected to ordeals that bruise his body: first a period of military training so harsh that his knees bleed, then a dangerous mission that leads him to prison, where he undergoes torture. Five months after joining the party, he is sent to the forest with about twenty other young people for military training.

These days of tribulation make Dhruwa 'very impatient to attack the enemy', but, to his disappointment, he is sent to 'collect' funds from shopkeepers in the district headquarters to help finance the party. There, he is caught by the police and thrown into prison but professes to be 'happy to have been arrested and proud to have been tortured' because, he says, 'prison, irons and torture are the school of revolutionaries'. In his case, this is particularly accurate, as he explains: 'It was by watching the police in prison that I really understood how the 303 calibre rifle works, how many parts it is made up of and how they are assembled.'

Upon his release from his gruelling stint in prison, Dhruwa is immediately taken into an armed operation with no prior warning, where he discovers the existence of a network of fighters who share coordinated actions and a secret language. Sent back to his original unit after three months, the young man is greeted by his friends who hand him a bottle of vitamins: 'I thought it was because I had lost a little weight in prison and no one told me anything. I did not know that I was going to take part in armed action.'

That same evening, he is taken to the forest by his comrades. When they reach a river, one of them shouts 'Kāle! [Blacky]' and a voice answers 'Sete [Whitey]'. Dhruwa writes:

> I was surprised, Why were they shouting Kāle and Sete in the night? Then my comrades came forward saying, 'Our friends are here.' It was only later that I learned that it was a coded language. We took out our weapons, put on our uniforms and hid our faces with black masks. At last, our commander gave us the details of the operation: 'The party has ordered us to carry out an action against Kunwar Manasing of Arghatos, who is a loan shark who exploits the people.... If he is at home, we will break his right arm, otherwise we'll take his papers'.

Dhruwa did not expect this: 'What was going to happen? How was this going to be? Many questions raced through my mind.'

Keeping Dhruwa in the dark like this was not limited to armed actions alone. In October 1999, after spending a year in the party, he went to the town of Butwal and was told that a certain Comrade Lakhan would like to see him. He was driven on a motorcycle to a big house.

> Who is this man and why is he calling me? I had no idea. I sat down beside him and he told me the details of the military campaign in Bam. I swallowed his every word with delight, but could not think of anything to say and just agreed: 'Good sir', 'It's good', were the only things that came out of my mouth. When I left his house, I felt very lucky to have met a great leader, but I still didn't know who he was or what his position was.

Dhruwa learns after the fact that he had in fact met Commander Badal. He experiences all of these moments as an intense mystery giving way to later revelation.

Six months after this, a period during which Dhruwa says that 'every day I had more responsibilities and I felt that the party trusted me more and more', he was sent on a mission to Arkhabang to prepare rations for thirty 'red fighters'. Dhruwa has no idea why they are there: 'I couldn't ask them, but I would have liked to know,' he writes. As they enlist him in their group for the operation, he learns from them that they are on their way to attack the Dhurkot police station.

During his journey, where Dhruwa experiences everything before knowing the reasons behind his actions, he becomes totally immersed in religious ignorance, taking part in the confessional 'purification' sessions which are designed to learn everything about him. The comrades are asked to disclose their mistakes and Dhruwa confesses that he discharged his weapon after the ceasefire and the surrender of the enemy, wounding a woman in the process. He would have to do push-ups to expiate his fault. The second purification he relates is more akin to an intimate confession. This time it all has to be written down, and Dhruwa, wanting to write that he had a sexual relationship, *yaun prem*, when he was in school, makes a spelling error that turns his fault into a 'mute love relationship', *maun prem*, making the entire assembly laugh, including a 'central member of the party' who asks him how it was. Publicly humiliated in this way, Dhruwa said nothing more, he recounts in his memoirs, which we can view as being another of those public confessions.

Dhruwa's last initiatory journey takes place as late as April 2001, four years after his engagement. Sent to the village of Kureli again without knowing why, he finally takes part in the assembly of the entire armed branch of the party, for its re-founding into the PLA. 'It was like a dream', says Dhruwa. He is by this point the head of an armed group, but still remains under the supervision of the political leader of his geographical sector, who asks him to write a diary so that he can read it every month. Dhruwa complies, even if his supervisor will in reality never ask to see his notebooks. These diaries will form the basis of his memoirs, which goes some way to explaining why they are written in such an intimate, confessional style.

At the request of the party, Dhruwa transferred from the armed wing to the political wing and became company commissioner during the Khara attack in May 2002. On this occasion, the passage of information followed a strict hierarchy, from the division commander to the company commanders, who in turn informed section commanders, who finally instructed their men. The attack was a failure and of the ninety members of Dhruwa's company, only 'twenty-five or thirty' survived. Yet Dhruwa continued his rise in the revolutionary army and became battalion commander in 2005. At the end of his journey, Dhruwa still retains the feeling of uncertainty that permeated his entire experience and which he sums up by the image of the warrior facing death: 'Is there a name written on the end of every bullet? And what is that name? Who can fight? And for how long? No one can say. Some bullets graze your ear, some take the hairs off your skin, but only one brings death and no one knows in which part of your body it will lodge.'

Dhruwa's account describes an initiatory journey into a parallel world, where every movement is controlled by an invisible power according to a plan known only to it. Deprived of his personal agency and individual identity, the revolutionary also loses his own intimacy, his emotions and even his faults, which he must share, with blind trust in his comrades, who, as yet more links in the party chain, become a reflection of personal milestones. Gradually, each of the new recruits is granted control over a small area, thanks to the multiplication of positions of authority, thereby redoubling the process of subjugation to higher powers. The party members end by reproducing their own experience among the people who, through abduction or forced appointment to a position in the party, in their turn lose control over their individual destiny and become involuntary members of the Maoist community of destiny.

The model village sacrificial ceremony

From 2001 onwards, the party became more powerful, with the continued growth of its armed wing, and the political bureau decided to set up parallel government in the base region. In the villages, people were appointed to be part of the 'people's government', regardless of whether they consented to do so or not. Fearing reprisals, everyone complied. The party then decided to transform certain places into 'model villages', where collectivisation and cultural revolution were particularly advanced, in order to serve as an example to other localities. Darling, the village where I had stayed for a long time for my doctoral studies, was chosen as one such model.

When I decided to go there in September 2005, I had not heard any news for two years. I knew that the valley was located on a Maoist corridor, but communications and mail had been cut off and I did not know that a people's government had been established there. After two days of walking, as I climbed the steep hill leading to the village, a young woman quickened her pace despite her heavy load of grass and offered to stop for a smoke. She unhooked the hemp headband that held her burden to her forehead, wiped her face with a flap of her skirt, and then, while exhaling the thick smoke of her first puff, announced point-blank: 'Our village has been captured.' – 'Captured! But by whom?' – 'By the Maoists of Darling. They came with weapons. It was a month ago. They rounded up the whole population and appointed the members of our village people's committee.' She then promptly replaced her headband and set off down a small side path. It was still four hours' walk to the Maoist stronghold that 'my' village had become. At the pass which demarcates the limit of its territory, there was no visible sign of the party, neither martyrs' gate nor red flag with the sickle, but the houses where we took a break for tea had been abandoned, with their shutters closed and their walls cracked, offering a rather gloomy welcome.

When I finally got to the hamlet where I had stayed for a long time, my arrival caused surprise and joy, but also concern. The neighbouring seamstress said to me, by way of greeting: 'They won't ask you anything, I'll tell them,' meaning that as a Dalit, she had a new authority in society. The old chief of the village arrived in due course, all smiles, before complaining that my arrival meant that: 'They won't let me sleep all night, that's for sure.' The context was peculiar enough that I understood what they were suggesting – the 'nothing to ask me' they were referring to was money, since the revolutionaries fed and armed themselves by taking donations. The 'they' who would not let the old chief sleep were the revolutionaries, who would inevitably come and question him on the reasons for my unexpected arrival, disliking the idea that someone had escaped their net. I learned fairly quickly, moreover, that I had not entirely managed to evade them, since a young man, whose face I remembered having seen somewhere, came to tell me that he had seen me eating a snack on the way a few hours earlier. Had he followed me to see where I was going, or was he simply taking the same path as I was? Not being in a position to enter investigative mode, I just sat and ruminated, confirming his observation with a friendly nod.

My friend, in whose yard I had already settled, came hurrying back from the fields, having been informed of my arrival. She began distributing instructions to the men around, in preparation for the sacrifice honouring the coming of a guest. Once the requisite chopping block, basin and cutlass had been assembled, they decapitated a goat, despite my protestations. We were then invited to the welcome meal, inside the house, and a tense atmosphere settled over the circle of gathered men. I knew them all, but now I did not know who was who.

Glasses of beer were passed around, and then the old chief handed me a leaf-cup full of grilled meat, while accompanying his gesture with a 'Here little sister, take your offerings (*prasād*)'. He insisted heavily on this word, so that I understood that he was being deliberately provocative in front of the members of the revolutionary government. Despite being unaware that there were bans on religious practices, because the media had not mentioned them, I immediately suspected that this was the case. I later learned that any ritual involving animal sacrifice was prohibited, as well as women's dances during the Tīj festival, ancestor worship, and even the thirteen days of funerals. As I began to inquire as diplomatically as I could about various members of the community and the new developments in the village, the old chief grew bolder and spoke of equality, reminiscing about the time I reminded him of, or that my presence allowed him to publicly evoke, when he was in charge of enforcing caste rules. He laughed as he recalled in front of the silent circle of Maoist cadres that time when 'even the little sister' knew that the consumption of buffalo meat was degrading. I soon learned that almost everyone in the village now ate not only buffalo but also cow meat, which was absolutely taboo in this still-Hindu kingdom.

At daybreak the next day, a stern-looking young woman burst into the closet that served as my bedroom and questioned me as I lay in a vulnerable position, scantily clad, tucked up in my sleeping bag. She wanted to see my papers, to know what path I had taken to get here and what exactly I had come to do. Like Dhruwa, I answered her without asking any questions, and only learned after she left that she was in charge of the whole sector. I went for a walk in the forest to clear my head after such a rude awakening. At the first clearing I came to, I met an old acquaintance, who literally threw herself into my arms, bursting into tears as she announced: 'They took my eldest daughter, it's been two months. I cry all day, in the morning I don't even want to get up. I would like to leave, but no one would even agree to buy our buffaloes.'

Her daughter, whom I had seen as a child, was among a group of seven teenagers from the village who had been abducted two months earlier by the

Maoists for the purposes of training. Abductions of teenagers had created a real climate of terror and any parents who could afford it sent them as far away to safety as possible, even at a very young age. Schoolchildren were liable to be kidnapped 'from class 7 onwards', villagers said, that is, around twelve or thirteen years old, and even the children of party members were not spared. Purna, the postman, who became a Maoist in 2003, had no idea where his daughter was in September 2005 and explained to me: 'They kidnapped her, what can I do?' as if he was not part of this organisation himself.[37]

However, during my stay, three teenagers abducted from another location were brought up to the village. They stayed there for several days for a revolutionary dance training given by a team of cultural warriors, including a dance teacher and some musicians. Most of the training took place in the courtyard of the former village headman, which conferred an official air to proceedings. The training session was being watched by a few onlookers from the overhanging terrace, and I went over to join them. Even though the villagers were suffering because their own children had been abducted, not one of them tried to communicate with the child-victims who had come to their village, nor to inquire as to where they had come from or how long they had been abducted. For these young people, there was no indication of any solidarity or even compassion from the population, whereas in fact the women of the house where I was staying were constantly lamenting their fate, but behind closed doors.

We soon learned that the teenagers had been brought here for the 'model village' celebration. Not having had the courage to go and talk to them myself,[38] I wondered why they had kidnapped and brought these particular young people to dance here, and not chosen a few young people from the village or, even more simply, had the members of the cultural troupe perform the dances. As the ceremony got underway, these questions were answered.

The ceremony had been loudly announced the day before and all the villagers had to attend, seemingly based on the model of the buffalo sacrifice, where participation was mandatory. On the esplanade – the place where the sacrifice now banned by the revolutionaries was once held – a table of honour, a banner and flags had been laid out in front of a row of benches, brought out of the school for the occasion. The ensemble faced the ruined town hall building, which had been destroyed by the revolutionaries' attacks, as well as the temple of the Goddess, which was permanently closed by a padlock but remained intact. The opposition between the old and the new government was thus drawn out in physical space. The entirety of the people's government, but also the cultural troupe and the person in charge of the region, the 'in charge' as she was known as, were lined up behind the table.

First there were congratulations shared by these representatives of the people among themselves, which took place in front of a 'people' who were less than attentive to proceedings, followed by long speeches which, despite their vehemence, did no better in capturing the crowd's attention. The children, who had been placed in school uniform in the front rows, took out their textbooks and began to mumble through their lessons, now turned to form a circle around me, their backs to the speakers. Old hands from behind my bench touched my shoulder to greet me, give me a cigarette, or ask me for one. I tried to answer them, all while catching snatches of the speeches, which spoke of the blood of the martyrs, of their dreams, of the strength of revenge. People squeezed under the unfurled umbrellas, crowded in shady corners and talked during the two long hours that the speeches lasted. Their end was marked by shots fired in the air by the militiamen, causing the little ones to flee, in a mix of both terror and delight.

Then the three young hostages came forward, all three dressed in the same new outfit, the two girls as well as the boy wearing black trousers and a red checked shirt. To the sound of the drum, guitar and harmonium (two instruments which were unknown in the village), they performed Maoist dances with typically Chinese choreography that they had learned in the days before, to everyone's delight. The first song was entitled 'The Fighter's Daughter' and spoke of a girl's determination to follow her father's example. The crowd had fallen silent, had stood up and come closer to get a better look, just as I had. Even the schoolchildren had put down their books and stopped chattering. They were watching, standing on the benches, their chins outstretched, and their eyes shining.

At the time, absorbed by the rhythm of the ceremony, which finally offered a little entertainment, I had not realised that these children were gazing upon frightened young hostages, who were offering them an image of what their own destiny could be. The connection was made clear to me by my young neighbour, who had become my 'partner-in-crime', since he had seen the red light of my camera on my lap at the beginning of the ceremony, which I wanted to record discreetly, and had not flinched after I held my finger to my mouth in a gesture of secrecy. He whispered in my ear:

> – 'Last year they came to my house and took my older brother. It was at night and they blindfolded him.'

– 'And what happened?'

– 'He doesn't know where he went, but he came back a week later and my parents sent him to India the next morning.'

The dances captivated the audience as they unfolded, and with them, the programme came to an end. It continued with an improvised party, where rifles were fired in the midst of the traditional Damāī band, who had taken over after the official ceremony had come to a close. Men threw themselves into the mêlée one by one, encouraged in their dance by the cries and chants of the spectators who enclosed them in a tight-knit circle, as is the custom.

The Maoist ceremony was therefore strangely reminiscent of the Dasaī festival, which had been banned by the people's government. It gathered together the same multicoloured crowd, under the same umbrellas. The preliminary phase of the sacrificial rite, consisting of daily readings, seemed here to be replaced by speeches, while the killing of the buffaloes was substituted by the dances of the captives. These seemed to have the same intensity and power of subjugation over the public as blood sacrifice. As the dances were performed by victims, this only served to strengthen the analogy. Finally, the compulsory nature of participation in the ceremony reinstated the much-decried sacrificial constraint of Dasaī. The younger ones, at whom the performance was especially targeted, displayed a mixture of excitement and dread, as potential victims of the spectacle they were being forced to watch.

However, the dance of the hostages also contrasted with the buffalo sacrifice in a number of significant ways. Whereas the latter engendered a violence aimed at the annihilation of opposing forces, the hostage dance depicted the party's capacity for incorporation of all the population in a seemingly harmless manner. The sacrifice of Dasaī summons different planes of reality that simultaneously come together to form an abundant and floating semantic field, because it is at one and the same time the expression of royal power and the repetition of the Goddess's deeds; because of the ritual use of a sword, in which one can see the king's *alter ego*, the weapon of the Goddess or even an entirely autonomous god; and because it targets a multitudinous animal, in which some recognise a demon, others an enemy and others still may even recognise themselves. The hostage dance seemed meaningless by comparison. Why kidnap children and take them so far away to make them dance? Do the victims represent something other than themselves?

Their anonymity was absolute and thereby introduced strangeness into the familiar world of the village. Admittedly, the ongoing war meant that wandering strangers were seen more often, but for these people, political affiliation took the place of identity. The hostage, on the other hand, bears witness to a power that is able to remove the individual from his or her territory, caste, family and all the ties that help to define them. Thus stripped of their personal attributes, she or he is shown as a human prototype, as *puruṣa* or *ecce homo.* Such stripping is the equivalent of death in Nepal. It was applied as a supreme punishment to those categories of people who it was forbidden to kill such as women and Brahmins, who were banished from the group and the territory instead of suffering the death penalty.

From the point of view of the individual, abduction or exclusion entails the same rupture of ties, but abduction goes further because it deprives the subject of any agency, turning them into an objectified, lifeless material only animated by an external force, in the manner of the *śakti*. The choice of dance, which engages all components of the body, is a remarkable expression of this power, especially since 'making dance' is a well-known idiom of power over others in this region, where shamans made witches dance in order to reveal their identity to all (at least, until the practice was forbidden by law in the nineteenth century) and where 'masters' cause mediums to become possessed by evil spirits and dance.

The force that simultaneously objectifies and makes the hostages act operates by a type of translation which is analogous to that exerted upon the animal during sacrifice. Here it is deprived of its life in order to be sent to another world, their existence being transposed onto a totally new plane, even sometimes being sent 'on a mission', as in the Brahmanic sacrifice. Like sacrificial violence, which is not violence, the hostage dance does not involve *visible* violence. The dance did cause palpable unease to ripple through the assembled crowd, however. This was most keenly felt by the youngest members of the group, who were placed in a position similar to that of the Indigenous peoples, forced by the Hindu power to celebrate their defeat at the buffalo sacrifice, and to laugh at the death of their parents. Here, the violence of the ceremony consisted in encouraging these teenagers to enjoy the spectacle of their own potential future, as hostages to be led against their will into the sacrificial camp.

Like the sacrifice of the buffalo, the dance of the victims is a targeted threat, but by specifically aiming at the youngest age group, who carries all the hopes for the future of the group on its shoulders, the entire group is affected. This is especially the case given that classificatory kinship rules mean that each member of the group is in fact a parent to a cohort of teenagers. The whole community is thus forced to watch the violent spectacle, deprived of agency, unable to intervene or even inquire about the identity of these children, where they come from and for how long they have been away from their parents.

This power is even stronger in that it makes the group complicit in the violence exerted on the young hostages, who have been brought captive from elsewhere specifically to celebrate the new status of their own village. This logic recalls the reproach made to the Untouchables that they exclude others from their cult, wherein they are made responsible for the very violence which is exerted upon them, or that they are at least participants in the violence which is directed towards them.

Spectators are thus offered a staged representation of the party's omnipotence over them and particularly its grip on the youngest class, who must sacrifice themselves in the People's War. Through this performance, the group witnesses its own sacrifice, understanding that they are to give the gift of their own children, who are to be led to the 'altar of the revolution'. For if, as the Maoists so often repeat, to enter the party is to offer oneself as a sacrifice, what does it mean to take others there by force, if not to actively lead them to sacrifice themselves? The theories of sacrifice have not given any name to this most important role – it is equivalent to the role of neither sacrifier (the one who gives his child) nor sacrificator (the one who puts them to death). It is a case of imposing this movement from beginning to end, and thus exerting a double violence upon the (sacrificial) victim and on the one who is turned into a sacrifier despite himself.

Notes

1. Martyrs, *lieshi*, emerged only after the war, in 1949, in response to the many human losses suffered (Hung 2008).
2. Pradhan uses the term *yagya*, which is commonly used in Nepali to refer to sacrifice in general, but refers more specifically to Brahmanical ceremonies involving offerings to fire.
3. Abbreviation of the Communist Party of Nepal (Maoist), commonly used to refer to the party.
4. These new principles were outlined in March 1995: 'Strategy and tactics' (1997).
5. For more details on the conception of war and violence in the Maoist movement in Nepal, see Lecomte-Tilouine (2009e, 2010a, 2010b).

6. This treaty, signed with British India, definitively fixed the borders of the country, with the exception of a part of the Terai which was returned by the latter to Nepal half a century later, as a gesture of gratitude for its military aid.
7. This name, which means the Path of Prachanda, was probably coined on the model of the Shining Path.
8. On the history of the Communist Party of Nepal, Rawal (2007); on the ideology of the Maoist party, Prachanda et al. (2004); on the transformations of the Communist party of Nepal (Maoist), Hachhethu (2008–2009); on the cultural revolution in rural areas, Lecomte-Tilouine (2010b), and for an overview of the movement, Lawoti and Pahari (2010) and Lecomte-Tilouine (2013).
9. School Leaving Certificate, obtained at the end of the tenth year. These restrictions were lifted after the outbreak of the People's War to strengthen the Royal Army.
10. This ban was lifted in 2004, showing that the reforms carried out by the revolutionaries contributed to normalise practices that had previously been prohibited.
11. The treatment of cows and Brahmins undoubtedly needs further exemplification. For example, K. Ogura's (2005) study of the attack on Beni shows that the 'volunteers' forced into combat by the Liberation Army did not include high-caste people.
12. The term *bhog* describes the semantic field attached to royalty well, since it encompasses pleasure, enjoyment, mastery, offering, blood sacrifice, copulation, reign and governance, according to the academy dictionary (Parajuli et al. 1983: 1027).
13. She was even accused of being behind the assassination of Rajiv Gandhi, as Coomi Kapoor wrote in *The Indian Express,* 13 December 1997: 'Just last week, Indo-Nepal relations came under a bit of a strain thanks to the Commission's inclusion of an intelligence report which refers to an unverified tip-off that Queen Aishwarya of Nepal had paid money for having Rajiv Gandhi assassinated.'
14. They said that she would have incurred the wrath of the crown prince by opposing his union with the girl he loved, but this version does not fit well with the fact that the prince first shot his father, and only shot his mother at the very last moment, when she came out to join him in the garden. According to another explanation, the queen caused the massacre by

opening a forbidden room in the temple of Gorakhkali in Gorkha the week before the event.

15. Some Nepalese consider that the massacre of the royal family had been announced by the god Bhimeshwar of Dolakha. This god sweats to prevent cataclysms. His right side concerns the royal family, the left the nation. He was seen to be sweating in January 2001, four months before the massacre. To put an end to his harmful influence, in July 2001, two men decided to transport water drawn from Pashupatinath to Bhimeshwar, to pacify it. The curse was such that they had to bring the water in reverse, driving their vehicles backwards over 138 kilometres of mountain roads, which they covered in 15 hours and 34 minutes, as reported in the press.
16. In many places, the former *mukhiya* headman retained a religious role while political power was transferred to an elected official (Lecomte-Tilouine 1993: 57–58). Likewise, the *mukhiya* was the land tax collector and retained this prerogative until the establishment of the cadastral survey, which was not completed until the late 1980s. Finally, caste rules, which were no longer legislated in 1963, continued unofficially, regulated by the 'big men' of each locality, among them the former *mukhiya*s. This contributed to the development of a local system of 'natural justice' that could be applied even in cases of homicide, and which later allowed the Maoist people's courts to take hold with relative ease.
17. On 6 April 1979, the Pakistani embassy in Kathmandu was attacked by students opposed to the execution of Ali Bhutto, and then a strike began at Tribhuwan University for the establishment of democracy within Nepal. In response, King Birendra held a referendum and won a majority for the continuation of the non-party system. The voting map shows that the mountainous and western regions were in favour of partyless rule, and that the Maoist revolution developed in more conservative regions, contrary to what a number of studies claim about the movement.
18. The *Maoist Information Bulletin* 3, 2002, among many others, attributes the new king with the qualities of extreme violence: 'As if to fill a set quota of human sacrifices each day, an average of two dozen men are brutally slaughtered by the royal butchers.'
19. 'Nepal King leaves bloody trail behind', *The Indian Express*, 28 June 2002. In an article entitled 'Nepal king offers animal sacrifice in Kolkata', the *Times of India*, dated the same day, reports: 'Unmoved by strong protests from animal rights activists, Nepal's King Gyanendra offered animal

sacrifice for the second consecutive Friday, when a goat was slaughtered after his prayers at the historic Kalighat temple here.'

20. Poem by Samir Yatri, published in the Maoist journal *Janaawaj.* The translation from Nepali, as well as all passages from publications in this language, is our own.
21. This success was attributed to fears that the party would resume its armed movement if it suffered an election defeat. A total of 19,600 combatants were identified by the United Nations in late 2006, a figure that was considered inflated by some, but which excluded combatants under the age of eighteen. After lengthy negotiations, they were integrated into the national army, thus permanently resolving the conflict. In total, 17,265 casualties and 1,327 missing persons were recorded, three-quarters of them by the security forces.
22. Mohan Bikram Singh, who founded the pro-Chinese Communist Party of Nepal in 1974, was celebrated for this gesture (Cailmail 2008–2009).
23. 'Abhimanyulāī salām' (Salute to Abhimanyu), poem by Shashikaran, 2005.
24. 'Ghaite shivirmā cahalpahal' (Tumult on the stretcher of the wounded), anonymous, 2002.
25. Poem by Lakshmi Gurung, 'Mṛtyulāī angalīsakekī chu' (I embraced death), 2003.
26. Poem by Sushil, 'Balidan' (Sacrifice) (2005).
27. Untitled poem by Simana Sharma, 2003.
28. As the commander of the 5th Division of the PLA, Comrade Abinash, reported during the operation against three police stations in Jelbang, where 'half a dozen policemen were burned to the ground': 'We revolutionary warriors then tied the death cloth on our foreheads, swore the oath "freedom or death" and launched the assault' (Abinash 2003: 4).
29. On this concept, Khosrokhavar (1998).
30. Untitled poem by Iswacandra Gyawali, *Janadesh* 12 (13) (2003).
31. Poem by Sailendra Ghimire, 'Ma tayari chu' (I am ready) (2005).
32. 'In the initial years of Prachanda the myth, politicians of all hues tended to dub rivals whom they loathed and feared as the 'real Prachanda'. For the political parties, the king was the 'real Prachanda', (Ghimire 2005). 'Even till the early 2000s ... idle speculation about the identity of the "real" Prachanda was ... quite common. Those bestowed that arguably ambiguous honour were a varied lot. The then prince Gyanendra ... the late Rishikesh Shah ... the renowned anthropologist, Dor Bahadur Bista....' (D. Thapa 2007).
33. On this opera: Stirr (2013).

34. The opposition between those who can see in the dark and those who are blinded in broad daylight feeds on the ancient forms of power in this region that the shamans call 'the blind country'. Only they are able to see the evil incarnate in witches, after an initiation where, from a perched tree, blindfolded, they publicly demonstrate their ability to see both the invisible and the future. On the shamanic initiation of the Magars in the Rukum region, see Michael Oppitz's remarkable documentary, *Shamans of the Blind Country* (1981) and Anne de Sales (1993).
35. The Maoist online newspaper *Revolutionary Worker* of 29 March 1998 reported that on 17 November 1996, armed police conducted a brutal search in Mirul village, and took five people to the forest for execution. Among them was a young Magar woman, Kumari Budha. She was carrying her two-year-old daughter on her back, who was thrown into a thicket and later found alive. The villagers introduced me to her during my visit to Mirul. Abinash's account of the events (2003: 51) depicts scenes of abject violence: 'They stripped Kumari Budha naked in front of her father and relatives. And, stripping her naked, the police and the Congress bastards took turns raping her, and then acting like wild beasts, they gouged out both her eyes. Finally, they set fire to her body, while she was only half dead.'
36. Kulman was one of the 3,000 volunteers requisitioned for the attack on Beni in 2003.
37. The following year I learned that she had become a party artist, but by 2009 she had been officially listed as a member of the PLA by the United Nations and I was able to meet her and her 'life partner' on leave from the military camp where they had been assigned to present their newborn child to their parents.
38. From these terraces, I decided to try to catch a moment of their training session on film but was quickly blocked by an old Dalit who indicated to me that this would not be well received.

Conclusion

We have proposed in these pages to consider sacrificial violence as a singularity – in other words, as an object that eludes analysis and that can only be approached through examining the set of relations that are tied up in it.

We have seen how violence, in its exemplary form of sacrifice and in its generalised form of the 'great sacrifice' of war, is intertwined with social organisation. The latter is born of sacrifice in the myth of the first sacrifice. Reciprocally, for the royal sacrifice, each group assumes the function proper to its class, as created by this mythical account of the first sacrifice. This circular movement expresses a tautological ideology that posits sacrifice as the essence of organised life and, in return, sacralises its sacrificial reordering.

Through the consecration of the violence it operates within, sacrifice presents itself as a model of *legitimate* violence. This violence is openly exhibited and may be denied as violence or else declared necessary. This does not mean, however, that sacrifice represents a lesser violence aimed at containing generalised violence. On the contrary, it is magnified and propagated during the buffalo sacrifice. Nor does its legitimacy make it a violence that is not perceived as such, at least by some categories of people in the assembly. In the royal ceremony, at the same time as the sacrifice directs violence outside of the group, in the execution of the animal *alter* and then in the war which follows it, it also exerts violence within it, through a whole range of procedures that we have encountered throughout this text, such as by exclusion, victimisation or threat targeted at specific categories of people within the group. Sacrificial violence thus takes on a dual manifestation within the group from which it emanates – at once unifying and divisive, inclusive and exclusive, it is exerted upon the community, carving out its partitions only to unfold outside of them. It thus expresses social violence and political violence in the same movement, each containing the idiom of the other at its heart, recalling the sacrifice in ancient India, in which each constituent part contained the whole. In this manner, both social structure and political activity inter-construct each other through violence, which is itself conditioned by the form that sacrifice gives it.

At the time of the royal sacrifice, caste society is reordered in the form in which the original, creative sacrifice brought it into being. The people are divided into specialised groups, but on closer inspection, these specialities undergo a translation from the civilian to the warlike – the Damāī tailors become drummers, the ringers and singers of battle; the Sārkī shoemakers become sheathers;[1] the Kāmī blacksmiths armourers; the Indigenous peoples and Kshatriyas fighters; the Brahmins priests of war.[2] Outside of this context, ringers and drummers return to their ordinary work of sewing, armourers forge and repair tools, sheath-makers return to shoemaking and the Brahmins to being domestic priests. However, most importantly, not all groups retain a caste speciality: thus the warrior class, which forms by far the most numerous group in Nepal – especially if one counts the Indigenous peoples in this class – has no specific task to perform in ordinary times. The sacrificial rite thus reorders caste society for war and itself takes on the form of a war: the execution of the buffalo causes all of the family groups to come together under their own standards, triggers the bringing out of weapons from the royal arsenal and sometimes even the release of the victim into an armed crowd, which transforms the sacrificial killing of an animal into a dangerous competition between men. The sacrifice itself is prolonged by the war dance, which brings together its circumscribed ritual form and its more generalised form, in the 'departure for war'.

In the sacrificial competition, as in the warlike extensions of the ritual, status is at stake. In the past, outstanding bravery in battle, even that of an Untouchable, could lead to his being promoted within the caste hierarchy, not only for the individual but also for his entire caste group.[3] The king thus reordered society and the world itself through the wielding of his sword, and, in turn, weapons offered an opportunity for social advancement, unparalleled in any other institution in the kingdom, to the subjects of the warlike sovereign. Similarly, as the sacrificial rite takes place, the very order of society is likely to be overturned because of ancient faults or events whose consequences are to be perpetuated for the rest of time. This means that the hierarchy of status founded by the myth of the first sacrifice may be relativised in relation to the royal sacrifice. The entirety of the ideal ordering may even be suspended by order of the king, who has the authority to overturn it for the duration of the sacrificial combat. The power that the king holds over the law, insofar as he is placed above it, and over the caste structure, of which he is the guarantor, is here affirmed by their negation during times of sacrifice and war, through the suspension of the usual laws and standard caste hierarchy.

In this respect, this translation which sacrifice brings to bear is also a displacement in time. This is not only because the Hindu caste organisation is based on the same structures it had when it was created but also because it reorders itself in the form of an archaic warrior society for the duration of the sacrifice. This sacrificial ordering is centred around and reinstates its local king when, in fact, most local kings lost their power at the end of the eighteenth century, as well as the tutelary gods of the community. This reordering also represents a return to the warlike past of the great epics, bridging the gap between mythic and real time. The killing of the buffalo reproduces this temporal connection between mythic time, which it reiterates with each death, as laid out in the epics, thereby giving the rite its own form in its 'shifted' temporality, and its present actualisation, which in turn mimics the bygone era of the ancient warlike kingdoms. The buffalo sacrifice also represents the crossroads between sacrifice and the 'great sacrifice' of war, sometimes borrowing the consecrated, concentrated form of the former, sometimes the dispersed, combative form of the latter. On this point, we diverge from Hocart (1938: 62), who considers that combat 'is not a primary attribute [of the king and the royal caste], but only a derivative'. The royal sacrifice not only retells the story of a mythic combat but also takes the form of a combat, as well as causing one to occur. Each part of this greater whole feeds back on the other parts, like a Möbius strip, neither side of which can be determined, for if war is a 'great sacrifice', must we not reciprocally consider sacrifice as a 'small war'?

In order to pick all of this apart, we must try to understand the royal sacrifice in two distinct stages, as well as through the effects it engenders in its participants: the first stage concerns the kid-goat offered by the family, who is comforted by the promise of ascending to the heavens before being slaughtered, during which the women and children often cry. The second stage is the execution of the royal or governmental buffalo, an act which frightens and terrorises more than it saddens. Indeed, each household's intimate offering of their most cherished animal is the prerequisite for the collective massacre of the most fearsome animal. In this way, we can see how this device whereby those closest to the family are sent to death in order to overcome a much stronger beast is not only a prerequisite for sacrifice but also, to a greater degree, for war.

To those who suggest that animal sacrifice could be substituted by offering flowers or coconuts instead, many Nepalis reply that sacrifice would simply lose its value. Life, they say, is 'priceless', *amulya*, and only a gift of the utmost force could be fitted to the proportion of sacrifice, or rather, to its disproportion, as sacrifice belongs to the realm of the absolute, where ethics give way to the heady unreason of faith or conviction. Sacrifice's capacity to transform the world as it is and to conquer even the most formidable forces is revealed in all its magnitude when it occurs without substitutes – in war. This is even more the case in revolutionary war, where each agent commits themself to sacrificing his or her life to overcome a violent organisation that is firmly rooted and fiercely protected to ensure its own survival.

The power of sacrifice therefore turns any violence inflicted during such revolutions into a supreme force, provided that it also violates the one who inflicts it. This principle is pushed to its limit in the reflexive form of the 'self-sacrifice' of the martyr. However, the apparently closed sacrificial loop of martyrdom does not fully erase the logic of the gift of an *alter*. This sense of making an offering is restored to martyrdom after death, couched as a sacrificial offering made by the person who originally gave the self-sacrifier life, that is to say, the mother of the martyr, thus reconnecting self-sacrifice with the figure of the sacrificial offering of the beloved, which causes extreme suffering. Reciprocally, this suffering inflicted upon the self which is engendered by sacrifice means that all forms of sacrifice are also self-sacrifice in their own way.

The revolutionary movement used the tropes of the field of violence and its consecrated form for their own ends, tracing out new guiding lines within it. It was therefore able to turn the repression of the people by the royal army into a vast human sacrifice orchestrated by the king against his own 'children', while simultaneously identifying each individual death as a glorious self-sacrifice offered by its combatants. In this way, the movement created a sacrificial matrix with two entry points which was impossible to stop, for it was fuelled just as much by its defeats as by its victories. In the revolutionary framework, death is transformed from being the passage to another existence, the final retribution for all the righteous or sinful actions one has accomplished in life, to becoming the determining moment of existence, either a victory which brings immortality to the self-sacrificing individual or else an erasing of the subject, a way to disappear into anonymity. Death thus became, as the Maoists so often stated, a 'moment of opportunity', so potent as to overthrow

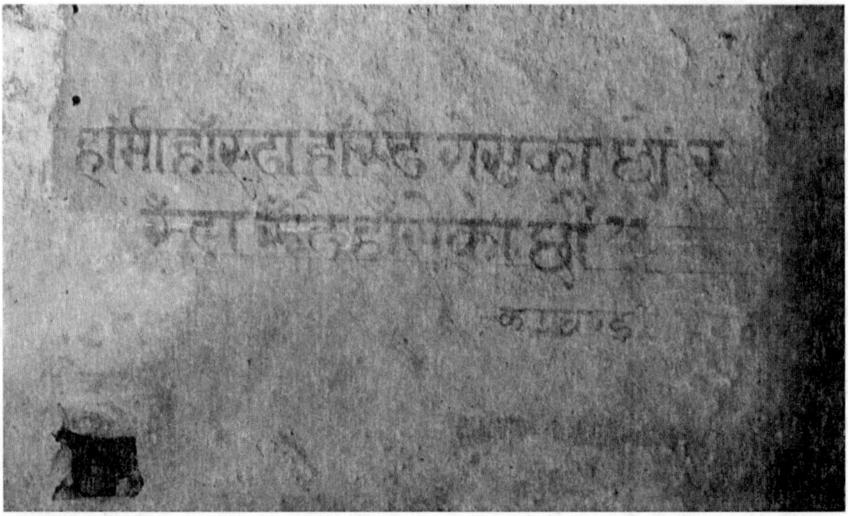

Figure C.1 'We cry while laughing and we laugh while crying', Comrade Prachanda

Source: Author.

the absolute power of death, by reappropriating it for their own ends (see Figure C.1).

At the same time as they undermined the sacrificial foundations of the caste organisation by denouncing its inherent violence, the revolutionaries revived the legitimacy of sacrificial violence by endowing it with a new transcendence and creative power. The ideal of the revolutionaries was the creation of a classless society, but in their fight against the feudal, patriarchal and hierarchised organisation of their society, they were forced to confront their own 'selfish tendencies', the accumulation of wealth, prestige and power, things which can only come at the expense of others. The Maoists were thus trapped in a web of their own making, unable to reach high enough to achieve their goals. While it is true that the values of renunciation, which had until that point remained purely idealised or only put into practice by a very limited number of individuals towards the end of their existence, were introduced to the people by the revolutionaries, for them to achieve not only collective but fully generalised self-sacrificial violence implied including every member of society, as was the case in the royal sacrificial violence.

Those who offered their lives for the revolution transmitted an energy to their comrades that encouraged them to fight and allowed them in turn to conjure up death, by following in their 'bloody footsteps' in the sacrifice of war. However, for the sacrifice to be total, the Maoists had to continually draft in new members from among a populace who for the large part wished to remain neutral. To attempt to realise this, they multiplied the number of ceremonies, the mechanism by which they immersed people in their circle of 'self-sacrifice'. This necessity gave them pause as to how to deal with the enemy, and the idea that they must 'make them understand' and include them in their struggle became stronger than their own denial of armed violence, which enticed them to simply 'clean them up'. Gradually, the 'evil camp' was thus reduced to the king, identified as the sole source of violence, in its social, political and warlike expressions alike. Royalty was reduced in this process to its simplest expression, as absolute monarchy, which was equally unacceptable for the orthodox Hindus, who are concerned with the complementarity of each class's respective functions, as it was for the educated population and the international community, who are attached to the democratic distribution of power. Like the sacrificial priests of ancient India, all the leaders of the major political parties in Nepal are Brahmins. When the king decided not to respect the rights accorded to their class, whose members had by this time exchanged religious rhetoric for political ideology, they formed an alliance with the Maoists in order to get rid of this polarising figure whom they considered was illegitimately occupying the space which should rightfully have been theirs.[4]

This modern-day scenario is reminiscent of the myth of King Vena, who was killed by the Brahmins for having prevented them from offering sacrifice to anyone other than himself. However, more than this figure, who is nowadays relatively obscure, it is the very unpopular demon-king known as Rāvaṇ that King Gyanendra came to embody, while, quite naturally, Prachanda was compared to the ideal Hindu king, Rām. The comparison was further reinforced by the fact that Prachanda, like Rām, was accompanied by his faithful ally Baburam Bhattarai, in the role of Lakṣmaṇ, and that they waged their war for almost ten years while 'in exile' in the 'forest', just like the heroic epic duo.[5] If we remember the mainstream readings of the buffalo sacrifice which firmly connect it with this epic, one cannot think of a better illustration of the possibility offered by the singularity of sacrifice not only to reverse directions but also to transpose one position onto another.

With the end of the monarchy, the royal sacrificial ceremony gradually lost its state sources of financing, but did not entirely cease to exist. As for the great sacrifice of war, this has now been entirely reabsorbed into its ritual archaic form, following the merging of the two previously competing forces – the royal army became the national army and the PLA was integrated into its ranks. These two models of sacrificial violence thus regained their circumscribed and matrix-like forms while retaining their potential to one day grow and encompass the entire social and political field once again.

In contrast to a textual approach that necessarily deals with what the elite says about sacrifice, ethnographic observation reveals the divisive effects of its violence and of the order it establishes. In the context of the villages, as in the former capitals of the Twenty-Four and Twenty-Two Kingdoms, women keep their distance from sacrifice and largely disapprove of it. They deplore the young age of the animals, the way they are bound, the anguish they show and simply the fact of killing, which often takes place in private, but is loud enough to be heard. The lower castes and the Indigenous peoples identify themselves with the victim, or at least consider that their role in the ritual is degrading. Many Brahmins or educated youths see animal sacrifice as a barbaric and backward practice, one which is unsuitable for their class and a source of dishonour for the gods. At the other end of the spectrum, there are those who are galvanised by sacrifice and find in it a way to show their strength and courage. There is also a whole crowd of people for whom the simple fact of eating meat is in itself a feast. However, none of these positions can be unequivocal or everlasting, given the contradictions of sacrificial violence, which the ritual devices knowingly play with. In the region of the Twenty-Two, buffalo sacrifice offers the Untouchables opportunities to momentarily transcend their lowly condition, while at the same time it is the only time they must comply absolutely with their obligation to publicly and collectively take on impurity for the other castes. As for the women, sacrifice places them in a condition of both suffering and rejoicing, by the killing of the animals they raise and love on the one hand and by the feasts that follow on the other. Whatever their reaction, sacrifice turns the villagers into spectators of an omnipotent force which extends over each of them, enjoining each to play their assigned role, sometimes in spite of themselves.

Ethnographic observation of what happens during the performance of the ritual thus allows for a variety of viewpoints to be considered simultaneously. This approach offers an access point into the derivatives of sacrifice, that is, all the phenomena that take place during the process and that constitute it. In much the same way as the trajectory of a movement says nothing about its speed or about the processes that go on during its trajectory, the sacrificial rite deserves to be considered not only in its final form but also in terms of the effects it produces while it is being carried out. When we take these effects into account, the real violence of sacrifice shatters the distance of the symbolic, because those metaphorical 'fountains of blood' do spurt out and really stain the audience. For many, sacrificial violence expresses the innate violence of the group, in that sacrifice is not only the organiser of society but also the revealer of its internal tensions and the faultlines which cross it. Long-term ethnographic research suggests that these faultlines crisscross many times, forming points where sacrifice is likely to be transformed into new practices, such as the offering of vegetable substitutes, or, on the contrary, as seen during the People's War, to develop into a vast, bloody counter-sacrificial system aimed at destroying the sacrificial organisation of the monarchy and of caste-based society. As such, we might describe sacrifice as a setting where the violent tension inherent to the organisation of the group is revealed through the public execution of a living being. This definition undoubtedly exceeds the original definition we used as a guideline at the beginning of this work. Sacrifice, like the violence that forms its core, divides and diffracts points of view. It is also ostentatious, and these two features, when combined, hold a mirror up to the group, showing them the violence at its core, the asymmetry of which is masked or naturalised by the relations that constitute it. The sanctification of the use of brute force brings together two seemingly mutually exclusive extremes, which opens the door for open and even contradictory interpretations of what is going on. This is despite the most logical reading of sacrifice being that it is an expression of the power held by a select few to force others to participate in roles that perpetuate their subjection. However, the oxymoron which defines the sacrificial principle, a formula of destroying in order to build, cancels the possibility of establishing any ontologies, as per Michel de Certeau (1982). Meaning is not reduced, but multiplied, as it leaves room for a wide range of emotions and identifications to take place when faced with this violence which imbues signs with force and transforms them into power.

Notes

1. In addition to scabbards, they were also specialised in the manufacture of leather protections for the body, skins for drums and saddlery.
2. The Brahmins are in charge of determining the most auspicious times for the rite or the battle, as well as the consecration of weapons and sacrificial victims.

3. An example is found during the first attack on Kirtipur by Prithvi Narayan Shah.
4. The Seven Party Alliance, signed in late 2005 between the seven main political parties of Nepal and the Maoist party.
5. Rām and Lakṣmaṇ are ideological twins here, a model of identity among party comrades. The complete allegory of the People's War as *Rāmāyaṇa* is described by Santosh Budha, in issue 1 of the magazine *Magarant*.

References

Note: The Vikram Era is noted VS [Vikram Sambat] in parentheses, with the corresponding year of the Common Era given in the main entry. The Nepali Maoist journals *Janadesh* and *Janaawaj* were posted without pagination on the website www.cpnm.org at the time of the conflict. The site has now disappeared, and the references taken from it are quoted with neither pagination nor link.

ABINASH. 2003 (2060 VS). *Jangko maidānmā* (On the Battlefield). Nepal: People's Liberation Army.

ACHARYA, Shankar. 2014. 'Dalits to Boycott Animal Carcass'. *The Kathmandu Post*, 28 October.

Ajanta Standard Dictionary Nepali–English. Edited by 'three authors'. Delhi: Ajanta Prakashan.

ANANTA. 2004. 'People's War in the 21st Century and Prachanda Path'. In *Problems and Prospects of Revolution in Nepal: A Collection of Articles by Com. Prachanda and Other Leaders of the CPN-Maoist*, edited by Prachanda et al., 214–225. Kathmandu: Janadisha Publications.

ANONYMOUS. 1992. 'Dasaī bahiṣkār ra pīḍit svar' (Dasaī Boycott and Oppressed Voice). *Lāphā* 1: 5.

ANONYMOUS. 1993. 'A Study of Para Village'. *Himalaya* 8 (2): 14–19.

ANONYMOUS. 1993. 'Hindu cāḍ Dasaī bahiṣkār garaun' (Let Us Boycott the Hindu Festival of Dasaī). *Lāphā* 7: 6.

ANONYMOUS. 1993. 'Magarāntī maulik paramparāgat cāḍparvaharu' (The Main Traditional Festivals of the Magar Country). *Lāphā* 7: 4–5.

ANONYMOUS. 'Sacrifice Sparks Debate'. *The Himalayan Times*, 4 October. Accessed 2 December 2019.

B. K., Amar Bahadur. 2008. 'Sanskritization and Caste Opposition: A Shift from Ritual to Politico-economic Power'. *Himalayan Journal of Sociology and Anthropology* 3 (November): 1–10.

Bajracharya, Manik and Axel Michaels. 2012. 'On the Historiography of Nepal: The "Wright" Chronicle Reconsidered'. *European Bulletin of Himalayan Research* 40: 83–98.

Baral, L. Sharma. 1964. 'Life and Writings of Prthinarayan Shah'. PhD dissertation. University of London.

Bataille, Georges. 1988 [1955]. 'Hegel, la mort et le sacrifice'. *Deucalion* 5: 21–43. Republished in *Œuvres Complètes* XII (Paris: Gallimard).

———. 1973. *Théorie de la religion*. Paris: Gallimard.

Bazin, Jean. 1998. 'Question de sens'. *Enquête* 6: 13–34.

Béteille, André. 1992. 'The Politics of "Non-antagonistic" Strata'. In *Society and Politics in India: Essays in a Comparative Perspective*, 122–139. New Delhi: Oxford University Press.

Bhandari, Jyoti. 2003 (2060 VS). *Prācīn mallakālīn ītihās, vibhinna vaṃśāvalī tathā devīdevatāharuko utpatti* (The History of the Ancient Malla Period, Various Genealogies and Origin Stories of Gods and Goddesses). Kanchanpur: Author.

Bhattachan, Krishna Bahadur. 2016. 'Let Us Celebrate Our Own Festivals'. *Indigenous Voice*, 4 October. www.indigenousvoice.com/en/let-us-celebrate-our-own-festivals.html, accessed 1 January 2024.

Bhattarai, Sewa. 2019. 'The Power and Pull of Pathibhara'. *Nepali Times*, 4 March.

Biardeau, Madeleine and Charles Malamoud. 1976. *Le sacrifice dans l'Inde ancienne*. Paris: PUF.

Bloch, Maurice. 1992. *Prey into Hunter: The Politics of Religious Experience*. Cambridge: Cambridge University Press.

Bodewitz, H. W. 1999. 'Hindu Ahimsa and Its Roots'. In *Violence Denied*, edited by J. E. M. Houben and K. R. Van Kooij, 17–44. Leiden: Brill.

Bonnechere, Pierre. 1999. 'La *machaira* était dissimulée dans le *kanoun*: quelques interrogations'. *Revue des études anciennes* 101 (1–2): 21–35.

Bordes, Rémi. 2005. 'Héros, bouffons et affligés. Anthropologie d'une poésie orale himalayenne (Doti, extrême Ouest du Népal)'. PhD dissertation. Université de Bordeaux 2.

Burgat, Florence. 2017. *L'humanité carnivore*. Paris: Seuil.

Burkert, W. 1986 [1972]. *The Anthropology of Ancient Greek Sacrificial Ritual and Myth*. Translated by P. Bing. Berkeley: University of California Press.

CAILMAIL, B. 2008–2009. 'Mohan Bikram Singh and the History of Nepalese Maoism', 'Revolutionary Nepal', special issue, edited by M. Lecomte-Tilouine. *European Bulletin of Himalayan Research* 33–34: 11–38.

CERTEAU, Michel de. 1982. *La fable mystique (XVI–XVIIe siècle).* Paris: Gallimard.

CHATAUT, R. D. 'Prabhas' 2001. *Dotyālī bṛhat śabdakoś* (The Great Dictionnary of Dotyālī). Kathmandu: Belu-Bishwa Smriti Pratishthan.

CHAUDHARI, Manoj Kumar. No date. *Shrī Gaḍhī Māī śakti pīṭh darśan* (Visit to the Seat of Power of the Honorable Mother of the Fort). Bariyarpur: Shri Gadhimai mul pujari parivar.

COBURN, Thomas B. 1984. *Devī Māhātmya: The Crystallization of the Goddess Tradition.* New Delhi: Motilal Banarsidass.

DELEUZE, Gilles. 1964. *Proust et les signes.* Paris: PUF.

DELEUZE, Gilles and Félix GUATTARI. 1980. '12. 1227 – Traité de nomadologie: la machine de guerre'. In *Mille plateaux*, 434–527. Paris: éditions de Minuit.

DELORT, Joseph. 1821. *Mes voyages aux environs de Paris.* Tome second. Paris: Picard-Dubois.

DETIENNE, Marcel. 1979. 'Pratiques culinaires et esprit de sacrifice'. In *La cuisine du sacrifice en pays grec*, edited by M. Detienne and J.-P. Vernant, 7–35. Paris: Gallimard.

DETIENNE, Marcel and Jean-Pierre VERNANT, eds. 1979. *La cuisine du sacrifice en pays grec.* Paris: Gallimard.

'DHRUWA' [BARAL MAGAR, Himmat] 2010. *Samar yātrā* (Journey into War), edited by Kalpana Kaucha Ritu. Kathmandu.

DIKSHIT, Sagarmani Acharya. 1958 (2015 VS). *Caṇḍīmā rājnīti* (Politics in the *Caṇḍī*). Pulchok: Jagadamba prakashan.

DONIGER O'FLAHERTY, Wendy. 1988. *The Origins of Evil in Hindu Mythology.* New Delhi: Motilal Banarsidass.

DUMONT, Louis. 1966. *Homo hierarchicus. Le système des castes et ses implications.* Paris: Gallimard.

DURAND, Jean-Louis. 1986. *Sacrifice et labour en Grèce ancienne. Essai d'anthropologie religieuse.* Paris/Roma: La Découverte/Ecole Française de Rome.

DUTT, Manmatha Nath. 1896. *A Prose English Translation of Markandeya Puranam.* Calcutta: Elysium Press.

FOUCAULT, Michel. 1973. *Ceci n'est pas une pipe.* Paris: Fata morgana.

———. 1994. *Dits et écrits 1. De la nature humaine, justice contre pouvoir.* Paris: Gallimard.

FREUD, Sigmund. 1960 [1912–13]. *Totem and taboo.* London: Routledge.

GABORIEAU, Marc. 1974. 'Les récits chantés de l'Himalaya et le contexte ethnographique'. In *Contributions to the Anthropology of Nepal*, edited by C. von Fürer Haimendorf, 114–128. Warminster: Aris & Phillips.

GHIMIRE, Sailendra. 2005. 'Ma tayari chu' (I am Ready). *Janadesh* 14 (7), January.

GIRARD, René. 1972. *La violence et le sacré*. Paris: Grasset.

———. 1985. *La route antique des hommes pervers*. Paris: Grasset.

GOVINDRAJAN, Radhika. 2018. *Animal Intimacies: Interspecies Relatedness in India's Central Himalayas*. Chicago: The University of Chicago Press.

GUPTA, Swati. 2019. 'Mass Animal Sacrifice Begins Despite Outcry from Activists'. CNN, 4 December, www.cnn.com.

GURUNG, Laksmi. 2003. 'Mṛtyulāī angalīsakekī chu' (I embraced death). *Janaawaj* 1 (43), January.

GUTSCHOW, Niels and Axel MICHAELS. 2005. *Handling Death: The Dynamics of Death and Ancestor Rituals among the Newars of Bhaktapur*. Wiesbaden: Harrassowitz Verlag.

GYAWALI, Iswaracandra. 2003. Untitled poem. *Janadesh* 12 (13), June.

HACHHETHU, Krishna. 2008–2009. 'The Communist Party of Nepal (Maoist): Transformation from an Insurgency Group to a Competitive Political Party'. 'Revolutionary Nepal', Special Issue, edited by M. Lecomte-Tilouine. *European Bulletin of Himalayan Research* 33–34: 39–72.

HANGEN, Susan. 2010. *The Rise of Ethnic Politics in Nepal: Democracy in the Margins*. London and New York: Routledge.

HEESTERMAN, Jan. 1993. *The Broken World of Sacrifice*. Chicago: The University of Chicago Press.

———. 1995. 'Warrior, Peasant and Brahmin'. *Modern Asian Studies* 29 (3): 637–654.

HÉRITIER, Françoise, ed. 2005 (1996 tome I and 1999 tome II). *De la violence: séminaire de Françoise Héritier*. Paris: Odile Jacob.

HEUSCH, Luc de. 1986. *Le sacrifice dans les religions africaines*. Paris: Gallimard.

———. 2000. *Les rois de Kongo et les monstres sacrés*. Paris: Gallimard.

HOCART, A. M. 1938. *Les castes*. Paris: Paul Geuthner.

———. 1970. *Kings and Councillors*. Edited by R. Needham. Chicago: The University of Chicago Press.

———. 1987. 'The Basis of Caste'. In *Imagination and Proof: Selected essays of A. M. Hocart*, edited by R. Needham, 95–108. Tucson: The University of Arizona Press.

HÖFER, Andràs. 1979. *The Caste Hierarchy and the State in Nepal. A Study of the Muluki Ain of 1854*. Innsbruck: Universitätsverlag Wagner.

HUBERT, Henri and Marcel MAUSS. 1994 [1899]. 'Essai sur la nature et la fonction du sacrifice'. *Année sociologique*, tome II. Republished in Marcel Mauss, *Oeuvres. 1. Les fonctions sociales du sacré*, 193–307 (Paris: Editions de Minuit); *Sacrifice: Its Nature and Functions*, translated by W. D. Halls (Chicago: Chicago University Press, 1964).

HUNG, Chang-tai. 2008. 'The Cult of the Red Martyr: Politics of Commemoration in China'. *Journal of Contemporary History* 4: 279–304.

HUTT, Michael. 2006. 'Things That Should Not Be Said: Censorship and Self-Censorship in the Nepali Press Media, 2001–02'. *The Journal of Asian Studies* 65 (2): 361–392.

ILO. 2005. 'Dalits and Labour in Nepal'. *Series 5*, ILO Nepal.

JACQUEMIN, Anne. 2014. 'Le sacrifice dans le monde grec et ses interprétations'. *Archimède* 1: 107–113.

JANKÉLÉVITCH, Vladimir. 1977. *La mort*. Paris: Flammarion.

JONES, Robert C. 2015. 'Animal Rights Is a Social Justice Issue'. *Contemporary Justice Review* 18 (4): 467–482.

JOSHI, Satyamohan. 1982 (2039 VS). *Nepāli cāḍ-parva* (Festivals of Nepal). Kathmandu: Nepal Rajkiya Pragya-pratishthan.

KANDEL, Uttam. 2009. *Jokhimkā pailā* (Risky Steps). Dadhing: Shahid Smriti Sancar Sahakari Samstha.

KHOSROKHAVAR, Farhad. 1998. 'Le modèle Bassidji'. *Cultures et Conflits* 29–30: 59-118.

KIERKEGAARD, Søren. 1983 [1843]. *Fear and Trembling*. Kierkegaard's Writings, VI, Volume 6: Fear and Trembling/Repetition. Edited and translated by Edna H. Hong and Howard V. Hong, 1–123. Princeton: Princeton University Press.

KRAUSKOPFF, Gisèle and Marie LECOMTE-TILOUINE, eds. 1996. *Célébrer le pouvoir. Dasai, une fête royale au Népal*. Paris: CNRS/MSH.

LAWOTI, Mahendra and Anup K. PAHARI, eds. 2010. *The Maoist Insurgency in Nepal: Revolution in the Twenty-First Century*. London: Routledge.

LEACH Edmund. 1976. *Culture and Communication: The Logic by Which Symbols Are Connected—An Introduction to the Use of Structuralist Analysis in Social Anthropology*. Cambridge: Cambridge University Press.

LECOMTE-TILOUINE, Marie. 1993. *Les dieux du pouvoir. Les Magar et l'hindouisme au Népal central*. Paris: CNRS.

———. 1996. 'Les dieux-sabres. Etude du Dasain dans une capitale sans roi (Isma)'. In *Célébrer le pouvoir. Dasaī, une fête royale au Népal*, edited by G. Krauskopff and M. Lecomte-Tilouine, 243–282. Paris: CNRS/MSH.

LECOMTE-TILOUINE, Marie. 2000. 'The Two Kings of Musikot'. In *Resunga, the Mountain of the Horned Sage*, edited by P. Ramirez, 143–170. Lalitpur: Himal Books.

———. 2003. 'The History of the Messianic and Rebel King Lakhan Thapa: Utopia and Ideology among the Magar'. In *Resistance and the State: Nepalese Experiences*, edited by D. Gellner, 244–278. Delhi, Social Science Press.

———. 2004. 'Les bardes hudke du Népal occidental, chantres de l'empire Malla?' In *De l'Arabie à l'Himalaya, hommage à Marc Gaborieau*, edited by V. Bouillier and C. Servan-Schreiber, 69–86. Paris: Maisonneuve et Larose.

———, ed. 2009a. *Bards and Mediums: History, Culture and Politics in the Central Himalayan Kingdoms*. Almora: Almora Book Depot.

———. 2009b. *Hindu Kingship, Ethnic Revival and Maoist Rebellion in Nepal*. New Delhi: Oxford University Press.

———. 2009c. 'The Dhuni Jagar. Possession and Kingship in Askot, Kumaon'. In *Bards and Mediums: History, Culture and Politics in the Central Himalayan Kingdoms*, edited by M. Lecomte-Tilouine, 78–106. Almora: Almora Book Depot.

———. 2009d. 'The Hudke Bard as Genealogist: The Raskoti Vamshavalis and Their Context of Performance'. In *Bards and Mediums: History, Culture and Politics in the Central Himalayan Kingdoms*, edited by M. Lecomte-Tilouine, 189–224. Almora: Almora Book Depot.

———. 2009e. 'Terror in a Maoist Model Village, Mid-western Nepal'. *Dialectical Anthropology* 33: 383–401.

———. 2010a. 'Fighting with Ideas: Maoist and Popular Conceptions of War in Nepal'. In *Armed Militias of South Asia: Fundamentalists, Maoists, and Separatists*, edited by C. Jaffrelot and L. Gayer, 65–90. London, Hurst/New York: Columbia University Press.

———. 2010b. 'Political Change and Cultural Revolution in a Maoist Model Village, Mid-Western Nepal'. In *The Maoist Insurgency in Nepal: Dynamics and Growth in the Twenty-First Century*, edited by M. Lawoti and A. Pahari, 115–132. London: Routledge.

———. 2012. 'Self-immolation by Fire versus Legitimate Violence in the Hindu Context'. *Revue d'Etudes Tibétaines* 25: 181–189.

———, ed. 2013. *Revolution in Nepal: An Anthropological and Historical Approach to the People's War*. Delhi: Oxford University Press.

———. 2016. 'The Untouchable Bard as Author of His Royal Patron: A Social Approach to Oral Epic Poetry in Western Nepal'. Special issue 'Authoritative

Speech in the Himalayas', edited by M. Lecomte-Tilouine and A. de Sales. *Oral Tradition Journal* 30 (2): 211–242.

LECOMTE-TILOUINE, Marie. 2018. 'Un barde parle de son art (Népal occidental)'. In *Musique et épopée en Haute-Asie*, edited by K. Buffetrille and I. Henrion-Dourcy, 93–116. Paris: L'Asiathèque.

LEMARDELÉ, Christophe. 2016. 'Le fait religieux sacrificiel comme révélateur de présupposés éthiques et théologiques'. *Cahiers d'études du religieux. Recherches interdisciplinaires* 15. http://journals.openedition.org/cerri/1535, accessed 12 December 2021.

LETIZIA, Chiara and Blandine RIPERT. 2023. '"Not in the Name of Dharma": A Judgment of the Supreme Court of Nepal on Mass Sacrifices at the Gaḍhī Māī Melā'. In *Animal Sacrifice, Religion and Law in South Asia*, edited by A. Good and D. Berti, 212–263. New York and Abingdon: Routledge.

LEVI, Jean. 2007. *Sacrifice et hiérarchie en Chine ancienne*. Nanterre: Société d'ethnologie.

LÉVI, Sylvain. 1898. *La doctrine du sacrifice dans les Brâhmanas*. Paris: Leroux.

———. 1905. *Le Népal. Étude historique d'un royaume hindou*. Paris: Leroux.

LÉVI-STRAUSS, Claude. 1949. *Les structures élémentaires de la parenté*. Paris: PUF.

———. 1962. *Le Totémisme aujourd'hui*. Paris: PUF.

MALAMOUD, Charles, ed. 1980. *La dette*. Purushârtha 4, Paris: EHESS.

———. 1989. *Cuire le monde. Rite et pensée dans l'Inde ancienne*. Paris: La découverte.

———. 2002. *Le jumeau solaire*. Paris: Seuil.

——— 2005a. *Féminité de la parole. Etudes sur l'Inde ancienne*. Paris: Albin Michel.

———. 2005b. *La danse des pierres. Etudes sur la scène sacrificielle dans l'Inde ancienne*. Paris: Seuil.

MARKALE, Jean. 1956. *Les grands bardes gallois*. Paris: Falaize.

MASKARINEC, Gregory. 2009. 'Conflicting Powers: Struggles between Rulers and Oracular Mediums in Jajarkot District, Nepal'. In *Bards and Mediums: History, Culture and Politics in the Central Himalayan Kingdoms*, edited by M. Lecomte-Tilouine, 55–61. Almora: Almora Book Depot.

MICHAELS, Axel. 1984. 'Siva's Wild and Wayward Calf: The Goddess Vatsala, Her Temple and Yatra'. *Kailash* 11 (3–4): 105–147.

———. 1994. 'The Legislation of Widow Burning in 19th-Century Nepal'. *Asiatische Studien* 48: 1213–1240.

———. 2016. 'Blood Sacrifice in Nepal: Transformations and Criticism'. In *Religion, Secularism and Ethnicity in Contemporary Nepal*, edited by

D. Gellner, S. Hausner, and C. Letizia, 192–225. New Delhi: Oxford University Press.

Michaud, Yves. 1978. *Violence et politique*. Paris: Gallimard.

Monier-Williams, M. 1899. *A Sanskrit–English Dictionary: Etymologically and Philologically Arranged with Special Reference to Cognate Indo-European Languages*. Oxford: The Clarendon Press.

Naraharinath, Yogi, ed. 1964 (2021 VS). *Gorkhā vaṃśāvalī* (Chronicle of Gorkha). Kashi: Aryabirsangh.

Oguibénine, Boris. 1994. 'De la rhétorique de la violence'. *Purushârtha* 16, 'Violences et non-violences en Inde': 81–96.

Ogura, Kioko. 2005. 'Realities and Images of Nepal's Maoists after the Attack on Beni'. *European Bulletin of Himalayan Research* 27: 67–125.

OHCHR. 2011. *Opening the Door to Equality: Access to Justice for Dalits in Nepal*. Nepal: OHCHR.

Oppitz, Michael. 2017 [1981]. *Shamans of the Blind Country*. Halle: Arthaus Musik [documentary].

Padhyaya, Shriyukta B. P. 1904 (1961 VS), *Caṇḍī (arthāt) śaptaśatī, Gorkhābhāshā ślokavaddha* (Caṇḍī or the Seven Hundred, Versified in Gorkhā Language). Baranasi: Durga Press.

Pandeya, Tarakant. 2006. 'Kavitā: swarup ra racanāvidhi' (Poetry: Form and Composition). *Naulo bihani,* October: 16–19.

Pant, Mahes Raj. 2016. Śāstramā bali (Sacrifice in the Normative Hindu Textual Tradition). *Rājdhānī*, October 5: *ka–kha*.

Parajuli, K. P. et al. 1983 (VS 2040). *Nepālī bṛhat śabdakoś* (Great Dictionary of Nepali). Kathmandu: Royal Nepal Academy.

Pariyar, Bishnu and Jon B. Lovett. 2016. 'Dalit Identity in Urban Pokhara'. Nepal, *Geoforum* 75: 134–147.

Pariyar, Sarita. 2018. 'The Old Weight of Caste'. *The Record*, 10 December. www.recordnepal.com.

Payen, Jean-Charles. 1979. 'Une Poétique du génocide joyeux: devoir de violence et plaisir de tuer dans la Chanson de Roland'. *Olifant* 6 (3–4): 226–236.

Phuyal, Sanjeeb. 2019. 'Why Is Dashain a Time of Great Rejoicing and Festivity for Nepalis'. *The Kathmandu Post*, 10 October, online. https://kathmandupost.com/national/2019/10/03/why-is-dashain-a-time-of-great-rejoicing-and-festivity-for-nepalis, accessed 1 January 2024.

Prachanda et al. 2004. *Problems and Prospects of Revolution in Nepal: A Collection of Articles by Com. Prachanda and Other Leaders of the CPN-Maoist*. Katmandu: Janadisha Publications.

PRADHAN, Hridaya Chandra Singh. 1970 (2027 VS). 'Yuddha ra yoddhā' (War and Warrior). In *Aphasos*, 33–51. Lalitpur: Sajha Prakashan.

PRASAD, Rajendra. 2008. *A Conceptual-Analytic Study of Classical Indian Philosophy of Morals*. New Delhi: Concept Publishing Company.

PRASAI, D. R. 2008. 'Nepali Festival: Dashain'. *Newsblaze,* 6 October. https://newsblaze.com/thoughts/opinions/nepali-festival-dashain_6611/, accessed 1 January 2024.

RAJAN. 2006 (2063 VS). *Mālemāvād ra pracaṇḍapathmā sainyavigyān* (Military Science in Marxism-Leninism-Maoism and Prachandapath). Kathmandu: People's Liberation Army.

RANA, Rathi Dhanshamsher J. B. 1975 (2032 VS). *Śāradīyadurgāpūjāpaddhati* (Manual for the Fall Worship of Durgā). Kathmandu: Nepal Rajkiya Pragya-pratishthan.

RAWAL, Bhim. 2007. *The Communist Movement in Nepal: Origin and Development*. Kathmandu/Achham: Forum CPN (UML).

'Recording Nepal Conflict: Victims in Numbers, 2011'. http://www.nepalmonitor.com/2011/07/recording_nepal_conf.html.

RIVIÈRE, Claude. 2003. 'Réalité et leurre du sacrifice'. *Social Compass* 50 (2): 203–227.

'SAHAYATRI', Saral. 2008. *Krāntīkā kathāharu* (Stories of the Revolution). Kathmandu: People's Liberation Army.

SALES, Anne de. 1991. *Je suis né de vos jeux de tambours*. Nanterre: Société d'ethnologie.

SCUBLA, Lucien. 1999. '"Ceci n'est pas un meurtre," ou comment le sacrifice contient la violence'. In *De la violence* II, edited by F. Héritier, 135–170. Paris: O. Jacob.

SHARMA, Khadananda. 1959. *90 sāl ko bhaicālā ko savāī* (Account of the 1934 Earthquake). Varanasi: Sarvahitaishi Kampani.

SHARMA 'DHAKAL', Nilahari. 1963 (2020 VS). *Juṭho sutak nirṇaya* (Treatise on the Forms of Impurity). Varanasi: Author.

SHASHIKIRAN. 2005. 'Abhimanyulāī salām' (Hail to Abhimanyu). *Janadesh* 14 (14): 15 March.

SHRESTHA-SCHIPPER, Satyabhama. 2003. 'Religion et pouvoir chez des indo-népalais de l'Ouest du Népal (Jumla)'. PhD dissertation. Université Paris X Nanterre.

SMITH, Brian K. and Wendy DONIGER. 1989. 'Sacrifice and Substitution: Ritual Mystification and Mythical Demystification'. *Numen* 38 (2): 189–224.

Smith, Emily. 2015. 'Challenging Tradition'. *Allanimals*, May/June: 34–35.

Staal, Frits. 1979. 'The Meaninglessness of Ritual'. *Numen* 26 (1): 2–22.

———. 1989. *Rules without Meaning: Ritual, Mantras and the Human Sciences.* New York: Peter Lang.

———. 1990. *Jouer avec le feu. Pratique et théorie du rituel védique.* Paris: Collège de France.

Stirr, Anna. 2013. 'Tears for the Revolution'. In *Revolution in Nepal: An Anthropological and Historical Approach to the People's War*, edited by M. Lecomte-Tilouine, 367–392. New Delhi: Oxford University Press.

Strenski, Ivan. 2003. *Theology and the First Theory of Sacrifice.* Leiden: Brill.

Subedi, Madhusudan Sharma. 1988 (2045 VS). *Śāradīya durgā pūjāvidhi* (Method of the Autumn Worship Addressed to Durgā). Lalitpur: Hindu Sadacar Pracarak Samuha.

Supreme Court of Nepal. 2016. *Gadhimai Verdict.* English Translation, The Jane Goodall Institute Nepal (Verdict of August 4, 2016, translation certified on August 8, 2019). https://www.kindmeal.my/download/jginepal/Gadhimai_Verdict-English.pdf, accessed 5 April 2022.

Sushil. 2005. 'Balidān' (Sacrifice). *Janadesh* 14 (40).

Taussig, Michael. 1987. *Shamanism, Colonialism, and the Wild Man: A Study in Terror and Healing.* Chicago: The University of Chicago Press.

Thapa, D. 2007. 'Artificial Intelligence'. *The Kathmandu Post*, 27 October.

Thapa, Pandav. 2004. 'Agokā muslobāṭ umriekā kavitāharu' (Poems Born of the Flaming Torch), part 1: *Janadesh* 13 (26) and part 2: *Janadesh* 13 (27).

Thapa Magar, M. M. 1993. 'Ke Dasaĩ Tihār Magarharuko cāḍparva ho?' (Are Dasaĩ and Tihār Festivals of the Magars?). *Lāphā* 7: 13–14.

Thapa Magar, Pradip. 1993. 'Dasaĩ bahiṣkār ko aitihāsik pṛṣṭhabhumi ke ho?' (How Was the Dasaĩ Boycott Introduced?). *Lāphā* 7: 12.

Thapar, Romila. 1995. 'L'histoire de Rama. L'élaboration continue d'une tradition écrite'. *Enquête.* http://enquete.revues.org/document317.html, accessed 1 January 2024.

Thorat, Amit and Omkar Joshi. 2020. 'The Continuing Practice of Untouchability in India'. *Economic and Political Weekly* 55 (2): 36–45.

Torri, Davide. 2016. 'To Kill or Not to Kill? The Issue of Blood Sacrifice and the Transformation of Ritual Patterns in Hyolmo Shamanism'. *European Bulletin of Himalayan Research* 47: 15–39.

Tull, Herman W. 1996. 'The Killing That Is Not Killing: Men, Cattle, and the Origins of Non-Violence ("Ahiṃsā") in the Vedic Sacrifice'. *Indo-Iranian Journal* 39 (3): 223–244.

TURNER, Ralph Lilley, Sir 1931. *A Comparative and Etymological Dictionary of the Nepali Language*. London: Trubner.

VAJRACARYA, Dhanvajra, ed. 1963 (2019 VS). *Paṇḍit Sundarānandaviracit Triratna-saundarya-gāthā* (The Beautiful Epic of the Three Jewels Written by Paṇḍit Sundarānanda). Kathmandu: Nepal Samskritik Parishad.

VARENNE, Jean. 1975. *Célébration de la Grande Déesse (Devî-mâhâtmya).* Sanskrit text translated and commented. Paris: Les Belles Lettres.

VARMA, Bhimabhakta Man Simha. No date. *Sadupadeś* (Instructions). Kathmandu: Bhimabhakta Man Simha Varma.

VERNANT, Jean-Pierre. 1976. *Religion grecque et religions antiques.* Inaugural lecture of the chair of comparative studies of ancient religions, Collège de France, Friday 5 December 1975. Paris: Maspero.

———. 1979. 'A la table des hommes. Mythe de fondation du sacrifice chez Hésiode'. In *La cuisine du sacrifice en pays grec*, edited by M. Detienne and J.-P. Vernant, 37–132. Paris: Gallimard.

VEYNE, Paul. 1988. *Did the Greeks Believe in Their Myths? An Essay on the Constitutive Imagination.* Translated by Paula Wissing. Chicago: The University of Chicago Press.

VINOT, Julien. 2004. 'La mort l'angoisse, le récit de la mort dans Aliscans'. In *Le récit de la mort. Ecriture et histoire*, edited by G. Jaquin, 79–91. Rennes: Presses Universitaires de Rennes.

WRIGHT, Daniel, ed. 1970 /1877. *History of Nepal.* Delhi: Cosmo Publications.

ZOTTER, Astrid. 2021. 'Who Kills the Buffalo? Authority and Agency in the Ritual Logistics of the Nepalese Dasaĩ Festival'. In *Nine Nights of Power: Durgā, Dolls and Darbārs*, edited by U. Hüsken, V. Narayanan and A. Zotter, 193–220. Albany: State University of New York Press.

Index